ELEMENTARY SCHOOLING
FOR
CRITICAL DEMOCRACY

SUNY Series, Teacher Empowerment and School Reform

Henry A. Giroux and Peter L. McLaren, editors

ELEMENTARY SCHOOLING
FOR
CRITICAL DEMOCRACY

Jesse Goodman

with assistance from
Jeff Kuzmic
and
Xiaoyang Wu

State University of New York Press

Published by
State University of New York Press, Albany

For information, address the State University of New York Press,
State University Plaza, Albany, NY 12246

Library of Congress Cataloging-in-Publication Data

Goodman, Jesse, 1948-
    Elementary schooling for critical democracy / Jesse Goodman with
assistance from Jeff Kuzmic and Xiaoyang Wu.
        p.   cm. — (SUNY series, teacher empowerment and school
reform)
    Includes bibliographical references (p.   ) and index.
    ISBN 0-7914-0859-0 (alk. paper). — ISBN 0-7914-0860-4 (pbk. :
alk. paper)
    1. Education, elementary—Social aspects—United States.
2. Democracy.   3. Harmony School (Bloomington, Ind.)—
Administration.   4. Education, elementary—United States—Aims and
objectives.   I. Kuzmic, Jeff.   II. Wu, Xiaoyang.   III. Title.
IV. Series: Teacher empowerment and school reform.
LC191.4.G66   1992
372.973—dc20   90-27262
                                                        CIP

10 9 8 7 6 5 4 3

This book is dedicated to
my father, Jack Goodman

CONTENTS

ACKNOWLEDGMENTS

Many individuals have contributed to the creation of this project. First, I need to recognize the contribution of Jeff Kuzmic and Xiaoyang Wu. Not only did their observations and personal involvement at Harmony confirm and challenge my own perceptions of the experiences that occurred in this school, but their insights into what we observed also added significantly to my own understanding and analysis. If readers feel that this book contains worthwhile information, then a significant part of the credit goes to Jeff and Xiaoyang. Of course, since I am the "sole" author and therefore made all final decisions about what would be written, I alone take responsibility for any of its shortcomings.

Second, I wish to acknowledge the support I have received from the series editors, Henry Giroux and Peter McLaren. Their belief in my work and the time they have spent helping me sort through this project exemplify the best spirit of critical collaboration. Forming a mutually supportive community of critical, democratic scholars is not simply a nice idea for these two individuals; it is something that they practice.

Most important, I wish to recognize the contribution of my spouse, Dona. Like the voices of many women in our society, hers has not been heard. Yet, it is she who gives life to many of the ideas in this book. Working with Dona to raise our two children has taught me more about educating and caring for children than perhaps I can ever articulate.

CREDITS

Some of the ideas that are presented in this book have been previously published in the following articles written by the author:

— (1989). Education for critical democracy. *Journal of Education*, 171 (2), 88-116.

— (1989). Student participation and control for democratic schooling. *Curriculum and Teaching*, 4 (2), 39-59.

— (1990). An educology of curriculum: Towards a connectionist curriculum for critical democracy. *International Journal of Educology*, 4 (1), 14-46.

— (in press). Theoretical and practical considerations for doing school-based research in a post-positivist era. *International Journal of Qualitative Studies in Education*.

FOREWORD
Education For Democracy

HENRY A. GIROUX AND PETER McLAREN

As we write this introduction, the United States is engaged in a war with Iraq. Government officials have informed the American public and the nations of the world that the United States is fighting in accord with its most sacred ideals. Consistently, the notion of democracy is invoked as an inviolable principle but rarely defined as a social or cultural practice. As an ideal, democracy is currently being used to legitimate the mobilization of a vast war machine in order to return to power an autocratic and oligarchic regime (that had remained in power by virtue of Western imperial might), from a usurper nation ruled by a ruthless military dictatorship that has been involved in genocidal attacks on its own Kurdish minority and constitutes a threat to its majority population and many of its aggrieved neighbors in the Middle East. Our description of this tragic state of affairs represents less a commentary on the paradoxical logic of warfare than a concern about how a nation understands democracy as both a defense against domestic and foreign tyranny and a collective struggle for freedom, especially when the term is used to justify the interests that support "our way of life," of which the control of oil resources figures prominently. What does democracy mean in the strong sense, when a government invokes the term to defend an oil-rich monarchy where the disparity among the wealthy and privileged and the local population is as vast as the Red Sea?

In the domestic sphere, how can the American public defend itself against its own ruling groups who seek to reduce the meaning and substance of democracy to the consumption of consumer goods, the formality of an electoral politics in which wealth and privilege become the primary determinants regarding who runs for office, or a wholesale celebration of individual choice as the basis for human agency, but one falsely abstracted from the dynamics of deep structural inequalities and power relations? We believe that there is a radical need to create a widespread public debate over the meaning of democracy. That is, there is a need for educators and others to rearticulate the tradition of liberty, equality, and justice with a notion of radical democracy. Democracy needs to be linked to citizenship as a form of self-management, self-articulation, and life praxis constituted in all major economic, social, and cultural spheres of society. As a practice, it involves employing the principles of freedom, equality, and justice as a basis for transferring power from those economic and political elites who control the commanding apparatuses of the state and civil society to the majority of the population who live out, in varying degrees, relations of subordination within the numerous public spheres that make up everyday life. Democracy becomes in these terms part of a significant restructuring of economic and social power so that power flows from co-operative efforts among groups who share a common concern for the social good and who stand for solidarity and dialogue rather than for structures of hierarchy and control.

Democracy is a terrain of struggle, but the struggle is not simply over restructuring power from elites to the various local publics, it is also part of a pedagogical struggle in which conditions can be created for students and others to invest in the debates over the meaning and nature of democracy as both a discourse and a critical practice. As a discursive conception, democracy is a multi-accentual sign within an ideological field where different interest groups compete over the meaning of the term and seek to organically link it to current historical and cultural developments so that certain preferred readings of the term become reflections of the nation's practical consciousness. Of course, the struggle over meanings and values will always be an intense, prolonged, and necessary contestation. It is part of the struggle for democracy itself. What is dangerous about this arena of struggle is not that a plurality of discourses may emerge, or that they will exhibit contradictory positions, but that, both in the public and private spheres of everyday life, premature closures may be placed on the process of articulation itself (see Hall, 1988). Furthermore, we believe that schools should be sites where students are invited to engage in the struggle against any premature closure of the democratic imaginary, wherever institutional, governmental, or popular limits to the meaning of freedom, dignity, and social justice are put into effect. In this view, democracy must be both understood and felt by teachers as part of a broader goal of creating political subjects who can take up the burden and responsibility of critical citizenship as cultural workers. Hence, both the political and pedagogical aspects of democracy must be linked to a discourse of critique and a project of possibility.

We believe that educators should be on the front lines of a reform movement to make critical democracy and citizenship a primary aim of American education. There is a need for educators to address how the purpose and meaning of critical democracy can be both elaborated and developed within concrete classroom practices. *Elementary Schooling for Critical Democracy* by Jesse Goodman (with assistance from Jeff Kuzmic and Xiaoyang Wu) provides an invaluable contribution to a theory and practice of education for critical democracy.

Elementary Schooling for Critical Democracy offers a way to reconceptualize the relationship between democracy and schooling in a manner that theorizes in an astonishingly clear way the actual practice of democracy as a pedagogical process. It is a book about one independent elementary school in the Midwestern United States that attempts to promote democratic ideals, values, and actions, but its importance is not limited to any one geographical location. Both the school itself, and Goodman's analysis of its strengths and shortcomings, offer an important message of hope for educators everywhere, regardless of their geographic location. Although this book is a case study of an independent school, it is a book that will have special importance for elementary school educators who work in public schools. The study itself has far-reaching implications for educators, cultural workers, and those who are responsible for school policy at state and federal levels. Most importantly perhaps, it provides a multiplicity of democratic images for those educators who, against great odds, have not ceased to give up the struggle for transforming the project of schooling to the search for building a world less burdened by oppression and human suffering.

There are a number of reasons why *Elementary Schooling for Critical Democracy* is a major contribution to the critical educational literature. First, Goodman works from a non-binary interactionist relationship between researchers and research participants. He astutely recognizes that critical research practice involves asking the question: What is the researcher's own enunciative place, his or her own politics of location? Goodman recognizes that current research practices too often ignore the materiality and contested social relations among students, teachers, administrators, parents, and community members but instead make appeals to objectivity, neutrality and political disinterest. But research practices that explore the daily exigencies of schooling—despite their emancipatory intentions—can never make a claim to offering researchers a transparent or transhistorical access to empirical truth. Forms of signification which are productive of research paradigms are never immune to political interests but are rather ideological outcomes that are always situated historically and within particular regimes of truth. Goodman astutely recognizes that all knowledge is an effect of social struggle within a conflictual terrain of economic, social, and political practices. However, it is to Goodman's credit that he is able to develop a methodology in which the observer is located directly within a socio-political context and is self-reflexive about his or her situatedness within such a context.

Second, in addition to being a keen observer of microsociological processes within the confines of the classroom and other social networks, Goodman has a particularly cogent understanding of both the history and practice of curriculum. He recognizes that issues of curriculum can best be conceptualized as a conflictual domain where various approaches to pedagogy proliferate. For instance, on one occasion he describes schooling as "a complex phenomenon that contains symbolism, rituals, myths, perspectives, and different modes of thought that must be deconstructed as a way of understanding what it means to teach and be taught." Goodman also recognizes that power operates through forms of school knowledge and practices in ways that exclude and silence groups on the basis of race, class, and gender. Schooling always privileges certain modes of intelligibility over others, and the purpose of critical educational theory, in Goodman's view, is to make explicit the assumptions that underlie such acts of privilege and the grounds that enable them to exist unchallenged. Goodman recognizes that, left unchallenged, schools too often become empires of consciousness that serve the interests of those who possess the power to narrate history. For students, they become agencies from whom permission must be sought and approval granted in order to be considered worthwhile individuals.

Third, Goodman's ethnography accommodates specific insights provided by some critical versions of feminist theory through his ability to evoke, demonstrate, and theoretically elaborate on the importance of power, subjectivity, and human agency as these intersect in the arena of school life. Fourth, Goodman clearly recognizes that constructing a curriculum for critical democracy means adopting a narrative understanding of democracy as an incomplete and unfinished story. In Goodman's view, given the current ideological pattern found in our society, educators need to consciously create a connectionist pedagogy in our schools that is forged within an ethics of solidarity and caring. Such a vision is a far cry from the narrowly utilitarian approach observed in many of today's public schools that operate within an instrumental rationality and discourse of individualism.

What is perhaps the most urgent aspect of this important volume is its ability to shed new light on the meaning of democracy and what this might mean for the rethinking and restructuring of schools as well as public spheres both directly and indirectly associated with the schooling process. For instance, *Elementary Schooling for Critical Democracy* suggests a reading of democracy that is anti-essentialist. Goodman works within a political imagery in which democracy is not a self-evident category with clearly demarcated categorical boundaries. It is a term that is deeply embedded in a range of conflicting discourses; it is constituted not through its univocal reflections on liberty and justice but through the tension of its multiple claims, possibilities, and existing social practices that are exercised under its name. This perspective is compatible with the recent insight of Zizek (1989: 98) who insists, after Laclau, that it is not "possible to determine a definite cluster of features, of positive properties, however minimal, which defines the permanent essence of 'democracy' and similar terms." Furthermore, argues Zizek, "the only way to define 'democracy' is to say that it contains all political movement and organizations which legitimize, designate themselves as 'democratic.'" That is, "in the final analysis, 'democracy' is defined not by the positive content of this notion (its signified) but only by its positional-relational identity—by its opposition, its differential relation to 'non-democratic'—whereas the concrete content can vary in the extreme."

Goodman clearly recognizes that the contextual specificity of democracy is important, and that it cannot be reduced to an a priori set of rules and regulations. This is an important insight because so much existing research on schooling and democracy operationalizes the term "democracy" in a way that totalizes the ideological field in the name of a selected reading of the term, and retroactively submits it to a previously established code. This can cause a misuse of the term "democracy" as it then becomes a master-signifier that conscripts the illusion that democracy, as it is equated with dominant readings of United States social life, exists as a force that possesses as immanent essence in capitalist social relations—something that has always existed from the beginning and is only "realized" in the historical phenomenon known as America. Such an uncritical understanding of democracy provides subjects with an already circumscribed place in the intersubjective network of existing social relations of the larger society. Viewed from such a perspective, the term "democracy" becomes the embodiment of its own immanent impossibility. This is disastrous for the construction of a critical democratic project since the meaning of democracy becomes reduced to what Aranson (1990: 39) calls "a set of specific rules within a clearly delimited sphere, without any reference to the partial institutionalization of autonomy (Castoriadis) or the institutional recognition of indeterminacy (Lefort)." However, the fact that democracy cannot, in Goodman's view, be realized through a list of empirical propositions, does not mean that democracy should be reduced to grasping at the vapors of good intentions or speculative political daring; rather, democracy must be forged in a project that, while necessarily provisional, is capable of giving concrete meaning to the everyday lives of historical subjects. What Goodman is able to do in order to challenge most school studies on democracy is to provide teachers with new and more specific categories for arriving at an understanding of democratic schooling outside the limp generalizations distilled from most liberal analyses of education. This serves to both increase and deepen the possibilities for creating what the author calls a "critical democracy."

Elementary Schooling for Critical Democracy charts out a theoretical/practical terrain that has an important purchase for understanding democracy as part of a broader notion of care, justice, and difference. There is no master narrative at work in this book, there is more importantly an attempt to reconcile the principles of difference, individualism, and freedom with cultural justice, social responsibility, and democratic public spheres. The cultural-economic organization of the social in school settings is a primary consideration of Goodman, especially as such organization becomes a social basis of consent that reproduces the dominative logic and social relations and divisions that exist within the larger society. Goodman is concerned with creating democratic spaces contemporaneously with collectivist practices. This means resisting forms of schooling in which inequality becomes a self-perpetuating and self-reiterating exercise, but rather creating sites that crystallize democratic values into a system that pits the role of the transformative intellectual against that of the vanguardist or elite cadre of curriculum or policy "experts." It means resisting the totalizing force of administrative life and the demobilization of political and racial identities. It implies that steps must be taken to reverse the effects of forms of human agency that, within the current historical trajectory, are receding into an objective realm of reification and turning students into receptacles to receive time, space, and knowledge, rather than agents with the critical means to produce them (Giroux, 1988).

Goodman recognizes that the current conservative backlash must be met with renewed efforts among the left, and left educators in particular. What makes Goodman's book particularly important is its stress on the incompatibility of democracy with racism, sexism, and poverty, and also the emphasis it places on the realm of the popular and its relationship to developing critical pedagogical approaches. We feel that the realm of the popular has important implications for teachers for a number of reasons. First, it is a recognition that in the world of the postmodern everyday, feeling is often valorized over meaning; emotions often exceed signification while the construction of mood displaces rationality. Popular culture is a world "overcoded by the excess of affectivity"—a perpetual opera whose mundane features make it all the more captivating (Grossberg, 1988). It is the popular that "quilts" students into particular ideological dispositions, attitudes, and social practices. The domain of the popular *inflects* meaning into an affective state—it shifts the semiotic register from sign to feeling (Grossberg, 1988). The power of popular discourses rests in the fact that they are able to refigure social formations through the mobilization of affect, that is, by mobilizing latent sentiments of affinity or by catalyzing a latent cleavage or disaffection among certain groups or segments of the social order. In other words, they forge or weld discursive articulations through the production of affective alliances connected to popular images and slogans rather than through a critical engagement with issues and a commitment to rethink core values and commitments in the spirit of radical social, cultural, and ethical renewal. That is, within the terrain of the popular, affective investments or feelings become "quilted" into various ideological alliances and struggles over meanings and practices. Attitudes and feelings are never fully stitched to any one ideological position or another in a unitary, monolithic, or fixed manner. There is always a surplus of meaning that remains unattached. To a certain extent, then, feelings and attitudes can be rearticulated and refigured through critical discourses available to teachers and students. What is important is that students are able to find explanations for the way that they feel about issues that are able to connect both the personal to the political, resulting in a sense of knowledgeable commitment to take an active role in the service of the public good. We are speaking here of a commitment that can serve as the *source* as well as the *effect* of feeling—one that is able to create through dialogue and criticism the ground for new democratic and transformative values and practices. If, as Grossberg (1988) notes, popular culture is a terrain of signification where meaning is inflected through images, music, and narratives as *feelings*, then schools should take up the challenge of *rearticulating such feelings into a purposeful social discourse that leads to democratic modes of sociality, forms of associative living, and emancipatory practices and leads to a celebration of the social value of community.* This is not to deny the possibility that the terrain of the popular cannot be a site of resistance in its own right, but rather to suggest that it can be used to forge a critical alliance with schools in order to both deepen and hasten the project of social and political transformation. As Goodman recognizes, schools need to be more than sites where students are unwittingly encouraged to live out their unfreedom under the assumption that they are participating in social relations that are formidably egalitarian. Following the lead of critical cultural theorists, we need to make the terrain of the popular the *place* from which we speak and struggle and not only the object of our analysis. This means that the popular and ordinary need not be exoticized as an object of critique but rather that the everyday world be brought into the classroom (through an affirmation and critical engagement with forms of mass entertainment, cultural forms of leisure, family and peer structures, sports, streetcorner styles and argot, religious traditions, beliefs, and practices, forms of sexuality and sexual preference, the world of work, advertising, and folk traditions, etc.) as the ground from which we speak to issues that forge our collective projects of possibility and life praxis (McLaren, 1986, 1989).

Goodman's book is not about false optimism but rather about radical hope. In this sense it offers a counter-narrative to so many critical approaches to schooling that betoken despair about the present and the future. It is a story about how a vision of transformative schooling can surmount the concrete limits imposed by objectified reality by helping children to construct their own realities and critical faculties in a project that escapes self-interest in order to be linked to broader social concerns. While radical hope often leads a subterranean existence, it continues to break through the surface of teachers' lives to assault historical reality with the intention of transforming it.

Goodman himself would be the last person to offer his work as a prescription for critical democracy. As Goodman advises, it is better for teachers and administrators to struggle though issues and obstacles for themselves and to create institutional spaces that grow out of their unique and particular situations. Teachers who read *Elementary Schooling for Critical Democracy* will find a wealth of ideas and perspectives for developing a critical praxis in the contextual specificity of their own institutional sites, and from the perspective of their own politics of location.

REFERENCES

Aranson, Johann P. "The Theory of Modernity and the Problem of Democracy." *Thesis Eleven*, no. 26 (1990): pp. 20-45.

Giroux, Henry. *Schooling and the Struggle for Public Life* (Minneapolis: University of Minnesota Press, 1988).

Grossberg, Larry. *It's a Sin* (Sidney, Australia: Power Publications, 1981).

Hall, Stuart. *The Hard Road to Renewal* (London and New York: Verso, 1988).

McLaren, Peter. *Schooling as a Ritual Performance* (London and New York: Routledge, 1986).

McLaren, Peter. *Life in Schools* (Albany, New York: Longman, 1989)

Zizek, Slavoj. *The Sublime Object of Ideology* (London: Verso, 1989).

PREFACE

Visions of what is considered "good education" are intimately rooted in the conscious and/or unconscious visions of what is considered a "good society." As stated in the first chapter, this book represents an attempt to create images of elementary schooling that can foster a more critical, democratic society in the United States. In particular, it suggests that the ideal democratic society is one that establishes societal structures such as schools that help balance two competing social values: individuality and community.

Since the book is concerned with the interaction of theoretical discourse and practice in schools, it may appeal to people with very different agendas. As a result, individuals may wish to approach the book differently. Those who want to be more fully informed about this author's vision of critical democracy and its relationship to educating young children will most likely want to read the book from beginning to end in the order that it is written. Those who are particularly interested in "school practices" may wish to begin their reading with the description of Harmony School in Chapter 2 (see page 48), continue through Chapters 3, 4, and 5, and then in order to put the portrayal of Harmony School into a more complete theoretical context, go back and read Chapters 1 and 6. Since the first two sections of Chapter 2 (pages 31-48) examine issues related to conducting social research in today's scholarly climate, those interested in school practices may wish to save this part of the book for their final reading.

In addition, some may feel that, because Harmony School is an independent rather than public school, what can be learned from this particular setting is extremely limited. To some degree, this concern is real; that is, the people who work at Harmony do not face a lot of the bureaucratic constraints, political pressures, or governmental interference that public schools face. However, this author has spent many hours teaching in and observing public schools, and there are many aspects of educating young children in Harmony that are readily applicable to public school settings, even under the current oppressive climate that surrounds public schooling in the United States today. In addition, it is important to remember that if we are ever going to substantively alter current practices in conventional schools, then it makes sense to take a careful look at schools that are unconventional. What is being suggested is that we can learn as much, if not more, from carefully examining the unique setting as we can from examining the generalized norm. The creative challenge for the reader of this book is to vicariously apply what she or he has read to his or her own specific situation, be it that of a single teacher in his or her own classroom, a small group of teachers who wish to form a "school within a school," a principal who wants to begin a process of restructuring his or her school, a curriculum director or superintendent who wishes to initiate a dialogue for change in his or her district, teacher educators who want to rethink the way in which preservice teachers are educated, or academics who are interested in developing their understanding of the role of schools in a democratic society.

1

Elementary Education and Democracy

As the title suggests, this book argues for and illuminates the way in which elementary education can serve as a vehicle for critical democracy. In doing so it draws upon the thinking of John Dewey and recent critics of schooling and society. However, its primary source of inspiration comes from the year we[1] spent observing the activities of a small group of elementary educators and children who work and play in an independent school that is actively searching for ways to create an elementary education for democracy. As a result, the focus of this discussion is on children, teachers, and administrators who act out their lives in day-to-day interaction. It is one thing to advocate a particular theoretical viewpoint, but it is another thing to establish an educational program for critical democracy within a given school and society. As Simon (1988: 3) states, "The move from visionary rhetoric to classroom reality, from curriculum critique to pedagogical possibility is rarely straightforward. But we know that to forsake such a journey is to continually postpone a serious exploration of 'what must be done.'" In fostering a vision of educational practice for critical democracy, it is important that we not overlook those who are currently involved in such actions. As Wexler and his colleagues (1987: 228-229) note, the type of pedagogy needed cannot "be theorized in the academy and successfully handed down to the classroom, with more than token effect. . . . To be authentic, demands for change must be heard in voices emanating from subjective life, and from collective action and movements." How might a school for critical democracy be structured, and what type of power dynamics might exist within it? What content might be taught, and what values might be embedded within the formal and implicit curriculum? What type of learning activities would dominate the instruction found in such a school? What dilemmas or struggles might teachers face as they try to manifest the goals of such a school? What factors might hinder the democratic empowerment of students and teachers within such a school? What aspects of this type of schooling could be transferred to other contexts, such as mainstream public or private schools? What material and ideological factors might inhibit this type of education from spreading beyond its current minority status within our society?

The goal of this book is not to emerge with some "model" or "ideal" for others to simply mimic, but to explore, as a "lived experience," the

1

possibilities and constraints for developing what some (Giroux, 1988b; Livingstone, 1987; Shor & Freire, 1987; Weiler, 1988) have called a critical or liberatory pedagogy. *Pedagogy* here refers to much more than mere teaching techniques. Rather, it presents a view of instruction within an institutional context that specifies a particular vision of ourselves and our relationship to others, what is considered worthwhile knowledge, the process by which one comes "to know" something, an appropriate physical and social environment within which education can occur, and the way in which schooling helps shape future directions for society. Simon (1988: 2) suggests that a critical pedagogy helps teachers and students

> to understand why things are the way they are and how they got to be that way; to critically appropriate forms of knowledge that exist outside of their immediate experience; to take risks and struggle with on-going relations of power from within a life-affirming moral culture; and to envisage versions of a world which is "not yet" in order to be able to alter the grounds upon which life is lived.

From this perspective, schools are forums for cultural politics that reflect, mediate, and potentially transform the societal order within which they exist.

This chapter examines contextual issues of critical democracy and elementary education. In doing so, it concentrates on the dialectical tension and balance between the values of individuality and of community that exist within the democratic ideal. Although the notion that schools in our society should help sustain and enhance a democratic way of life has a long and accepted history, this chapter provides a brief reexamination of this ideal in an attempt to flesh out the above tension as it becomes manifested within an educational context. As part of this discussion, this chapter examines fundamental presuppositions, as well as previous radical educational reform efforts.

CRITICAL DEMOCRACY

As previously stated, the concept of critical democracy is drawn primarily from John Dewey's political philosophy, particularly as reflected in his publication *The Public and Its Problems* (1927), which examines the relationship between democracy, the state, and the public.[2] For most Americans democracy is an often used but taken-for-granted concept. As Dewey (1927: 170) observes,

> The words "sacred" and "sanctity" come readily to our lips when such things [aspects of our political and social system] come under discussion. They testify to the religious aureole which protects the institutions. If "holy" means that which is not to be approached nor touched, save with ceremonial precautions and by specially anointed officials, then such things

are holy in contemporary political life. As supernatural matters have progressively been left high and dry upon a secluded beach, the actuality of religious taboos has more and more gathered about secular institutions, especially those connected with the nationalistic state.

This reified image of American democracy is rooted in the republican form of government that serves as our state apparatus. Democracy as practiced in the United States is seen as inherently good and has something to do with choosing representatives, having faith in the will of the majority, providing certain checks and balances, and protecting the right to express minority viewpoints. For most citizens, democracy is equated with notions of freedom as reflected by the way our public and private institutions currently operate. At most, democracy as we generally understand it needs only minor modifications, such as voting rights acts or court rulings outlawing segregation, to preserve its virtue. Perhaps the most noticeable part of our democracy is that it calls for relatively little effort on the part of the average citizen (voting).

In *The Public and Its Problems*, Dewey (1927) challenges the viability of this seldom questioned concept of democracy. First, he takes special notice that the "state" (as we have come to know it) is, in actuality, a modern phenomenon. The way in which we have organized ourselves into given societal arrangements and have developed institutions by which to govern ourselves is not the product of some metaphysical destiny but has emerged historically from concrete social, political, and economic forces. As a result, it is within our ability (although difficult) to transform what is taken for granted into more humane and just arrangements.

In many of his writings, Dewey makes a sharp distinction between democracy as a living, social arrangement and democracy as a form of government. From Dewey's perspective, all states have governments that represent *some* people. The problem stems from setting up certain types of institutional arrangements to make the public as fully represented as possible. Dewey calls attention to the fact that in our society democracy is associated with strictly *political* institutions and realms of thought. As a result, it is limited to "a specified practice in selecting officials and regulating their conduct as officials. This is not the most inspiring of the different meanings of democracy. . . . But it contains about all that is relevant to *political* democracy" (1927: 82). He goes on to question whether this modern, distinctly political democracy actually is capable of serving the public interest, as liberal political theory suggests. In particular, Dewey draws attention to the way in which politics, culture, and economics have become fused in our society.

[Liberal democracy] emancipated the [upper and upper-middle] classes whose special interests they represented, rather than human beings

impartially. . . . The notion that men are equally free to act if only the
same legal arrangements apply equally to all—irrespective of differences
in education, in command of capital, and the control of the social environment which is furnished by the institution of property—is a pure absurdity,
as facts have demonstrated. (Quoted in Manicas, 1985: 141)

He goes on to illustrate the way in which economic powers within society
effectively narrowed our notion of democracy and the "proper" role of
government to political aspects of society, thus protecting the interests of
relatively few privileged (and therefore powerful) citizens by shielding their
interests from public scrutiny and debate.

Thus fear of government and desire to limit its operations, because they
were hostile to the development of the new agencies of production and
distribution of services and commodities, received powerful reenforcement.
The economic movement was perhaps the more influential because it
operated, not in the name of the individual and his inherent rights, but
in the name of Nature. Economic "laws," that of labor springing from natural
wants and leading to the creation of wealth, of present abstinence in behalf
of future enjoyment leading to creation of capital effective in piling up still
more wealth, the free play of competitive exchange, designated the law
of supply and demand, were "natural" laws. They were set in opposition
to political laws as artificial, man-made affairs. . . . The economic theory
of *laissez-faire*, based upon belief in beneficent natural laws which brought
about harmony of personal profit and social benefit, was readily fused with
the doctrine of natural rights. (Dewey, 1927: 90-91)

From Dewey's (1927: 108-109) perspective, because our concept of
democracy is limited to particular forms of political institutions, the public
at large has been effectively removed from genuine democratic processes.

The modern economic regime control present politics . . . [to ensure]
that the main business of government is to make property interests secure.
. . . The same forces which have brought about the forms of democratic
government, general suffrage, executives and legislators chosen by majority
vote, have also brought about conditions which halt the social and humane
ideals that demand the utilization of government as the genuine instru-
mentality of an inclusive and fraternally associated public. . . . The
democratic public is still largely inchoate and unorganized.

For most, democracy has become viewed as an artifact (governmental
agencies) or a set of cultural rituals (passively observing or voting in elections)
rather than a dynamic process in which the public actively participates on
a daily basis and which involves face-to-face contact.

Dewey's critique of liberal democracy has been echoed and enriched
by several political theorists during the last two decades. For example,

Habermas's (1970, 1973, 1975) analysis of Western industrial societies identifies the rise of an "instrumental rationality" (rooted in positivism) that has effectively removed substantive political and ethical thought and discourse from public consideration. According to Habermas (1970: 112-113), this rationality

> reflects not the sundering of an ethical situation but the repression of "ethics" as such as a category of life. The common, positivist way of thinking renders inert the frame of reference of interaction in ordinary language, in which domination and ideology both arise under conditions of distorted communication and can be reflectively detected and broken down. The depoliticization of the mass of the population, which is legitimated through technocratic consciousness . . . reflects . . . a new . . . disempowering institutional framework and systems of purposive-rational action that have taken on a life of their own.

Building upon this critique, Hanson's (1985) historical analysis of American political discourse reveals a significant closure in national political debate during this century. As the underlying structure of a corporate-dominated, consumer economy became ever more entrenched, meaningful dialogue over the nature of American democracy atrophied.

> The role of liberal regimes in preserving and promoting the private accumulation of wealth has retreated behind a facade of administrative neutrality. . . . [and] is insulated from any fundamental scrutiny. . . . With the assumption by the state of responsibility for economic and social stability, the ideal of a good and just society has been replaced by that of a self-regulating, cybernetic social system. Politics has given way to administration, and policy discussions have been reduced to considerations of economic necessity and technical feasibility. Consequently, the range of perceived and allowable collective action has been considerably reduced, to the point where genuinely ethical and political questions concerning the ends of such action are suppressed. (Hanson, 1985: 378)

One does not have to be a political scientist or sociologist to witness the lack of depth in political discourse in our society. Even during electoral campaigns, the problems facing society are often taken for granted and the main difference between candidates or political parties is their style and the proposed technical solutions to these problems, which tend to be packaged in a manner that can be easily consumed, much like microwave dinners. Hanson's (1985) analysis illustrates the way in which national political parties no longer debate what a democracy ought to be, but only which and to what degree various interest groups receive their "fair share" as political consumers.

Several analysts elucidate the way in which people are disenfranchised from more democratic participation in their lives. For example, Braverman (1974) and others (Burawoy, 1979; Wood, 1982) illustrate how workers have increasingly lost their "voice" in determining the substance of their labor. At the turn of the century in the United States, the nature of work began to change dramatically. The cottage industries or small craft shops quickly disappeared as urban factories developed and produced new and larger quantities of goods. Individual craftspeople simply could not procure their goods at competitive prices. Although a few denounced this progress for turning the individual worker into a mere cog in a big machine, the nation as a whole became mesmerized by the potential productive output of this rapidly growing industrial development. As urbanized industry continued to mushroom and hence become more complex, new ways to organize labor became necessary. These decisions were left to "efficiency experts" who applied principles of "scientific management" to increase production, rather than to the workers themselves (Edwards, 1979; Gordon, Edwards, & Reich, 1982; Mouzelis, 1967; Wiebe, 1967). This lack of any significant democratic participation in the workplace has resulted in the deskilling of workers and the degradation of work in general.

Both racism and sexism also have contributed significantly to a narrowing of democracy in our society. For example, Barrett (1979) examines the way women have been concentrated into particular kinds of work (clerical work, nursing, domestic service, education) rather than others (medicine, law, politics, business, building trades). Occupations designated as "women's work" usually offer lower wages, less desirable working conditions, less occupational autonomy, and less status than occupations identified as "men's work." As a result, those who do "women's work" are relatively powerless in our current political democracy. It is important to note that efforts to challenge these patriarchal circumstances have been directed primarily at helping women (mostly from white, upper, and upper-middle economic classes) gain access to traditional male occupations rather than at reducing the distinction between "women's" and "men's" occupations. Similarly, it is widely acknowledged today that, in spite of gains made in civil rights, people of color are still largely disenfranchised from the political, economic, and cultural power centers of our society. Affirmative action programs are currently under attack, and overt racism is once again being manifested in many communities and college campuses. Efforts to promote equality among the races through school desegregation have, for the most part, failed (Hochschild, 1984; Oakes, 1985). Hochschild's (1984) review of this research illustrates the way in which our liberal democratic structures and procedures (strategies of incremental change) have inhibited true democratic transformations for people of color in our society. Weis's (1985) research illuminates the way in which young blacks must reject their own cultural background to "succeed" in society, and thereby risk ostracism by their families and friends. The failure of educational programs to respond critically to the lives of "disadvantaged" young Afro-Americans interacts with their urban cultural ethos to form a vicious cycle of continued oppression and disempowerment. Democracy can exist only in a society that is fundamentally free from racism and sexism.

Given the above critiques, there is nothing inherently complex about the concept of critical democracy.[3] It presents both a vision of an ideal (and hence never completely realized) society and a process by which this vision can be pursued. First, as might be expected, critical democracy refers to much more than political institutions.

> A democracy is more than a form of government; it is primarily a mode of associated living, of conjoint communicated experience. The extension in space of the number of individuals who participate in an interest so that each has to refer his own action to that of others, and to consider the action of others to give point and direction to his [or her] own, is equivalent to the breaking down of those barriers of class, race, and national territory which kept men from perceiving the full import of their activity. (Dewey, 1966: 87)

As a form of associative living, critical democracy implies a significant expansion of democratic participation in the multiple realms of social life in which one takes part. As Dewey (1927: 148) states, "Democracy is the idea of community life itself." Institutions, whether public or private, would be organized around giving their members a "voice" in setting and implementing their goals (Barber, 1984; Pateman, 1970). As such, democracy implies a commitment to a broad-based distribution of knowledge and promotion of communicative experiences. In establishing criteria for democracy, Dewey (1966: 83) asks, "How numerous and varied are the interests which are consciously shared? How full and free is the interplay with other forms of association?" He goes on to state that creating a democracy entails "perfecting the means . . . of communication . . . so that genuinely shared interest in the consequences of interdependent activities may . . . direct action" (Dewey, 1927: 155).

Although expansive knowledge distribution and communication are essential to increased democratic participation beyond the strictly political arena of society, they are not enough. Critical democracy also implies a moral commitment to promote the "public good" over any individual's right to accumulate privilege and power (Barber, 1984; Dahl, 1982; Gran, 1983). In this sense, it suggests strong values for equality and social justice. As a result, critical democracy presupposes that social arrangements will be developed within a socio-historical context. When groups of people have suffered historically from economic, social, and/or psychological oppression, there is an accepted responsibility to alter current societal arrangements to redress previous inequalities, whether these are based upon class, race, religion, ethnic heritage, gender, or sexual preference. Critical democracy also suggests the extension of this responsibility beyond the borders of a particular state; that is, it recognizes the interdependency of all life forms on this planet, and therefore implies a commitment to the welfare of all people and other living species that inhabit the earth.

It is important to note that critical democracy does not imply a simplistic view of a harmonious, utopian society. Peck (1987) suggests that in their desire for bonding, many groups of individuals establish communities under the false assumption that once a group is established, all conflict between people will evaporate in the face of human love. He goes on to illustrate, however, the way in which these groups acually create neurotic and sometimes destructive "pseudocommunities" that lack authenticity. "The basic assumption of pseudocommunity is that the problem of individual differences should be avoided. The boring mannerliness of pseudocommunity is a pretense devoted to fleeing from anything that might cause healthy as well as unhealthy conflict" (Peck, 1987: 109). Barber (1984: 132) notes that within a critical democracy "conflict is resolved in the absence of an independent ground through a participatory process of ongoing, proximate self-legislation." Crenson's (1983) study of an urban community suggests that a strong sense of community is not achieved through the homogeneous consensus of its members. To the contrary, democratic participation increases as residents confront ways to improve conditions in their immediate environment, often causing social discord in the process. According to Crenson, "good neighborhoods" emerge and participation is energized when diverse interests and hence conflict are manifested among neighbors who personally know each other.

As Ventriss (1985) notes, critical democracy implies that citizens will struggle with the meaning of such philosophical and practical concerns as democratic theory, civic virtue and responsibility, social equity, group conflict and cooperation, community structure, institutional organization, individual rights, the public interest, and the distribution of power. In this sense, critical democracy is not simply a set of institutional changes, however far-reaching. As Dewey (1927) notes in his view of the "Great Community," democratic empowerment also involves a corresponding transformation of human practices and modes of consciousness. Underlying many of these concerns is the dialectical tension that exists within a critical democracy between the values of individuality and of community. This dialectical tension is at the core of this book's thesis; therefore, a brief examination of it is required.

INDIVIDUALITY AND COMMUNITY

In order to sustain a critical democracy within society, the balance between the values of individuality and community must be maintained. On the one hand, individuals within a critical democracy must be not only free but also actively supported in their efforts to "self-actualize" (Fromm, 1956; Maslow, 1976). One's ability to focus on one's desires, fears, hopes, dreams, and creativity in order to existentially "know oneself" is important for any society that wishes to promote freedom and human dignity. In addition, society needs to provide opportunities for individuals to lead self-determined lives. Having occasions for individuals to pursue their inner callings, to achieve beyond typical expectations, and to have those achievements recognized is also a sign of a dynamic, democratic society. Finally, within a critical democracy there is an active tolerance of individual uniqueness and self-expression (religion, ethnic heritage, race, gender, sexual preference, emerging life-styles, social and political ideas, and creative and performing arts). Human diversity is appreciated.

However, the value of individuality must be equally balanced by an ethos of community. As Barber (1984: 100) states,

> [Individual] freedom is a social construct based on a rare and fragile form of human mutualism that grants space to individuals who otherwise would have none at all. . . . the will [individual spirit] unimpeded by external obstacles is not free in any recognizable human sense until it is informed by purpose, meaning, context, and history. Solitude, when it is not simply an illusion, is not freedom but misanthropy. Self-direction brings freedom only when the self is emancipated from mere impulse and appetite, when it is associated with intention and purposes that by their nature can only arise within the guiding limits of a society and a culture. To be unimpeded and infinitely mobile is not freedom but deracination, unless by *free* we mean only "homeless."

Each individual's self-actualization can be fully realized only within a just and caring society. Individual goals must be balanced by deep and sincere attitudes of altruism, compassion, cooperation, and civic responsibility and the social structures that support them. *Freedom* within this context suggests nonexploitative psychological, social, and economic relations and the belief that our individual identities cannot be seen as separate from the organic, interdependent system of humankind, what Maslow (1976: 179-180) calls our "specieshood."

Democracy cannot survive in societies if the dialectical tension between individuality and community gets out of balance. As Lesko (1988: 10) notes, "Individuals need to be concerned with the public realm [community], and a just society needs strong, autonomous individuals to keep it responsive, self-critical and dynamic." When the value of either individuality or community significantly supersedes the other, then the one which dominates distorts the democratic ideal. For example, if tilted in the direction of individuality, an ideology of individualism emerges. This ideology suggests that individual self-interest is the essential principle upon which society is based. Autonomous individuals are seen as existing prior to and separate from social arrangements, and are thus seen as more important than societal associations. In fact, individualism legitimates a view of society as little more than a stage upon which the individual "acts" to obtain his or her desires. The public sphere is, for the most part, an abstraction; only the aspirations of the individual are real. As a result, "society" can be justifiably manipulated by the individual for his or her benefit. Naturally, individualism assumes that the solitary soul is entitled to all prosperity that can be identified as resulting from his or her achievements. As a result, the societal rewards (economic advancement, social status, social mobility) for self-centered achievements are great, and the forfeitures for more communal endeavors are apparent to those who do not choose to work for personal advancement. From this perspective, society improves when individuals are free to pursue their own, idiosyncratic interests with minimal restrictions. In this manner, individualism implicitly justifies a moral posture of selfishness. As Wood (1972: 127) states, "An 'individualistic' society . . . is characterized by privatization and atomistic social relations, which, if not synonymous with egoism . . . always threaten to degenerate into it." If society tries to restrain the efforts of the individual, it is perceived as oppressive and villainous.

Similarly, if the value of community dominates in a given society, it is transformed into an ideology of social conformism. This ideology suggests that the needs of society as a whole are so important that autonomous individuals are a potential threat by their mere existence. From this perspective, the only good is the "common good." Pursuing personal interests or any diversion from fulfilling the common goals of society is viewed as "self-indulgent vanity." In order to promote this sense of common purpose, there is a clearly defined and uniform understanding of how people should look, how they should act, and what they should think. Deviance from the norm is seen as unnatural or treasonous. Passive obedience to authority is elevated to the level of moral obligation. Social conformism justifies prohibitions against examining ideas openly and critically on the grounds that some ideas will clearly undermine the social fabric (often presented in nationalistic or religious terms) that holds society together. Since individuals do not exist in any meaningful way outside of society, the "social order" must be defended (through fear, intimidation, ostracism, or even death) against deviant views and actions. As Mayer (1955) illustrates, when social conformism is highly successful, it is capable of convincing the vast majority of those who live within it that the protection of society against people who are "different" is at the crux of their personal freedom, as in the case of Germany's National Socialism during the 1930s and 1940s.

Striving for balance between individuality and community is central to establishing a critical democracy. The suggestion that elementary schooling can be used to help advance this democratic ideal in our society cannot be considered in a vacuum: that is, all practices, both real and proposed, must be seen in light of a particular socio-historical context. Since the purpose of this book is to explore the way in which elementary education can foster critical democracy in the United States (and possibly other similarly structured societies), it is necessary to briefly relate the previous discussion to the American experience.

THE RISE OF INDIVIDUALISM IN THE UNITED STATES

The dominance of individualism at the expense of community as a social value in the United States has been substantiated by a diverse body of historical, philosophical, anthropological, sociological, psychological, and educational research (Damico, 1978; Dewey, 1930; Elshtain, 1981; Huber, 1971; Lasch, 1978; Lesko, 1988; Lukes, 1973; Nisbet, 1990; Peck, 1987; Sennett, 1977; Varenne, 1977; Wood, 1972). Dewey (1930: 13) notes that our society often recognizes the importance of community values:

> We praise even our most successful men, not for their ruthless and self-centered energy in getting ahead, but because of their love of flowers, children, and dogs, or their kindness to aged relatives. Anyone who frankly urges a selfish creed of life is everywhere frowned upon.

However, his examination of the social and economic institutions and cultural values that underlie our daily interactions reveals "that the personal traits most prized would be clear-sighted vision of personal advantage and resolute ambition to secure it at any human cost. Sentiment and sympathy would be at the lowest discount" (Dewey, 1930: 12). More recent analyses suggest that the dominant purposes and goals among Americans (especially among middle- and upper-class whites, that is, those with the most power) are expressed in individualistic terms. For example, Nisbet's (1990) examination of postwar society illuminates the way in which individualism and the quest for status have flourished in the United States while those components of society that foster the development of community, such as the family, certain religious organizations, labor unions, and social service agencies, have been considerably weakened. Bellah and his colleagues (1985) suggest that although values of civic responsibility are strongly felt in fragments of our populations, the vast majority of our present-day society lacks a meaningful "language" that clearly reflects a desire to work for the public good. President

Reagan's 1980 campaign slogan, "Are you [as an individual rather than the country as a whole] better off today than you were four years ago?" is illustrative of the individualistic orientation of our society. Lasch (1978) suggests that the American preoccupation with individual advancement has escalated dramatically in the past few decades, resulting in a "culture of narcissism." To fully appreciate the influence that individualism has over our society, however, an overview of those factors which have contributed to its rise is necessary.

Heritage

The liberty to control one's own life is perhaps the most widely acknowledged and passionately felt American value. Personal initiative to obtain privately motivated goals is a value deeply rooted in our heritage. Huber's (1971: 10-11) study of "American success" illustrates the beginnings of individualism upon this continent.

> The idea of success was a force which drove men on to build America. At the center was the individual. Self-confident in his God-given rights, he entered a free world of expanding opportunities. . . . Under American conditions . . . there developed a hunger for wealth. It was not the sensuous hunger of an oriental potentate, but a moral hunger fed on the awareness that one's self-esteem depended on the results.

Many immigrants who initially settled on this continent did so in the name of personal liberty and the right to build one's "own empire."

In his midnineteenth-century study of the United States, Alexis de Tocqueville devotes attention to the "individualism" that he saw as the essence of "American democracy."

> [Americans] owe nothing to any man, they expect nothing from any man; they acquire the habit of always considering themselves as standing alone, and they are apt to imagine that their whole destiny is in their own hands. Thus not only does democracy make every man forget his ancestors, but it hides his descendants, and separates his contemporaries from him. . . . As for the rest of his fellow citizens, he is close to them, but he does not feel them; he exists only in himself and for himself alone; and if his kindred still remain to him, he may be said at any rate to have lost his country. (Tocqueville, 1948: 99)

Early American authors such as Ben Franklin, Walt Whitman, and Ralph Waldo Emerson often acclaimed the development of "the self" over society. "The union is only perfect when all the uniters are isolated. . . . Each man, if he attempts to join himself to others, is . . . diminished. . . . The Union must be ideal in actual individualism" (Emerson, 1929: 318). Individual liberty, separation from past traditions and social arrangements, and personal freedom to "prosper" without restrictions were promoted as the founding values of American democracy and rooted the ideology of individualism deep into our psychic soil.

Corporate Economy

Although individualism is tied to our national heritage, several analysts suggest that its dominance crystallized during the rapid growth of industrial capitalism in the early part of this century. In discussing the reason behind this rise of individualism, Dewey (1930: 9) notes, "Anthropologically speaking, we are living in a money culture. Its cult and rites dominate." As Lukes (1973: 26) suggests,

> It was in the United States that "individualism" primarily came to celebrate capitalism and liberal democracy. It became (by the early twentieth century) a symbolic catchword of immense ideological significance, expressing all that has at various times been implied in the philosophy of natural rights, the belief in free enterprise, and the American Dream . . . advancing a set of universal claims seen as incompatible with the parallel claims of the socialism and communism of the Old World.

Corporate capitalism justified an ethos of unlimited personal gain with "the claim that private accumulation leads to public welfare" (Lukes, 1973: 30). Industrialists such as Andrew Carnegie, John D. Rockefeller, Henry Ford, and Andrew Mellon became America's heroes—proof that any individual could achieve greatness in a "system of Individualism which guards, protects, and encourages competition" (Clews, 1907: 1).

This emerging corporate structure drastically altered the nature of work by emphasizing specialization, the division of labor, and the solidification of economic classes. Prior to this development, it was widely understood that interdependence and economic interrelatedness were needed for the production of goods. Individuals often became skilled at many different crafts. However, under industrial advances and incorporation, specialization was needed to maintain a competitive edge. Work was segmented into different tasks, and workers were seen as fragmented abilities (Braverman, 1974; Edwards, 1979; Gordon, Edwards, & Reich, 1982). Contractual relations among individuals served as the model for the new industrial society. These relationships minimized one's connection to the past and future. Only an individual's capabilities at any one moment were deemed important. Each person was viewed as essentially unrelated to a social group or society at large.

This corporate ethos legitimated individual competition as an ethical basis for economic productivity and gained support during this same time period from the theory of social Darwinism. As Hofstadter (1945: 174) notes, this theory proposed that those individuals who "won" within a competitive social framework were examples of our species' continuing evolution.

> American society saw its own image in the tooth-and-claw version of natural selection, and that its dominant groups were therefore able to dramatize this vision of competition as a thing good in itself. Ruthless business rivalry and unprincipled politics seemed to be justified by the survival philosophy. As long as the dream of personal conquest and individual assertion motivated the middle class, this philosophy seemed tenable, and its critics remained a minority.

Although most businessmen did not rationalize their personal success by social Darwinism, some major industrial leaders invoked this theory to defend their elimination of competition and consolidation of businesses under a single corporation. Take, for example, the often quoted statement by John D. Rockefeller, Jr.:

> The growth of a large business is merely a survival of the fittest. . . . the American Beauty rose can be produced in the splendor and fragrance which bring cheer to its beholder only by sacrificing the early buds which grow up around it. This is not an evil tendency in business. It is merely the working out of a law of nature and law of God. (Quoted in Huber, 1971: 66)

Darwinian individualism encouraged the majority of our population to take this economic structure largely for granted.

> And if the culture [sic] pattern works out so that society is divided into two classes, the working group and the business (including professional) group, with two and a half times as many in the former as in the latter, and with the chief ambition of parents in the former class that their children should climb into the latter, that is doubtless because American life offers such unparalleled opportunities for each individual to prosper according to his virtues. If few workers know what they are making or the meaning of what they do, and still fewer know what becomes of the work of their hands—in the largest industry of Middletown perhaps one-tenth of one percent of the product is consumed locally—this is doubtless because we have so perfected our system of distribution that the whole country is one. And if the mass of workers live in constant fear of loss of their jobs, this is doubtless because our spirit of progress, manifest in change of fashions, invention of new machines and power of overproduction, keeps everything on the move. Our reward of industry and thrift is so accurately adjusted to individual ability that it is natural and proper that the workers should look forward with dread to the age of fifty or fifty-five, when they will be laid on the shelf. All this we take for granted; it is treated as an inevitable part of our social system. To dwell on the dark side of it is to blaspheme against our religion of prosperity. (Dewey, 1930: 10-11)

Even when the "dark side" was recognized, it was often presented as a necessary evil as reflected in the philosophy of social Darwinism. For example, in one of his most famous articles (published in the *North American Review* in 1889), Andrew Carnegie noted that in an individualistic economy some men accumulate fortunes because of their "natural talents," and that society pays a large price as a result: the division of economic classes is rigidly formed. Because of competition, employers are forced to hold wages down, and in some instances fire unnecessary workers. As a result, there is often tension between the owner and his work force. As companies grow larger, employers and employees become strangers and are often distrustful of each other. However, he went on to state that

> the advantages of this law [social Darwinism] are also greater still, for it is to this law that we owe our wonderful material development. . . . While the law may be sometimes hard for the individual, it is best for the race, because it insures the survival of the fittest in every department. (Quoted in Huber, 1971: 69)

Thus, the basic structure of a corporate economy legitimates, depends upon, and promotes the ideology of individualism. Not only is economic individualism (the encouragement of competition, specialization, and the division of labor) good for society in general because it increases the production of goods, but it also reflects our natural evolution as a species.

The adulation of competitiveness so apparent during our early industrial growth has become somewhat muted, and as Hofstadter (1945: 174) suggests, the middle class eventually "shrank from the principle [social Darwinism] it had glorified, turned in flight from the hideous image of rampant competitive brutality, and repudiated the once heroic entrepreneur as a despoiler of the nation's wealth and morals." However, in the present-day era of yuppies, insider trading, and flagrant unethical and in some cases illegal use of political influence for personal gain, it is *easy to see why* Hofstadter (1945: 175) also notes that the "critics of Darwinian individualism" have been relatively ineffective in altering the material and political structure of society. The "win-lose" approach to social proceedings that is reflected in individualism remains intact.

Patriarchy

Patriarchy has also played an important role in the promotion of individualism. *Patriarchy* refers to a system of thought and subsequent actions that sanctions male authority over women. In society, patriarchy is characterized by particular economic, cultural, and psychological relationships among men of all classes, races, and ethnic groups that formally and informally oppress women and men who do not conform to and reflect a masculine rationality, physical appearance, and style of behavior (Hartmann, 1984). As several analysts have noted, patriarchy promotes a set of manly values (competition, individual achievement, aggressiveness, objectivity) while at the same time implicitly repudiating alleged feminine values of subjectivity, empathy, caring, and bonding (Belenky, Clinchy, Goldberger, & Tarule, 1986; Elshtain, 1981; Gilligan, 1982; Noddings, 1984; Spender, 1980). For example, Hubbard (1979) exposes the way in which Darwin's theory of evolution justified the superiority of this masculine ethos.

> Woman seems to differ from man in mental disposition, chiefly in her greater tenderness and less selfishness. . . . Man is the rival of other men; he delights in competition, and this leads to ambition which passes too easily into selfishness. These latter qualities seem to be his natural and unfortunate birthright. . . . [Men have had] to defend their females, as well as their young, from enemies of all kinds, and to hunt for their joint subsistence. But to avoid enemies or to attack them with success, to capture wild animals, and to fashion weapons, requires the aid of the higher mental faculties, namely, observation, reason, invention, or imagination. . . . Thus, man has ultimately become superior to woman. . . . (and if men did not genetically pass along some of their mental abilities to their daughters as well as their sons) it is probable that man would have become as superior in mental endowment to woman, as the peacock is in ornamental plumage to the peahen. (Quoted in Hubbard, 1979: 19-20)

Smith's (1978) analysis of symbolic communication within society illuminates how patriarchy has excluded women from having equal access in creating our intellectual and moral culture. Gilligan's (1982) research suggests that if the "voice" of women were included in our understanding of ethical action and societal arrangements, then the values of community (altruism, caring, civic responsibility, compassion, human connection, and safety from violence) would be significantly stronger in our society than they currently are. As Dietz (1985: 34) states,

> Feminist historians have discovered that women develop distinctive organizational styles and generate reform movements, act collectively and in distinctively democratic ways, agitate for social change and challenge political corruption. . . . If we are to [improve society] . . . we would do well to look to our [women's] history, our organizational styles, and our distinctive modes of political discourse.

Since Western civilization has been dominated by a male consciousness for several thousand years (Elshtain, 1981; Janssen-Jurreit, 1980; Keller, 1985; Smith, 1978; Spender, 1980), it is not surprising that our conception of societal relations reflects a masculine ethos which in turn legitimates and fosters the same set of values as individualism.

Popular Culture

The final factor that has contributed to firmly establishing individualism as a societal creed is our popular culture. Durkheim (1933) and more recent analysts (Bellah et al.,1985; Giddens, 1971; Giroux & Simon, 1988; Vivas, 1955) acknowledge the integral role that art, religion, popularized philosophical themes, and other cultural practices play in establishing society's "moral order," through which societal values are declared "right" and "natural." Illustrations of the way in which our popular culture has championed individualism are not difficult to locate.

Huber (1971: 11) documents the manner through which Christianity during the colonial period of our nation's history "encouraged the accumulation of wealth [and] worked in harness with economics toward the goal of individual success." Popular religion helped Americans resolve the dilemma of Christian values that call people to have concern for the welfare of their neighbors versus capitalism's call for personal reward through active competition against one's fellow human beings by assuring people that their prosperity was a form of "God's work" because their wealth was being used for good purposes (the building of a Christian society). Since the 1930s, religion has been used not merely to justify the accumulation of wealth but also to obtain riches. If one *truly believes*, one can expect prosperity. From this perspective, "getting ahead in order to get right with God [was supplanted by] getting right with God in order to get ahead" (Huber, 1971: 332). Jim and Tammy Bakker, Jimmy Swaggart, Jerry Falwell, Oral Roberts, and other televangelists have, of course, turned this utilitarian interpretation of religion into a "performing art."

As industrial capitalism emerged, a secularized amorality or "radical subjectivity" (Sennett, 1977: 22) replaced Christianity as philosophical guidance for many individuals' personal actions. Under this personality ethic, individual ambition no longer had to be morally justified. Personal achievement was considered a manifestation of a "healthy personality." Dale Carnegie's (1936) *How to Win Friends and Influence People* became a prototype for an entire genre of popular literature that claimed to help individuals "get ahead." As illustrated in his book, learning effective communication and interpersonal skills is not seen as a way to increase communication and interpersonal harmony but as a means to manipulate others to satisfy one's own desires. With the proliferation of the "pop psychology" manuals and courses now in vogue, the social Darwinist proverb "survival of the fittest" has been replaced by more innocuous aphorisms such as "Do your own thing," "Look out for #1," or the army's latest contribution, "Be all that you can be." However, the basic message is the same: individual success and accomplishment is what life is all about.

This value of individual achievement has been supported through our popular arts, entertainment, and literature. The preeminence of the individual who "wins out" over social groups and forces is a conventional plot of print and visual media. Images of "superheroes" who are capable of "standing alone and winning" against overwhelming forces fill the pages of popular literature and scenes from films. Contemporary folk heroes such as athletes, entertainment stars, and political personalities give credence to the belief in an individualistic route to success and provide proof that this is a country where "anyone" can "make it." Popular television shows such as "Lifestyles of the Rich and Famous" and "Dynasty" lead us to believe that our society's greatness lies in the fact that it provides opportunities for individuals to gain power and wealth.

The Ironies of Individualism

There are a number of ironies implanted in American individualism. While generating an image of individual autonomy and uniqueness, insofar as this ideology has reflected and helped maintain a corporate economy, it has encouraged a state of social conformism. As Dewey (1930: 36) notes,

> The United States has steadily moved . . . to a condition of dominant corporateness. The influence business corporations exercise in determining present industrial and economic activities is both a cause and a symbol of the tendency to combination in all phases of life. Associations tightly or loosely organized more and more define the opportunities, the choices and the actions of individuals.

He goes on to suggest that although this "corporateness" brings us into association with others, these associations lack any sense of true community. We work side by side, day by day, yet few of us feel a genuine connection. What is left is an existence of conformity. Our corporate institutions keep us together but also keep us apart in that the motives and incentives that underlie these institutions are individualistic. At the same time these institutions are often indifferent (or antagonistic) to the individuality of those who work in them.

> The growth of corporateness is arbitrarily restricted. Hence it operates to limit individuality, to put burdens on it, to confuse and submerge it. It crowds more out than it incorporates in an ordered and secure life. . . . An economic individualism of motives and aims underlies our present corporate mechanisms, and undoes the individual. (Dewey, 1930: 58-59)

Since only a very few individuals can actually manifest their unique thoughts, values, or artistry within this corporate structure, the vast majority are left huddled together in a passive uniformity.

> Hence, the irony of the gospel of individualism. . . . One cannot imagine
> a bitterer comment on any professed individualism than that it [individu-
> alism] subordinates the only creative individuality—that of mind—to the
> maintenance of a regime which gives the few an opportunity for being
> shrewd in the management of monetary business. (Dewey, 1930: 91)

As corporate capitalism has grown, it has absorbed many areas of social
life to fit a relatively narrow pattern of marketplace relationships. Today,
as in Dewey's time, much of our life is reflected in economic metaphors
of working, buying, selling, and ownership. We become deluded into
thinking that our individuality is part and parcel to what we own. While
flaunting our ability to choose from an abundance of commercial goods,
we channel our desires into a relatively narrow range of how life could be
lived as we come to identify ourselves as primarily "consumers" (Adler,
1977; Ewen, 1976; Ward, Wackman, & Wartella, 1977). Ewen (1976:
214-215) asserts,

> In the years following World War II, . . . the injection of corporate bonding
> into the interstices of existence was altering and attempting to safely
> standardize the common perception of daily life. While heralding a world
> of unprecedented freedom and opportunity, corporations . . . were
> generating a mode of existence which was increasingly regimented and
> authoritarian. If consumer culture was a parody of the popular desire for
> self-determination and meaningful community, its innards revealed the
> growing standardization of . . . what was to be consumed and
> experienced.

As our personalities become aligned with the needs of our corporate
economy, our "individuality" is, in part, reduced to choosing the brand of
beer or cigarette that "singles us out from the crowd." Dewey (1930) attacked
the ideology of individualism for its mythical powers. While creating a
compelling image of the solitary individual making the most of his or her
life, societies based upon individualism actually provide few opportunities
for most people to manifest this individuality. It is a significant paradox that
individualism and social conformism coexist as parts of the same social order
in advanced corporate societies such as the United States.

A second irony embedded in America's individualism is found in the
myth that it provides an opportunity for each person to become "self-
actualized." Sennett and Cobb (1972) argue that since success in our society
is presented as the result of one's own doing rather than in a context of
social class, race, and gender which results in an unequal distribution of
power and privilege, the self-esteem of working-class people (and other
nonwhite, poor, and female persons) is implicitly and insidiously undercut.
Since "upward mobility" is presented in our culture as the rule rather than

the exception, one's failure to succeed is tacitly connected to one's personal shortcomings, not to class, race, or gender inequities. Since our society is inherently disparate along the lines previously mentioned, many individuals who are unable to obtain "upward mobility" are left with a feeling of personal failure. The realization of one's dreams, aspirations, and self-actualization is indubitably easier for those in our society who are already privileged than for those who happen to be born nonwhite, working class, homosexual, handicapped, or female. However, individualism obscures the reality of social privilege and power from our consciousness, thus making it more difficult to understand ourselves and grow.

A final irony found in individualism is that, although it promotes the view that we can determine our destiny, its emphasis on individualistic solutions to societal problems restrains us from doing so. Many people feel dehumanized and without a sense of personal identity in their encounters with social institutions (schools, workplaces, shopping centers, governmental institutions). In response, they withdraw from public spheres and devote their energies to highly personal projects. Moustakas (1961: 25) paints a grim picture of what is happening to many within our society.

> The individual no longer has an intimate sense of relatedness to the food he eats, the clothing he wears, the shelter which houses him. He no longer participates directly in the creation and production of the vital needs of his family and community. He no longer fashions with his own hands or from the desires of his heart. Modern man does not enjoy the companionship, support, and protection of his neighbors. He has been sharply cut off from primary groups and from family and kinship ties. He lives in an impersonal urban or suburban community where he meets others not as real persons but according to prescribed rules of conduct and prescribed modes of behavior. He strives to acquire the latest in comfort, convenience, and fashion. He works in a mechanized society, in which he is primarily a consumer, separated from any direct and personal contact with creation. Modern man is starving for communion with his fellow man and with other aspects of life and nature.

In spite of this desire for communion, the impersonality of our major institutions and social arrangements is often taken for granted as "natural." As we grow to distrust and recoil from the public arenas of life, we become increasingly isolated and begin to believe that "what is" cannot be transformed (Lasch, 1978; Sennett, 1977). Although many of us intuitively know that "something is missing," individualistic responses to societal alienation hinder us from working collectively to build an alternative social order and to take control of our mutual destiny.

Summary

This abridged account situates individualism deep within the political and social fabric of our society. Our heritage, economic structure, system of patriarchy, and mass culture all contribute to the growth and entrenchment of individualism as a national ideology. Although this ideology is offered as a source of personal liberation, in many ways it prevents most individuals from achieving genuine self-knowledge (which implies a fundamental connection to other human beings) and authentic power over their lives. By fostering the perception that there is an essential opposition between one's personal advancement and a commitment to the public good, individualism erodes the possibilities for genuine democracy.

Although individualism reigns in our society, it is crucial that we also emphasize that it is not an all-pervasive ideology. As Varenne (1977) notes, just as individual autonomy has its roots in the American tradition, so does a sense of neighborliness, civic concern, and a desire to "fit into" one's social group. Although the social value of community is not as strongly felt in our society as other values, its presence is recognizable. First, various immigrant groups struggle to maintain their community values in the face of pressures to assimilate, and there is evidence that not all members of ethnic groups have adopted white, upper-middle-class values of individual achievement over community responsibility (Feldstein, 1979; Hostetler & Huntington, 1971; Kleinfeld, 1979; Rodriguez, 1982). In addition, there have been periods in our history when people have strongly advocated establishing a greater community ethos within our society. The union movement during the 1930s, the civil rights activities that began in the 1950s, the 1960s peace movement, and most recently the feminist movement are just a few examples of efforts to reduce the power of individualism in our society. It is important to avoid viewing society as monolithic. At any given time, there are individuals and groups of people who work consciously to build a more balanced society that appreciates both individuality and community.

INDIVIDUALISM AND ELEMENTARY SCHOOLING

Contemporary Americans live much of their lives in formal institutions that exist outside of family structures. For the vast majority of citizens, most of the waking hours are spent in work sites or schools. Even much of our recreational time is spent in formal organizations (Boy/Girl Scouts, Lions Club). Institutions can be seen as "worlds" within themselves. As Berger and Luckmann (1967: 59) state, "Institutions, by the very fact of their existence, control human conduct by setting up predefined patterns of conduct which control it in one direction as against the many other directions that would theoretically be possible." As might be expected, institutions reflect and to some degree mediate the values and social relations found in a given society.

One of the most important institutions within an industrialized society such as ours is school. All citizens spend a considerable amount of their childhood inside school buildings. Schools teach children about society through subjects such as social studies, science, and literature. However, the form and structure of schools also teach children about societal values and arrangements. Given this situation, elementary schools play an important role in supporting and promoting individualism within the United States.

Individualism is both reflected and nourished in most elementary schools through their organizational structure and curricular content and form. Almost without exception, elementary schools assume that learning is an individual experience. "Individualizing instruction" is a popular educational goal. In recent years, there have been several programs developed for elementary schools that systematically "individualize" classroom learning (Talmadge, 1975). PLAN (Program for Learning in Accordance with Needs) is representative of this popular system of instruction.

> The basic building block in PLAN is the TLU ("Teaching-Learning Unit"), which includes instructional objectives associated with recommended learning activities and criterion tests. A guidance system uses data on students and draws upon a bank of available TLU's to recommend an individualized program of studies (POS) for each student. The POS is individualized on the basis of both the number and type of activities the student pursues. A computer facility is used in PLAN to collect information concerning the progress and performance of students from terminals located in the participating schools. This information is processed for feedback to students and teachers and is stored for record-keeping purposes and for use in the management aspects of the system. . . . The development of PLAN was not based on any one particular learning or instructional theory. It was founded, rather, on the belief that an educational program should use the individual student and his needs as the basis for a complete educational system. (Flanagan, Shanner, Brudner, & Marker, 1975: 136, 139)

Although not all elementary schools have adopted such an extreme form of individualized instruction, most follow similar practices. Elementary students spend the vast majority of their school day working at individual desks in single rows, answering questions and problems in separate workbooks or worksheets, individually taking tests, and asking questions related to their individual concerns in order to finish prescribed schoolwork (Goodlad, 1984; Sarason, 1982). In this sense, individualized instruction has little to do with developing the individuality of students, that is, with responding to each child's unique learning style, recognizing and giving voice to the personal knowledge base that each student brings to school, and consciously promoting each child's originality, creativity, thoughtfulness, and efficacy. Rather, as practiced in most schools, individualized education refers to an instructional design that separates each child's learning from that of his or her classmates and focuses on his or her particular achievement in standardized curriculum content. Instruction is individualized in the sense that if a child shows a weakness in a particular "skill," there are specialized drills and tests that focus the student's learning tasks upon his or her "deficiency" until it can be "mastered" (Carlson, 1982).

This isolated learning supports a competitive learning environment. There are few activities which necessitate cooperative learning in most elementary classrooms. The contributions or ideas of one's classmates are rarely seen as important to one's own learning. Rarely do students develop the feeling that they are studying or exploring subject matter "together," as a class or group. Because of tracking in such subjects as reading and math (which dominate the school day), each child is painfully aware of his or her individual "standing" in the class (Oakes, 1985). Henry (1956) suggests that in most schools one student's success is inherently connected to another student's failure. Consequently, students learn to work within an adversarial atmosphere. They are taught that the only thing that is important in school is their own achievement.

Individualism is also reflected in the form and content of the elementary curriculum found in most schools. Subjects such as history typically present a view of life as something in which only a few individuals (usually white men) actually participate. In most elementary schools, knowledge is broken down into "skills" that are taught outside of an intellectual context. Reading, writing, and math are emphasized over substantive content, reflective thinking, or artistic talent (Goodlad, 1984). As a result, elementary education takes on a narrow, utilitarian orientation. These skill "subjects" are broken down further into individual segments or "objectives," which are then taught and tested separately. For example, reading in most elementary schools is not viewed as a holistic activity that involves the child's imagination and his or her relationship to people, books, knowledge, or language; rather, it is defined as the summation of discrete phonics, comprehension, contextual, and structural analysis skills. These skills are further broken down into hundreds of specific subskills that are taught and tested separately. Instead of being viewed as subjectively created and integrated, knowledge is conceived as something existing outside of the human mind that can be understood only by being tested within a controlled setting. Lukes (1973: 110) refers to this perception of knowledge accumulation and generation as "methodological individualism," and it has served as the guiding principle in our conceptualization of how knowledge should be treated within schools.

As many analysts have documented (Apple, 1979, 1986; Callahan, 1962; Giroux & Penna, 1977; Haubrich, 1971), elementary schools have adopted the bureaucratic organizational system found in corporate business. To a great degree, schools are structured in such a way as to promote a division of labor within a hierarchical system. Principals manage the physical plant and staff; teachers teach the curriculum content; psychologists test children; special education teachers teach children with special needs; social workers deal with the children's emotional or family problems as they are related to pupil performance in the schools; and students "consume" school knowledge as they work on their assignments. In addition, teachers work in segregated classrooms and rarely have opportunities to actively communicate or participate in educational decisions with their colleagues. As Sarason (1982) notes, teachers often cite this professional isolation as a central aspect of their job experience.

Individualism is also reflected in most elementary schools through the adoption of an "official" policy of moral relativism. Although there are clearly subtle systems for the social control of "acceptable" school knowledge and values (Anyon, 1979; Apple, 1986; McLaren, 1986; Popkewitz, 1987), schools present themselves as "neutral" institutions in which all beliefs are considered of equal value. Numerous individuals advocate that schools should have no role in helping children determine what is right or wrong. Schooling should be limited to simply teaching the skills and basic cultural information that individual children will need to compete in society. From this perspective, education promotes the supremacy of individual opinion over the struggle to establish a set of values to promote the common good.

Through an emphasis on competition, individual achievement, utilitarian skills, the atomization of knowledge, separation of labor, and official moral relativism, individualism has become an underlying foundation for our society's schooling. In this manner, individualism is persuasively woven into our children's consciousness; that is, traditional school practices take on a quality that makes them "commonplace" and thus not easily available for analysis (Sarason, 1982). As in society, the individualism upon which schools are based often promotes an organizational and curricular structure that ironically results in the establishment of social conformism. Although isolated in their work, all children actually do the same type of work, study the same content, and are expected to learn in a similar fashion (memorization and drill) and at a designated pace. In addition, dress codes often limit what students can wear, and censorship limits students' intellectual ideas in most schools. In this sense, individualistic schools contribute to teachers' and students' alienation from themselves as individuals, from others with whom they work, and from the work in which they are engaged (Greene, 1973; Macdonald & Zaret, 1975; Pinar,1975). However, just as in the larger society, there are teachers and schools that consciously work towards a more balanced, community-orientated education for children (Kleinfeld, 1979; Kuzmic, 1988; Lein, 1975; Mayhew & Edwards, 1966; Teitelbaum, 1987; Wu, 1988).

CRITICAL DEMOCRACY AND RADICAL EDUCATIONAL REFORM

Popkewitz (1983) convincingly argues that formulating a vision of what education "should be" cannot be accomplished without addressing the type of society in which one hopes to live, or, as Dewey (1966: 97) states, "The conception of education as a social process and function has no definite meaning until we define the kind of society we have in mind." For the purpose of this project, the image of a critical democracy has been developed to give form to the nature of the society we wish to help establish; that is, our desire is to address practices of elementary education that will prepare children for a society in which citizens are intellectually aware of the world around them, are capable of taking an active role in promoting democracy in all spheres of social life, are encouraged to develop their unique individuality, and can exhibit a vital concern for not only their own well-being but also the well-being of all people (as well as all other species of animals and plants) who live on our planet.

The paradox that individualism and social conformity coexist as part of the same social and economic order in our society makes developing strategies for its transformation difficult. Clearly, the education of children by itself cannot produce the type of alterations necessary to transform our society from a liberal, political democracy into a critical democracy. Political analysts such as Barber (1984), Boyte (1980, 1984), and Gran (1983) illustrate several strategies within various spheres of society that can help move our society towards critical democracy. As Barber (1984) notes, the central task of those interested in establishing critical democracy is to invent processes, organizations, and forms of citizenship that nurture political judgment, democratic talk, deliberation, and public action. Eventually, fundamental changes in all our economic and social institutions will be needed to build a critically democratic society. However, Dewey (and other, more recent critics such as Paulo Freire [1973]) argues that the key to transforming society lies in transforming the consciousness of its citizens, which can be successfully accomplished only through education as opposed to imposition. Although imposing change might alter societal structures, it also distorts human intelligence and thus ends by preventing the establishment of genuine democracy.

> Doctrines, whether proceeding from Mussolini or Marx, which assume that
> because certain ends are desirable therefore those ends and nothing else
> will result from the use of force to attain them is [sic] but another example
> of the limitations put on intelligence by any absolutist theory. In the degree
> in which mere force is resorted to, actual consequences are themselves
> so compromised that the ends originally in view have in fact to be worked
> out afterwards by the method of experimental intelligence. (Dewey, 1946:
> 139)

Dewey goes on to argue that children's education must play a central role
in this societal metamorphosis. Children "are not as yet subject to the full
impact of established customs"; therefore, "the chief means of continuous
. . . social rectification lies in utilizing the opportunities of educating the
young to modify prevailing types of thought and desire" (Dewey, 1922:
127-128). In acknowledging the need to transform society through the
modification of our public consciousness, it is essential that we see children's
education at the core of democratic activity *prior to* changes in other spheres
of society, *during* any changes that take place in these spheres, and *after*
social and economic institutions have been fundamentally altered.

In building a critical democracy, there is clear need for radical educational
reform. As Graubard (1972: 7) states,

> An approach to school reform that can reasonably be called *radical* does
> not concern itself much with moderate changes of technique. The emphasis
> is on the process of socialization and the kinds of character traits and values
> that are encouraged; the functions like "tracking" children to fit along social
> class lines to future job possibilities; the detrimental effect of the authoritarian
> techniques of public schools on qualities like intellectual curiosity. To see
> that schools need *radical* reform depends on a perception of deep and
> pervasive harm that can be ascribed to the dominant structures, values,
> and techniques of the existing schools. The idea is not, as in the most
> moderate sense of reform, that we need to improve our techniques
> somewhat in order to better accomplish what is already being done.

As previously mentioned, it is not possible to address educational reform
outside of a particular social, political, and cultural context. Therefore, the
reform of elementary schooling to foster a critical democracy in the United
States must confront our national preoccupation with individualism.

However, Cagan's (1978) analysis suggests that much of what passes
for "radical school reform" proposals (either within public schools or in the
creation of alternative private schools) fails to adequately address the
dialectical tension between the social values of individuality and community.
The response by many radical reformers to the hierarchical authoritarianism,
regimentation, and repressiveness found in traditional schools has been

incomplete or misguided in that it has fallen back upon the same individualism dominant within our society which inhibits more democratic forms of social arrangements to emerge. As Gross and Gross (1969: 14) point out in their book, *Radical School Reform*, "In social relations, radical means libertarian: an affirmation of the autonomy of the individual against the demands of the system." For example, in many alternative educational settings the sole emphasis is on catering to the individual child's interests and needs. A. S. Neill (1977: 114), a leading spokesperson for radical education reform, clearly articulates this orientation.

> We must allow the child to be selfish—ungiving—free to follow his own childish interests through his childhood. When the child's individual interests and his social interests clash, the individual interests should be allowed precedence. . . . I believe that to impose anything by authority is wrong. The child should not do anything until he comes to the opinion—his own opinion—that it should be done.

For many radical educators, any restrictions (except in situations that involve the safety of children) on an individual student's ideas or behavior are seen as inimical to "self-development." Freedom is viewed as the absence of external control over the individual.

Given this orientation, the notion that schools (or other institutions that have responsibility for children outside the immediate family) have the right to deliberately influence the values of children is an anathema to many concerned with the radical reform of education. As Graubard (1972: 222) notes,

> Reacting against authoritarianism and boring, sterile, simple-minded, and often propagandistic subject matter, some new schools people took their affirmation of freedom to imply never interfering with children, never asserting values and priorities with the knowledge that one was quite possibly influencing the young people, condemning the ideas of authority and the idea of the significance of subject matter—"the process of learning is what counts."

In reviewing the literature on radical school reform, one is struck by the insistence on personal liberty and the lack of attention given to the need for educating children in a manner that will develop their compassion, altruism, cooperation, civic responsibility, and commitment to work for the general welfare of our planet (Graubard, 1972; Gross & Gross, 1969; Silberman, 1973). Rather, the emphasis often is on simplistic rejection of that which is "bad," such as formal knowledge, skills, authority, or structure, and praise for that which is "good," such as individual freedom, creativity, or decision making. By locating liberty within a strictly anti-authoritarian context, many proponents of radical school reform project an educational agenda and structure that very much conform to and legitimate the individualistic ideology that dominates our society.

Cagan (1978) notes that conscious effort to influence the values and character of children should be undertaken only if there are compelling reasons. The impact of individualism, as a national ideology, upon our society and children provides such compelling reasons. If elementary schooling in the United States is to be reformed to promote critical democracy, then its organization and practices must be deliberately established to cultivate a "connectionist" perspective among its administrators, teachers, and students—that is, a perspective that places one's *connection* to the lives of all human beings and other living things on our planet at the center of the educational process.[4] Children need clear and consistent educational experiences that emphasize the social bonds and responsibilities that citizens exhibit in ideal democratic societies. The purposes for learning that are expressed to students must be situated in terms that highlight our concern for the collective good, rather than our concern simply to "get a job" or "beat Japan." The radical reforming of schools needs to be centered on helping children understand the ways in which life on this planet is interconnected and interdependent, and that in caring for others we are caring for ourselves. It is highly unlikely that a focus on personal freedom and liberating children from adult authority, as currently reflected in many radical school reforms, would adequately instruct children towards this connectionist perspective.

While legitimating the need to consciously structure children's education in order to develop a connectionist perspective among them, as Cagan (1978) cautions, it is important to avoid setting up school arrangements and practices that result in social conformism. For example, some schools that place great emphasis on the value of community (such as those found in the Soviet Union, China, or fundamentalist religions) have, in fact, established educational practices that promote social conformism (Bronfenbrenner, 1970; Kessen, 1975; Peshkin, 1986; Rose, 1988; Yesipov & Goncharov, 1947). Requiring unquestioned obedience and passive acquiescence to adult authority at all times, equating patriotism with the value of community, creating cult figures such as Joseph Stalin, Mao Tse-tung, or a particular religious leader to be blindly revered, stressing rote memorization and "correct" answers to even moral questions, and placing so much value on group solidarity that the individual who disagrees becomes "silenced" through intimidation are some of the instructional practices found in these schools that result in an education for social conformism rather than for critical democracy. To be genuinely effective and democratic, the effort to influence children's values in the direction of a connectionist orientation must be done in an atmosphere in which children can freely examine and express their convictions without fear of intimidation or banishment and in surroundings where children listen thoughtfully and critically to the convictions of their classmates and teachers. While recognizing the need to deliberately promote a moral agenda that accentuates community values in our society, we must also hold children's individuality, self-confidence, and participation in their own education in high esteem.

REFLECTIONS: LEARNING FROM EXPERIENCE

In a society that takes the values of self-interest and individual achievement for granted, a critical pedagogy that fosters a connectionist perspective reflects a radical alternative to the status quo. However, merely calling for schooling that will move our society towards a more equalized position vis-à-vis the dialectical tension between individuality and community does not address the need for a clear discourse on the programmatic elements and issues needed to spawn these more balanced young people. Most of the literature that calls for critical approaches to pedagogy remains on an obtuse level of abstraction, with few images from which to gain a true understanding of the authors' meaning and intent. As Ellsworth (1988: 2) notes, "This language [is] more appropriate (yet hardly more helpful) for philosophical debates about the highly problematic concepts of freedom, justice, democracy, and 'universal' values than for thinking through and planning classroom practices to support a political [and social] agenda." It is with these thoughts in mind that the present book is written. By locating this discourse within the lived experiences of the educators and students at Harmony School, we can enhance our insight into creating a pedagogy for critical democracy.

It is important to emphasize that we did not go into Harmony with a rigid, predetermined working definition of education for critical democracy. Initially, we were simply interested in observing the type of education that existed in an elementary school that expressed a desire to create educational experiences suited for a "democratic" society and that saw itself as providing alternatives to the traditional practices found in most schools. Our own understanding of critical democracy and the importance that the values of community and individuality played in establishing the democratic ideal emerged from our working with Harmony's teachers and students.

As will be discussed in the next chapter and as Cagan (1978) notes, the type of education being called for here is perhaps "easier" to establish in independent schools than in most of our current public schools. Creating an elementary education for critical democracy in public schools would be difficult without major shifts in our societal priorities, values, and resources. As we spent time observing Harmony's elementary school on a day-to-day basis, it became clear that students were being provided with an education balanced between the values of individuality and community. Students were encouraged to grow as unique individuals, to become thoughtful and active participants in their own learning and the learning of their fellow students, to cultivate a sensitivity to their own interests and needs as well as to the lives of their fellow students, and to develop their sense of social concern and responsibility. However, as previously mentioned, because of the power of individualism in the United States, it is our contention that schools such as Harmony need to emphasize values of community more than those of individuality; that is, radical educators need to consciously create a connectionist, rather than balanced, education if they are to counterbalance the dominance of individualism and effectively nurture critical democracy in our society. Although not ideal, schools such as Harmony do provide examples of educational practices that can be examined by educators in a variety of public and private settings who are interested in developing a connectionist pedagogy. In order to address this purpose, the remaining chapters will examine several issues. The next chapter explores how we can learn about elementary schooling for critical democracy by focusing on the social reality within a specific school. The following two chapters examine questions of power and control within this educational institution. The subsequent chapter investigates issues of curriculum and instruction, and a final chapter attempts to synthesize the previous discourse and to outline the possibilities for, and constraints upon, establishing an elementary pedagogy for critical democracy within our present societal context.

2

Learning from Reality:
Harmony School

As mentioned in the first chapter, establishing an elementary pedagogy for critical democracy will probably be ineffective if it is simply theorized in the halls of academia and then handed down to practicing teachers. Conceptions of needed pedagogical reforms will be most beneficial if grounded in the subjective voices of those involved in democratic educational actions. This book, however, is not an empirical study of a "democratic school." There is no attempt to "prove" that Harmony School is "better" than all other schools. It is not being suggested that Harmony should serve as a model to mindlessly mimic. Rather, this book represents an attempt to address those structures, practices, and issues of elementary education that will encourage the establishment of critical democracy in society and that are grounded in the lives of real people. Since much of what is being analyzed in this book is based on our experiences in a given school, we are called upon in this chapter to articulate our theoretical presuppositions concerning the nature of this social reality and the orientation used to learn from it. In addition, this chapter introduces the particular setting that is used as the focus for our learning, Harmony's elementary school. Finally, it presents an overview of the individuals who spent time in Harmony and the methods used to understand what was happening in this particular educational setting.

THEORETICAL CONSIDERATIONS IN A POSTPOSITIVIST ERA

A few years ago, N. L. Gage, who was honored with the 1988 Distinguished Contributions to Educational Research Award by the American Educational Research Association for his prolific, quantitative analyses of teaching, wrote an article in which he reviewed the "paradigm wars" that occurred during the 1980s and 1990s within education from the perspective of one who is speaking in the year 2009. In this piece, Gage (1989) outlines three possible scenarios that describe the outcomes of these "wars." In the first, positivist research quickly withers away in light of the criticisms brought upon it by "antinaturalists," "interpretivists," and "critical theorists." In the second, positivist researchers find a way to merge their interests, methodologies, and presuppositions with those of the three groups of scholars from the previously mentioned schools of criticism. The result is a blending of what at one time were seen as mutually exclusive paradigms into a unique, synthesized form of inquiry.[1] In the final version, the "wars" continue. What is particularly noteworthy about this article is the missing scenario. Here we have N. L. Gage, a longtime positivist researcher and one of the most internationally recognized scholars in education and psychology, who does not envision the reemergence of positivism as the *dominant* research paradigm within education or other social sciences in the foreseeable future. Of course, Gage's futuristic portraits merely reflect the simple phenomenon that the positivist perspective of social reality and ways to study this reality have been on the defensive in education and other social sciences for more than a decade. Ten years ago, Putman (1981: 74) alleged that we were beginning to see the "demise of a theory [positivism] that lasted for over two thousand years." A few years later, Fiske and Shweder (1986: 16-17) declared,

> There was once a time, not so long ago, when the very idea of rationality was equated with the results and findings of positive (i.e., objective) science. The results of positive science were considered worthy of respect because scientists had possession of a unitary method for discovering truths, and they knew how to employ that method to discover useful knowledge. Over the last several decades, that picture of science and the equation of science and rationality have taken their lumps. [Today, there are a] wide range of alternative positions concerning science and the subjectivity/objectivity that one might credibly adopt in a postpositivist world.

Lather (1988b) draws attention to the fact that during the last five years there has been an explosion of ideas and practices in our effort to know, understand, and learn from social reality. *Phenomenology, hermeneutics, interpretive, naturalistic, feminist, critical,* and *constructionist* are just a few terms that describe the "frames of reference" through which it is possible to examine social reality. She goes on to note that currently there is also a proliferation of "post" frames, such as *postmodernism* (Hassan, 1987; Lyotard, 1984), *post-Marxism* (Althusser, 1969), *postcritical* (Wexler, 1988), *postenlightenment* (Rajchman, 1985), and *postparadigm* (Caputo, 1987). In rejecting the positivist view of social reality as well as the purpose for examining this reality, social scientists are faced with an expansive propagation of contending ideas that raise serious questions regarding the legitimacy and authority of scholarly practice (Marcus & Fischer, 1986). Anderson (1989: 250) states that

> what characterizes the present postpositivist world of the social sciences is a continued attack on positivism with no single clearly conceived alternative. Within disciplines and fields generally, broad paradigms and

grand theories are increasingly found lacking in their ability to provide guidance in asking and answering persistent and seemingly intractable social questions. . . . Thus the current situation, although chaotic, is also full of opportunity.

A number of educational scholars and other social scientists seem electrified by prospects of reorienting themselves and the work of other academics in what is becoming an era of "postpositivist" scholarship (Fiske & Shweder, 1986).

Lather (1988b: 1) insightfully comments that although the proliferation of these contending notions of what it means to "do social science" is exciting, it is also, as she states, "dizzying," especially to those of us whose primary interests do not fall within the field of philosophy of science. Today scholars not only are faced with questions about how to generate projects worthy of social inquiry, how to enter particular educational settings, and how to find good informants who work in these settings, but must also question the rationality that they use in developing their own presuppositions concerning social reality, the ethics of their work, the power relationships between themselves and those people whom they observe, and the eventual reporting of their experiences.

Although these added concerns make it more difficult for the social observer, academics who wish to share what they have learned from their observations of social reality are responsible for communicating the frames of reference through which they experience the social world being portrayed and discussed. As Namenwirth (1986: 29) argues, this synthesis is necessary because

> scientists are no more protected from political and cultural influence than other citizens. By draping their scientific activities in claims of neutrality, detachment, and objectivity, scientists augment the perceived importance of their views, absolve themselves of social responsibility for the applications of their work, and leave their (unconscious) minds wide open to political and cultural assumptions. Such hidden influences and biases are particularly insidious in science because the cultural heritage of the practitioners is so uniform as to make these influences very difficult to detect and unlikely to be brought to light or counter-balanced by the work of other scientists with different attitudes. Instead, the biases themselves become part of a stifling science-culture, while scientists firmly believe that as long as they are not *conscious* [her emphasis] of any bias or political agenda, they are neutral and objective, when in fact they are only unconscious.

A commitment to conduct "openly ideological" scholarship (Lather, 1986a) requires us to articulate the frames of reference that influenced the orientation we used to learn from the social reality found in Harmony's elementary school. As will become evident, a synthesis from several distinctive frameworks was more helpful to us than any one tradition.

Popkewitz (1981: 158) notes that many social scientists have utilized Thomas Kuhn's (1970) concepts of 'paradigm' and 'scientific revolutions' as a "legitimizing function" that provides "a language, a method, and a focus for reappraising the history and present conditions of the social discipline." The work of social phenomenologists offered one of the first alternative paradigms to positivism advanced by academics. Individuals such as George Herbert Mead, Alfred Schutz, and Max Weber rejected the positivist view that social reality was controlled by "laws" similar to those found in the physical sciences (Berger & Luckmann, 1967). According to this view, psychological laws control the behavior of people, who in turn set up social systems that reflect these laws (Homans, 1967). Given this orientation, society consists of unified arrangements and values, and tensions are viewed as the result of personal recalcitrance against societal standards. Conflict is seen merely as an inability of the individual to integrate himself or herself into the normative order. Thus people are viewed as passive actors who are socialized into a consensual, societal framework. The role of the scientist is to prove the existence of these preexisting laws so that society can be organized in a more effective and efficient manner, that is, in accordance with the laws of "human nature."

Against this background, social phenomenologists present a contrasting view of people as active agents in the creation of their own social reality. Societal arrangements result from an interaction between inner dispositions of individuals and external forces that limit what one can possibly do within a given social context (Blumer, 1969). Individuals do not merely respond to external stimuli; they *interpret* the world around them and then act upon their unique interpretations. People are free to create their own world because they are able to symbolically communicate to others and themselves, thus giving meaning to their environment. Consciousness is never fixed or static. As people participate in social relationships, they are open to modifications in the way they experience reality. Social reality emerges as a network of interrelated consciousness. Through the processes of both primary and secondary socialization (Berger & Luckmann, 1967), people acquire a sense of reality, and through continued interpretation, they perpetually reproduce and transform their social world (Cicourel, 1973; Mead, 1934). As a result, conflicting interpretations and thus interests are seen as normal aspects of social reality.

Given this set of ideas, the primary focus for the study of social reality is to understand the *meaning* that people give to their actions and the actions of others who share their world. Although social reality can exist only within human experience, this does not mean that the exploration of this reality is limited to the isolated consciousness of each individual. Blumer (1969: 22) expands upon this point.

> One errs if he thinks that since the empirical world can exist for human beings only in terms of images or conceptions of it, therefore reality must be sought in images or conceptions independent of an empirical world. Such a solipsistic position is untenable and would make empirical science impossible. The position is untenable because of the fact that the empirical world can "talk back" to our pictures of it . . . in the sense of challenging and resisting, or not bending to, our images or conceptions of it. This resistance gives the empirical world an obdurate character that is the mark of reality.

Blumer goes on to suggest that adhering to scientific protocol, testing hypotheses, replicating controlled studies, and using standardized operational procedures distances the observer from the social world and therefore makes it impossible for him or her to truly understand reality. Instead, he argues that one comes to know social reality through prolonged and intimate participation in it.

> If one is going to respect the social world, one's problems, guiding conceptions, data, schemes of relationship, and ideas of interpretation have to be faithful to that empirical world. This is especially true in the case of human group life because of the persistent tendency of human beings in their collective life to build up separate worlds, marked by an operating milieu of different life situations and by the possession of different beliefs and conceptions for handling these situations. One merely has to think of the different worlds in the case of a military elite, the clergy of a church, modern city prostitutes, a peasant revolutionary body, professional politicians, slum dwellers, the directing management of a large industrial corporation, . . . and so on endlessly. . . . To study them intelligently one has to know these worlds, and to know the worlds one has to examine them closely. No theorizing, however ingenious, and no observance of scientific protocol, however meticulous, are substitutes for developing a familiarity with what is actually going on in the sphere of life under study. (Blumer, 1969: 38–39)

This orientation allows one to meet the basic requirements of science: to directly confront the social world being studied; to raise abstract questions about this world; to discover relations between categories of data; to formulate propositions about these relations; to organize these propositions into analytical schemes that others can understand; and to test the questions, data, relations, propositions, and analyses through renewed examination of the social world.

Viewing the social world as a complex interaction of reflexive subjects rather than mute objects upon which the scientist turns his or her objective gaze was at the core of our efforts to learn from the social reality in Harmony's elementary school. However, this frame of reference alone has some serious shortcomings. First, by emphasizing the subtle texture of subjective meaning that actors use to make sense of their world, we may in fact be limiting our understanding of what actually constitutes social reality. Although we are not discounting the importance of actors' conscious perceptions of their and others' experiences of the social world, this world is more than mere configurations of subjective meanings. If the focus remains solely on the conscious awareness of the actors, no means remain for distinguishing between that which *seems* to be the case for the actor and that which *is* the case. To dwell on actors' consciousness may conceal the extent to which such consciousness is regulated by underlying structures and social relationships. After all, actors may or may not be conscious of these structures and their influence upon themselves and others who share their world. They may subconsciously take them for granted or simply not recognize their existence. Therefore, the observer of social life must not simply base his or her understanding of a given world on the awareness of the actors. Group life can be fully understood only in terms of its embeddedness within a social, political, and historical context. The frame of reference that emerges from the work of social phenomenologists does not encourage us to ask questions such as why certain institutionalized meanings dominate within a given milieu rather than others or the extent to which the interpreted meanings of the actors are socially regulated by underlying societal structures and ideologies. For example, McLaren (1987) notes several limitations in Peshkin's (1986) recent ethnographic study of a fundamentalist Christian school. Although it insightfully illustrates educational practices leading to rigid social, moral, and intellectual control of students in the name of "salvation" and the way intolerance is systematically taught to children in the name of God, Peshkin's study fails to illuminate the way in which the teachings of this school reflect the secular, conservative ideology that dominates our society, which in turn keeps current relations of power and privilege intact. As a result, Peshkin's ethnography fails to uncover the more insidious dimensions of this type of education.

A second shortcoming of this frame of reference is the lack of attention it gives to the relationship between the observer and those being observed. As Dreyfus and Rabinow (1983: 180-181) state,

> As long as the interpretive sciences continue to search for a deep truth, that is, to practice a hermeneutics of suspicion . . . while insisting that the truths they uncover lie outside the sphere of power, these sciences seem fated to contribute to the strategies of power. They claim a privileged externality, but they actually are part of the deployment of power.

Similarly, within positivism, a number of "qualitative inquirers" have advocated for the standardization of data gathering and analysis methods to ensure that what is being reported is the "truth." For example, Lincoln and Guba (1985) have developed several methodological practices (audit trails, auditor's verification, triangulation of data) to ensure the "trustworthiness" of data collection and analysis. LeCompte and Goetz (1982) answer the charge that phenomenological science is "soft" by articulating steps that should be taken by scholars to ensure that their ethnographic research can meet the rigorous criteria of reliability and validity. Miles and Huberman (1984) articulate a set of "qualitative" research techniques that will prevent researchers' self-delusions and keep them from inserting their own bias into the research process. If these techniques are followed, then researchers can have faith that their work will be judged "truthful" in the eyes of skeptical readers. The assumption is that the researcher plays the role of neutral adjudicator of what is going on in a given setting without realizing that his or her own observations, questions, analysis, and theorizing contain implicit political content. In situating the researcher in the role of a privileged, external observer who is politically neutral, social phenomenology in some instances has merely become a form of clandestine positivism. As Hall (1985: 103) argues, "Ideas don't just float around in empty space. . . . they are materialized in, they inform, social practices. . . . In other words, there is no social practice [including research] outside of ideology." Social phenomenology has generally failed to address the way in which our own work as observers of social reality supports particular social and political interests at the expense of others.

These shortcomings raise the question of what it means to study social reality in an unjust and often uncaring world. Claims of value-neutral knowledge production camouflage the social, political, and psychological interests intrinsic to all human actions, including the work of academics and other "producers" of social knowledge. Popkewitz (1984: 50) calls for the creation of a science that is

> concerned with how forms of domination and power are maintained and renewed in society. The intent of the research is not just to describe and interpret the dynamics of society, but to consider the ways in which the processes of social formation can be modified. Finally, it posited the social world as one of flux, with complexity, contradiction and human agency.

As a result, the social observer is situated directly within a socio-political context. Popkewitz and others call upon academics to conduct their work within a theoretical, emancipatory framework. In this sense, one actively seeks to find ways of linking group life in a particular setting to the systems of power and privilege within the broader societal context within which it exists.

The researcher needs to distinguish between the meaning of a given reality as it appears to the actor and the meaning of the situation as it seems to the observer. This distinction will often be in terms of the conceptual framework which the researcher has developed in his or her effort to make what she or he has observed comprehensible. In this sense, research is seen as a form of praxis (Lather, 1986b). The goal is not to simply report "what's out there," but to analyze this reality in ways that empower us, as human beings, to work against those social, economic, cultural, and psychological constraints and ideologies (class, gender, race) that keep us from creating a more just and caring reality. As Fay (1987: 75) states, the aim of critical social researchers "is to help people not only to be transparent to themselves but also to cease being mere objects in the world, passive victims dominated by forces external to them."

Although this contextual awareness was extremely valuable to us in our work at Harmony, it also contained a few potential drawbacks. First, critical studies of social reality have tended to concentrate on the existence of patterns and structures within social arrangements, thus ignoring the unique individual or small-group experiences of the people who live within these arrangements. This tendency often results in the development of relatively rigid abstractions and notions of "the way things are," rather than sensitive understandings of the dynamics of social life (Wexler, 1983). Although critical ethnographies recognize that those being observed are social beings who construct various meanings in interaction with others, they frequently fail to fully probe and thus translate the complexity and subtlety of the participants' experiences and views (Anderson, 1989).[2] Too often, the voice of the actors being observed is largely muted as critical researchers "race" to develop and then become enamored with their own theorizing (Christian, 1987). Bowers (1982) argues that critical observers of social reality frequently become overly concerned with developing abstruse theoretical systems of thought in deriving their understanding of the social world. He goes on to suggest that this concern has "prevented them from testing their theory against the phenomenological world of people involved in concrete social and cultural relationships" (1982: 546). Participants' experiences are viewed as if from a television set and as such get contained into relatively cosmetic representations for more abstract theoretical insights (Wexler, 1983, 1987).

Although one must develop a theoretical framework to comprehend social life, one must place this theory in proper perspective. Not to do so presents an image of the researcher as one who has special insight into truth. One example of this potential drawback can be found in the Marxist notion of "false consciousness." False consciousness suggests that actors in a given social context have been so completely socialized by dominant, ruling-class ideology that they are unable to recognize their own oppression, let alone the oppression of others. It suggests that people who do not understand reality as Marx did suffer from *deficient* thinking, rather than merely having an alternative understanding of life's experiences. Christian (1987: 59) presents another example of a *false consciousness mentality* (although she does not use this specific term) as a foundation for theorizing.

In the race for theory, [some] feminists, eager to enter the halls of power, have attempted their own prescriptions. So often I have read books on feminist literary theory that restrict the definition of what *feminist* means and overgeneralize about so much of the world that most women as well as men are excluded. Nor seldom [sic] do feminist theorists take into account the complexity of life—that women are many races and ethnic backgrounds with different histories and cultures and that as a rule women belong to different classes that have different concerns. Seldom do they note these distinctions, because if they did they could not articulate a theory.

For academics (or anyone else) to place their own understanding in such a privileged position is morally unjustified and politically dangerous. Berger (1975) argues that the concept of false consciousness lays claim to a cognitively privileged status which allows "intellectuals" to designate "truth." He and others (Hall, 1985) go on to suggest that no one (including academics) can claim to possess "true consciousness." All of us are simply trying as best we can to make sense of this experience of living. As Lather (1986b: 267) states, "Data must be allowed to generate propositions in a dialectical manner that permits use of a priori theoretical frameworks, but which keeps a particular framework from becoming the container into which the data must be poured." Although critical scholarship has provided many insights into the way we should approach research, it cannot remain useful if it is presented as a "rescue mission" that saves us from our own ignorance.

Although research that aids in the construction of a more just and caring society was central to our work, it was crucial for us to employ self-reflection in our efforts to interpret the social life found in Harmony. This reflexivity is necessary in order to guard against imposing meaning on phenomena rather than constructing meaning through negotiation with those being observed (Lather, 1988b; Rajchman, 1985). Lather (1988b: 12) draws upon the work of poststructuralists as she explains that

research [is] an enactment of power relations; the focus is on the development of a mutual, dialogic production of a multi-voice, multi-centered discourse, a particular moment of textual production that says more about the relationship between researcher and researched than about some 'object' capturable via language.

Given this orientation, there is no "final knowledge," no "grand theory" that explains life's happenings, whether it be positivism, liberalism, or

Marxism. Rather than creating unified theories, human beings create "discourses" which construct and constitute social reality. From this perspective, language (as well as other forms of texts), rather than material conditions, exerts primary power in manifesting a given social reality. For example, Foucault concentrated his attention on the discourses of those individuals who are often ignored in social science—the weak, poor, and humble (what he referred to as "subjugated knowledges")—rather than those with power and privilege (Dreyfus & Rabinow, 1982; Rajchman, 1985). Foucault's work centered on how systems of ideas emerge as systems of power. Whether these ideas concern, for example, sexuality or surveillance, they become discourses which construct and influence human beings within societal settings. These discourses are connected to social conditions that define what is "true" at any given moment in history (Foucault, 1977, 1979). Whether the goal of research is to predict, understand, or empower and liberate, all forms of knowledge are discourses that we, as human beings, have created in order to discover "truths" about ourselves, and the process by which this discovery takes place also impacts upon these developing discourses (Rajchman, 1985). From this perspective, the goal is to conduct research through a reflexive process in which science can continually deconstruct the realities it helps to create. Reflexivity erodes the authority of our own academic discourse in order to challenge current relations of power, legitimacy, and domination. In our efforts to discuss and illuminate life in schools, there is a recognition of our own vulnerability to conceive, understand, and write about what we have observed.

Although at Harmony we recognized our intellectual vulnerability, we were not ignorant of voiced concerns that this position eventually leads to intellectual and moral relativism (Phillips, 1987). Lyotard's (1984: 82) notion of the "postmodern condition" suggests an era in which we "wage war on totality." His analysis suggests that because of recent developments in science, technology, and the arts, people's reliance on fixed philosophical and moral foundations is eroding. Unifying notions such as 'liberation' are seen as merely alternative forms of oppression. Lyotard (1984) presents a view of postmodernism without any intellectual or visual substructures upon which people can confidently act. It is an era in which the only thing that remains constant is change. He argues that knowledge and the meaning people give to that knowledge can no longer be securely connected to totalizing sociological or historical theories. As D'Amico (1986: 136) states, for some individuals, "the central continuing postmodernist theme is a radical relativism."

Although aspects of postmodernist discourse seem to encourage "irrationalism, antipathy to science, and nihilism" (D'Amico, 1986: 136), this issue of relativism can be addressed in a number of ways. One place to start is to question what exactly relativism means within the context of academic discourses. For some scholars the loss of authoritative theorizing suggests that if we cannot know anything with certainty, then we can know nothing. For example, Bloom (1987: 379), in his now famous assessment of higher education and the social sciences, castigates poststructuralism as

> the last, predictable stage in the suppression of reason and the denial of the possibility of truth in the name of philosophy. . . . There is no text, only . . . cheapened interpretation [which] . . . liberates us from the objective imperatives of the texts which might have liberated us from our . . . narrow horizon.

From Bloom's perspective, questioning the legitimacy of authoritative knowledge has significantly undermined our efforts to intellectually progress as a culture and species. However, framing the postmodernist antipathy for teleological theorizing as crude relativism misses the point. As Eisner (1983: 2) illustrates, discrediting the notion of absolute knowledge does not result automatically in the loss of reasoned analysis.

> Because different theories provide different views of the world, it does not follow that there is no way of appraising the value or credibility of a view. First, we can ask what a particular theoretical view enables us to do, that is, we can determine its instrumental utility. Second, we can appraise the consistency of its conclusions with the theoretical premises on which they are based. Third, even if those conclusions are logically consistent with their premises, we may reject the premises. Fourth, we can determine whether there are more economical interpretations of the data than those provided by any particular theoretical view. Fifth, we can judge the degree to which it hangs together. And sixth, we can assess the view on aesthetic grounds: How elegant is the view? How strongly do we respond to it?

The fact that grand theories are inherently problematic does not mean that all thoughts are equally arbitrary. As will be discussed later, in addition to the criteria mentioned by Eisner, we can make distinctions between types of grand theories and grand narratives and can examine these ideas in light of their ethical and moral foundations. Theorizing in itself is not the problem as long as it maintains its essential vulnerability. From the poststructuralist perspective, theories that assume positions of legitimacy do so within a specific socio-historical time and place. Lather (1988a: 7) states, "What is destroyed by the post-structuralist suspicion of the lust for authoritative accounts is not meaning, but claims to the unequivocal dominance of any one meaning." This orientation keeps researchers' thinking in process by disrupting our notions of reality and helping us see knowledge creation as an act of mental play as well as of serious reasoning. Rather than viewing this destabilization as muddled thinking or deficient scholarship, researchers can observe school life with fresh minds and eyes.

In addition to recognizing that in rejecting the supremacy of grand theories we will not destroy our ability to make rational and moral judgments, it is also worthwhile to view the charge of "relativism" as an expression of power relations within academic settings. Relativism is an overriding concern only within an intellectual context in which academics search for a privileged position as the grantors of certainty. For example, a number of feminist writers (Harding, 1987a; Lather, 1988a; Yeatman, 1987) suggest that this intense apprehension over relativity is in reality an effort on the part of white, class-privileged men to maintain their positions as authoritative knowledge givers and to avoid normative debate over this power within a context of equity, justice, caring, and democracy. As Harding (1987b: 10) asserts in her analysis of "doing" social science,

> Historically, relativism appears as an intellectual possibility, and as a "problem" only for dominating groups at the point where the hegemony of their views is being challenged. . . . The point here is that relativism is not a problem originating in, or justifiable in terms of, women's experiences or feminist agendas. It is fundamentally a sexist response that attempts to preserve the legitimacy of androcentric claims in the face of contrary evidence.

Drawing upon Adrienne Rich's work, Spender (1982: 35) succinctly states, "Objectivity is the name we give to male subjectivity." Concern for establishing a foundational body of knowledge, way of thinking, or methods of science may in fact reflect a masculine, Western cultural ethos. Charges of "relativism" then are used not as a way to illuminate the weaknesses of alternative perspectives, but merely as a weapon to maintain this patriarchal hegemony.

Although charges of "relativism" should be seen as problematic, it is important to emphasize that in rejecting "grand" or "total" theories of social reality it is not being suggested that scholars' work must remain trapped in theoretical minutia that can have no value outside of a highly specific time and cultural setting. Postmodernists' rejection of all foundational thinking can lead, unimpeded, to a glorification of novelty for its own sake. When one removes all social, historical, and moral reference points from which to analyze social reality, there is a danger of falling into what Hall (1986: 47) refers to as "the tyranny of the New." Hall (1986) goes on to suggest that this glorification can then become (somewhat ironically) an ideology of the "new," rather than freedom from ideology. Manthorpe (1990: 117) raises an important point regarding relativism in her analysis of feminist science: "This [relativism] would not simply be an epistemological problem, but a political one, for, in the absence of any criteria of validity which had been mutually agreed, it would only be the most powerful social groups who could successfully defend their interpretation of truth." Giroux (1988a: 16) suggests that we view "total theorizing" as a heuristic device rather than as an ontological category. In this way, the researcher can examine particularistic phenomena in light of a larger context "in which it is possible to make visible those mediations, interrelations, and interdependencies that give shape and power to larger political and social systems." This perspective would allow scholars to examine the relationship between micro and macro "worlds" within a social and historical context while at the same time maintaining their subjective and intellectual vulnerability. Kellner (1988: 253) distinguishes grand theories from "grand narratives" and suggests that whereas the former subsume and thus distort reality into a totality of thought, the latter facilitate scholars' efforts to tell a "Big Story, such as the rise of capital, patriarchy, or the colonial subject." If we condemn all forms of universal thinking outright, then we run a significant risk of not being able to adequately examine social reality in its full complexity.

In summary, it is difficult these days to situate one's theoretical orientation with a single adjective (*phenomenologist, feminist, Marxist*). Lather (1988b) notes that, given the current dialogue, the theories themselves are better off referred to in the plural (*feminisms, phenomenologies, Marxisms, postmodernisms*). In carving out a theoretical stance vis-à-vis the conduct of research in schools, we found it necessary to draw from several traditions. Each frame of reference discussed offered us a way of viewing and understanding reality. Each contributed to our analysis of what we observed and the manner in which this analysis was eventually written. These frames of reference assisted us in our efforts to decode social reality. Given the issues previously discussed, there were particular facets of social life found in Harmony's elementary school that were particularly helpful as we initially attempted to decode the social realities found there.

DECODING SOCIAL REALITY

Conceptualizing an elementary education for critical democracy within a societal context which accentuates individualism presents issues of both practice and theory. As mentioned in the previous chapter, schools have considerable power in establishing the social expectations and human talents needed for a given society. At the same time, a particular educational setting can be created that will challenge societal norms and provide young people with alternative values and abilities. These unique schools can provide educators with opportunities to carefully consider the type of pedagogy needed for critical democracy. However, directly asking a given teacher or student to reveal his or her image of schooling for democracy is not likely to yield many insights. The education of children is a complex phenomenon that involves organizational structures, personal identities, interpersonal dynamics, and symbolic communications. An understanding of what happens in a given school is not readily accessible by simple or direct means. As a result, education as a lived experience must be sought through observations of people as they engage in various types of communicative experiences, as they manifest their personal identities, and as they create structures, rituals, and symbols that express values and ideas. One way to explore this complex interplay of human experience is to focus one's observations and analysis on those aspects of the school which reflect its basic foundational values and knowledge base. In our situation, it seemed particularly worthwhile to examine the myths, rituals, perspectives, and modes of thinking of those who made up Harmony School's elementary program.

Myths

One way to gain insight into the social reality of a given school is through the stories that people tell. Human beings often speak in narrative form. "People tell stories to help order their world" (Lesko, 1988: 24), and each adult and child in Harmony had "a story to tell." In small communities, these oral tales (although more ambiguous and rambling than written communication) often become the central means by which people make sense of their lives (Gee, 1989a; White, 1981). In these more intimate settings, shared experiences frequently form the basis of collective stories, which are then used as the basis for group identity.

As stories are told and retold, they can become myths that play a powerful role in establishing the social life of a given group (Campbell, 1988). Myths, as used in this instance, are collective stories in which certain aspects are given greater significance in order to enhance some real event and thus influence the way people see their world and live their lives (Barthes, 1972). In some cases, these collective stories become distorted because certain elements are left out or certain details of what actually happened are altered for the purpose of symbolizing values or intentions. Myths sweep the obscurity of reality aside in an effort to present a particular view of events and the meaning of those events for all to understand.

School administrators, teachers, and students create collective stories which, if important enough, become myths. For example, Harmony School recently bought an unoccupied school building from the local school district. We were told that this building was bought by the students, and technically it was. The building was sold for ten dollars, and one hundred students donated a dime each for its purchase. A plaque with each child's name was prominently displayed on one of the walls of the school. The message of this story was to emphasize that Harmony was the students' school. In reality, the building underwent a $400,000 renovation which was raised through a building fund drive. The school is not legally owned by the students, their parents, or teachers. Nevertheless, the story of buying the building had become a powerful myth which was used to express a value deeply felt among the people who worked and went to school at Harmony.

To examine the stories and myths in a school is to probe its embedded values and visions of education, society, and the roles of individuals within these contexts. Repeated stories and myths help create and maintain the status quo of a given institution or society, and thus they also can help us identify the views and actions of dissident actors.

Rituals

In addition to telling stories, groups also "communicate" through ritual events. McLaren (1986: 35-37) cogently argues that rituals are a necessary focus for observation if one hopes to understand school life.

> As organized behavior, rituals arise out of the ordinary business of life. In opposition to the widespread opinion among many scholars and laymen that rituals have generally disappeared in contemporary society, rituals are always and everywhere present in modern industrial life. . . . Rituals are more than mere signs or symbols in some kind of sociocultural semaphore. On the contrary, they form the warp on which the tapestry of culture is woven, thereby "creating" the world for the social actor. . . . A group or community's rituals become . . . the symbolic codes for interpreting and negotiating events of everyday existence. . . . Rituals are inherently social and political; they cannot be understood in isolation from how individuals are located biographically and historically in various traditions of mediation (e.g., clan, gender, home environment, peer group culture). Ensconced in the framework of both private and institutional life, rituals become part of the socially conditioned, historically acquired and biologically constituted rhythms and metaphors of human agency.

Rituals contain properties such as special timing, a particular order of events, style of behavior, collective setting, and repetition (Moore & Myerhoff, 1977).

Because of their collective nature, rituals transmit a group point of view. Like myths, they are often created to express a particular meaning in symbolic form (Grimes, 1982). Although rituals often contain overt messages, their symbolic form leaves their meaning open to interpretation by those who observe or participate in them (Moore & Myerhoff, 1977). For example, Harmony School begins each year with a three-day camping trip. This ritual was established by the faculty the very first year in order to, as Dan, Harmony's curriculum coordinator, stated, "help establish a sense of family within the school, that is, to allow the children and faculty to develop relationships with each other as people rather than as teachers and students." However, this message was never overtly stated during this three-day period. Although the children and faculty did use this trip as an opportunity to develop a sense of camaraderie, a few simply looked at it as an opportunity to play for a few more days before, as Peter, a fourth-grade student, stated, "real school begins" (all children's names are fictitious).

Although their meanings can be open to interpretation, rituals are used as a means of social control. They can serve to legitimate and make reasonable social expectations (Geertz, 1973), they can exert direct control over people's behavior (Van Gennep, 1960), and they can reaffirm community beliefs and social roles (Bateson,1958). Although rituals often contain "should" or "ought" messages that "put us in our place" (McLaren, 1986: 38), some are established as catalysts for transformative experiences (Turner, 1969). Take, for instance, the traditional Native American ritual of the "Vision Quest," in which a young man goes off by himself for up to four days in order to seek his "vision" of who he is and what his purpose on earth is to be (Neihardt, 1959). Similarly, Harmony School developed, according to Dan, its sixth-grade graduation project as a "rite of academic and social passage" ritual which included a ten- to twenty-page written research report on a topic of each student's choice (with approval by and direction from each student's two-member faculty research committee), the oral presentation and a visual display of the students' projects as part of the graduation ceremony, a review of the students' efforts towards building a sense of community within the school, and ten hours of community service (see Chapter 5). Such rituals often contain an aura of drama about them through which they exert influence upon those who directly and indirectly participate (Courtney, 1982).

As points of drama, rituals are keys to our understanding of what it means to participate in the group life of a given community or institution. The complexity of rituals allows participants to create meanings from them, and their repetition establishes them as focal points for group identity and values. As such, rituals provide valuable opportunities to observe school life as a dynamic event.

Educational Perspectives

Along with myths and rituals, people's perspectives offer another avenue for decoding social reality. The concept of perspectives captures the ideas, behaviors, and contexts of a particular act. Becker and his colleagues (1961:34) define a perspective as

> a coordinated set of ideas and actions a person uses in dealing with some problematic situation, to refer to a person's ordinary way of thinking and

feeling about and acting in such a situation. These thoughts and actions are coordinated in the sense that the actions flow reasonably, from the actor's point of view, from the ideas contained in the perspective. Similarly, the ideas can be seen by an observer to be one of the possible sets of ideas which might form the underlying rationale for the person's actions and are seen by the actor as providing a justification for acting as he does.

Perspectives differ from more abstract constructs such as attitudes or beliefs in that they include people's actions rather than merely their dispositions to act. Perspectives, according to Becker's definition, are context bound; that is, they are specific to particular situations and do not necessarily reflect more general, abstract ideologies in which people might believe.

Educational perspectives take into account how the situation of school and the classroom is experienced; how this situation is interpreted given the individual's background of experiences, beliefs, and assumptions; and how this interpretation is manifested in actions. In this situation, we were particularly attentive to the educational perspectives of Harmony School's administrators, teachers, and students regarding the purpose of schooling, the knowledge taught in school, the type of instructional strategies employed, the ways in which people learn, the various roles that people play, the relationships among people within their peer groups and across lines of authority and power (administrator/teacher, teacher/student, administrator/student), and the organizational structure of the school. Educational perspectives offer us occasions to carefully examine the complex relationship between people's beliefs, ideas, and perceptions and the way these are then manifested through actions within a given social context. As a result, focusing on educational perspectives allows us to closely examine social reality at both a conceptual and material level.

Modes of Thinking

Myths, rituals, and perspectives contain underlying modes of thinking that are socially and historically constructed (Durkheim, 1957). Examining people's styles of thinking can provide deeper insight into their lived experience within a given social context. As Lesko (1988) notes, observing the systems of thought among a group of people can help one determine the depth of their interpersonal connections. Research suggests that modes of thinking might be associated with class, race, and gender. For example, Givon (1979), Heath (1983), and Gee (1989a, 1989b) suggest that methods of thinking in communities of "strangers" (as exemplified in the language and thought patterns of many white, upper-middle-class people) tend to be analytic, explicit, logical, impersonal, and directive. In communities of "intimates" the thinking and hence language of people tend to be more contextualized, personalized, and metaphorical. Meaning is conveyed more implicitly than explicitly.

Some studies on women's thinking indicate that gender plays a role in determining what mode of thinking is legitimated within a given social context. Masculine thinking tends to validate objectivity, utility, sequential logic, efficiency, categorization, factual knowing, and evaluation, whereas a feminine mode of thinking tends to encourage intuition, synthesis, subjectivity, and understanding (Belenky et al., 1986; Noddings, 1984). By attending to the modes of thought that are manifested in a given social context, one is potentially able to gain insight into the underlying characteristics of its makeup. In schools populated by "strangers," where a "masculine consciousness" might dominate, one could conceivably expect to find a mode of thinking that is often abstruse, competitive, impersonal, and individualistic. In schools populated by "intimates," or where "women's consciousness" is manifested, one might be expected to find a mode of thinking that is contextualized, nonadversarial, and personal.

Summary

In our effort to learn from the social reality at Harmony School, we viewed schooling as a complex phenomenon that contains symbolism, rituals, myths, perspectives, and different modes of thought that must be deconstructed as a way of understanding what it means to teach and be taught. As a result, our approach was to examine the statements and actions of the administrators, teachers, and students as individuals and as part of a collective whole and then place this examination within the broader context of societal relations. By linking an analysis of the micro to the macro structural arrangements, our discussion will address issues and practices leading to a more comprehensive understanding of elementary schooling for critical democracy. However, before these issues are examined, it is necessary to briefly introduce Harmony School and the people who work under its roof.

HARMONY'S ELEMENTARY SCHOOL

As one might suspect given the discussion in the first chapter, locating a school that attempts to promote democratic ideas, values, and actions among its staff and students is not easy in a country that finds itself in the middle of what Shor (1986) refers to as a "conservative restoration." As Finkelstein (1984: 280-281) notes,

> For the first time in the history of school reform, a deeply materialist consciousness seems to be overwhelming all other [educational] concerns.
> . . . Contemporary reformers seem to be recalling public education from its traditional mission—to nurture a critical and committed citizenry that

would stimulate the processes of political and cultural transformation and refine and extend the workings of political democracy. Reformers seem to imagine public schools as economic rather than political instrumentalities. They . . . call public school to industrial and cultural service exclusively . . . to enhance the process of industrial development, and to extend the competitive reach of America's economic, cultural, and social elites. . . . Americans for the first time in a one-hundred-and-fifty-year history, seem ready to do ideological surgery on their public schools—cutting them away from the fate of social justice and political democracy completely and grafting them instead onto elite corporate, industrial, military, and cultural interests.

Although we were able to locate individual teachers during the last few years who tried to teach in ways consistent with democratic values and goals (Goodman, 1987, 1988b), finding an entire elementary school within reasonable traveling distance from home was more difficult. Unable to locate a public school, we broadened the search to include independent schools. Eventually, a school in Bloomington, Indiana, was brought to our attention, and within a few months we were given permission (by the administrators, teachers, students, and parents) to spend a year observing Harmony's elementary school.

The Town

Bloomington, a town of approximately 60,000 people, is located in the southern part of Indiana. It is probably most noted for its college basketball program and coach, a country-rock musician who lives nearby, and a "coming of age" movie that featured a popular local bicycle race. Its economic base is dominated by Indiana University (students make up half of the town's population) and several industrial corporations (Otis Elevator, Westinghouse, RCA, Goodyear) which have factories in the area. At the present moment there is nearly full employment; however, many of these jobs do not pay substantial wages or include health or life insurance. According to the U.S. Commerce Department, in 1980 Bloomington and the surrounding county had the lowest yearly income per person in Indiana. Approximately 3.5 percent of the population earned over $50,000 each year, and 22.5 percent earned less than $4,000. Politically, the town tends to vote Democratic in an otherwise staunchly Republican state. Although most residents tend to be moderate to liberal in their political and social views, there is a small but visible progressive element within the town's population made up of many individuals who stayed in Bloomington after going to the university during the late sixties and early seventies. Few minorities live in the area. The population is overwhelmingly white and middle class (people of color make up nearly 7.5 percent of the population). The primary source of cultural diversity comes from foreign students (and their families) attending graduate school. However, Bloomington is noted as a place that tolerates personal and cultural diversity. On any given Saturday night, one can see a wide variety of fashion and life-styles being displayed, from punk rockers to ex-hippies to yuppies to farmers on the main street of town.

Although Bloomington is seen as an enclave of liberal tolerance, at the same time there is an active, conservative element within the community, some of whose members have extreme views. For example, in 1987, a group of Christian fundamentalists put enough pressure on the owners of the local shopping mall to cancel the inclusion of a Spiritual Fair (fortune telling, Tarot Card reading, astral projections) from their annual Halloween program because they felt these activities were not "godly." At times within the last decade, overt racism, sexism, and anti-Semitism have been manifested within the community (yelling racial slurs at Afro-Americans, sending hate mail to Jewish and feminist leaders and professors, raping women). As in many communities around the country since the "Reagan Landslide," there have been increased physical assaults directed towards Afro-Americans and other minorities on the college campus and in the community. Given its mixture of people, occupations, services, and life-styles, Bloomington might be considered in many ways to be unique and at the same time a "typical" town in the United States, if there is such a place.

The School

Harmony was founded in 1974 as an alternative high school. After several requests by individuals in the community, the director, Steve Boncheck, obtained a federal grant and started the elementary school in the fall of 1977. Legally, Harmony is an independent corporation. Steve is the president of the board; Dan Baron, the school's curriculum coordinator, is the secretary; and Haines Turner, a retired professor of labor education, is the treasurer. These three individuals are legally responsible for determining what happens to Harmony. In addition to these officers, Harmony has an "advisory board" of eighteen interested adults from various backgrounds within the local community.

The elementary school was located in a local church building until 1986, when it moved (along with the high school and the newly established middle school) into a two-story, brick public school building that was built in the 1920s. Located in a middle-class residential neighborhood, the building, playground, and parking lot occupy approximately three-fourths of a city block. At the time of our study, the elementary school contained a lower program (grades 1-3) that was located on the first floor of the building (along with space that was rented out to the Head Start program) and an upper program (grades 4-6) that was located on the second floor along with the middle and high schools. Each classroom in the lower elementary program contained a newly built loft. The rooms all had large windows, high ceilings, and natural oak woodwork, as was the style when the building was originally built. The furniture in the classrooms varied depending upon the teacher's preferences and typically included three or four tables at which four to six students could sit and several beanbag chairs. Two of the rooms had sofas in them and one or two long tables. There were no rows of individual children's desks in any of the rooms. Each room had a teacher's desk that was often difficult to locate because it blended into the surroundings of the class.

The ethos that guides the educational practices at Harmony is continually evolving. Initially, Harmony was established simply as a "humane" alternative to the public schools. At its inception, Steve gave the new elementary school teachers five "rules of thumb" upon which to base their educational program.

1. The teachers should be available to the students and family twenty-four hours a day, twelve months a year, in order to facilitate working with the "whole child."

2. The school should not artificially separate children from each other, or limit their development because of age any more than is absolutely necessary. Students should be encouraged to move at their own pace and at the same time help other students both academically and socially who are either older or younger than themselves. The program should be established to promote a sense of big brothers and big sisters within the school.

3. The program should provide flexibility for teachers to tailor their methodology to the particular learning style of the students. Teachers should not have a "pure ideology" but should feel comfortable using any methodology that works, whether that be rote memorization, open concept, Montessori, or whatever else will help students learn.

4. The school should be a microcosm of the community. In the selection of students, diversity is crucial, and ability to pay should be of minimal importance in determining enrollments.

5. Teachers and students should respect each other as equals. Everybody should participate in decision making together.

Although Harmony School has never developed an all-encompassing theory of education, over the years a democratic ethos has slowly emerged as a guide within the school. Some faculty members have spoken of an "old Harmony" that lacked organization and clear goals. Dan, the curriculum coordinator, has mentioned that one of the main differences between Steve and himself is that he has felt the school needs to have a more articulate philosophy upon which to base its continuing development. He has often spoken of the need for "praxis" within schools, that is, practices that emerge from a sound theoretical analysis of education and society.

Today, Harmony's democratic ethos is verbalized in several ways. For example, a recently published brochure states that Harmony was created in order to "foster the skills necessary for active and constructive participation in our country's democratic process." In his article, "A Case Study of Praxis," Dan writes, "We seek to encourage the learner to be an active discoverer of knowledge as well as a critic of social injustice" (Baron, 1979: 48). During job interviews with two prospective candidates, teachers were observed describing the school's primary goal as "liberating," "enlightening," "emancipating," and "empowering." Issues of democracy and power are often the topic of faculty meetings. Take for example, the following interchange during the first all-faculty meeting of the year:

> Alison, one of the high school teachers, brought up the issue of cigarette smoking. At the end of last year, the teachers developed a policy on who could smoke and where they could smoke, but this policy had never actually been voted on by the students. She felt that this had to be done at the first high school meeting. Michele, the first-grade teacher, voiced her concern about this proposal. "What if they vote to smoke whenever and wherever they want? What they vote on affects more than just themselves. There are younger children who might be negatively influenced by high school kids smoking." Alison felt that the high school students would take Michele's concern into consideration and come up with a policy sensitive to younger children. She stated that if Harmony is committed to empowering students, then the staff need to trust their decision-making abilities and the results of the democratic process. Jim, one of the lower elementary teachers, questioned if students should have the right [through mere voting] to do something on school grounds that is definitely harmful to their health. Steve mentioned that the entire society was struggling with who should be allowed to smoke and where they should be allowed to smoke. At this point several teachers spoke to the issue of how much power they felt students should be able to exercise. Do teachers have the right to veto "unwise" decisions that students make? Should they exercise reasoned control over what issues are brought before students for their voting? Various opinions were expressed. Most everyone agreed that teachers should not veto votes once taken, but some adult control over appropriate issues was necessary. For the most part teachers of younger children felt that they had to exercise more oversight over what students could vote on, whereas teachers of older students felt that students could make sound decisions about a much wider range of issues. Consensus was never fully reached, but most agreed that there was a relationship between the age of the children and the extent of the decision-making power they should assume. The discussion ended with agreement that the issue of student

empowerment and the democratic process used in the school would have to be continually reexamined. (Summary of field notes)

Although faculty members often expressed different viewpoints on specific topics, their commitment to the democratic mission of the school was clearly evident.

In particular, the dialectical tension between the values of individuality and of community was explicitly or implicitly addressed in almost every question that came before the staff. For example, even the decision regarding whether individual students could choose not to go on the fall semester's three-day field trip to Indianapolis reflected this tension.

The next item on the agenda was to discuss Bruce and Jack, who had expressed a desire not to go on the fall trip. A couple of faculty members mentioned that these students often didn't want to participate in any of the school's activities. For example, neither had signed up to participate in the school's winter talent show, and this pattern of not wanting to participate had been going on for a couple of years. There was general concern about the possible alienation these students might be feeling and talk about scheduling a meeting with these students' parents in the near future. Jim brought the discussion back to particulars when he stated that students should be given a choice of whether they want to go on the trip. Bart agreed, stating that he didn't want to deal with "unmotivated" kids. "If a few kids don't want to be there, they can make it terrible for everyone." Julie noted that the school goes on weekly trips around Bloomington, and wondered if Bart's and Jim's opinions should apply to those situations. Jo jumped in and stated, "I think they should go. Bruce and Jack always complain about doing things, and then once they do them they're usually glad they did. Besides, I see these trips as school. We don't give them the choice about going to class. Allowing a couple of children to not go would be giving the wrong message to the other students." Julie and Michele agreed, feeling that allowing Bruce and Jack this choice would "open up a can of worms. What if a lot of students decided they didn't want to go?" Jim responded by saying, "In that case maybe we made a mistake in making the decision in the first place." He went on to note that in the past students had some say in where the school went on trips. Barb noted that several students were disappointed that they were going to Indianapolis. Last year when they went to Chicago, there wasn't any resistance. Julie pointed out that sometimes it's good for children to see that what they take for granted (Indianapolis) might have something very special to offer. She predicted that the students would love this trip. She said that this trip would offer them some unique experiences, and that the students would gain a much deeper appreciation of what Indianapolis has to offer. She felt it was also good for the students to see that initial impressions do not always tell the whole story, and that sometimes it's important to investigate possibilities. After about 30 more minutes of discussion, the staff agreed that in the future they would make sure students were more involved in deciding where to take trips, but that for now students would be required to go on this trip. Finally, they agreed that Julie should talk to Bruce and Jack individually to see if they were simply complaining as they often did or if there were compelling reasons for their resistance, in which case they might consider setting up alternative plans for them. (Summary of field notes)

Balancing the interests of the individual against those of the school as a community and determining what actions are in the best interests of individual students and students as part of a collective group were common underlying issues that emerged in faculty meetings. The tension that existed between the values of individuality and community could be easily observed in the school's structured experiences, established rituals, and myths, as well as in the spontaneous events that occurred among the faculty and students.

The Staff and Students

As will be discussed in the third and fourth chapters, faculty members and students at Harmony exert considerably more power over decisions regarding school policy, curriculum, and instruction than their public school counterparts. As a result, their personal backgrounds and perspectives are more clearly manifested through their work. In a significant way, Harmony School's program reflects a composite picture of those teachers and students who work in it at any given moment. In its first year of operation, Harmony's elementary school had five teachers and twenty-five students. During the year we observed, the school had six teachers, two administrators (Steve and Dan), and roughly sixty-six students. Of the original six individuals who were involved in the creation of the elementary school, four still worked at Harmony, although not all in the elementary school. Harmony was a popular place to send children to school, as is indicated by the fact that for every child who was enrolled in the elementary school another child was on a waiting list for admission.

The staff of the elementary school came from various social and economic backgrounds, although each was white and (economically speaking) roughly middle class. However, four of the teachers, along with Steve and Dan, might be seen as "downwardly mobile"; that is, they grew up in traditional upper-middle-class families where the father (who was the primary wage earner) was a doctor, lawyer, or business executive. As adults, these individuals all lived at a lower standard of living than the one in which they were raised. All but one of the elementary faculty mentioned being influenced by the call to service that emerged from the Kennedy administration and/or the subsequent "counterculture" movement (Roszak, 1969) during the late 1960s and early 1970s. From talking to individuals about their family backgrounds, we were reminded of Keniston's (1968: 66) research into the lives of young people growing up during the above mentioned time period.

> Whatever the contradictions in some of these families, they are less impressive than the consistent orientation to principle. Somehow these parents communicated, often without saying outright, that human behavior was to be judged primarily in terms of general ethical principles; that right conduct was to be deduced from general maxims concerning human kindness, honesty, decency, and responsibility; that what mattered most was the ability to act in conformity with such principles. Whether the principles were religious or secular, the atmosphere within these radicals' families during their early years was one in which ethical principles occupied the highest position.

According to Keniston (1968), these families encouraged their children to assess their actions in terms of moral principles rather than to merely conform to given rules of conduct or follow traditional forms of thought. The eight staff members involved with Harmony's elementary school reflected this commitment to examine their actions in terms of human and social values. Unlike many of their contemporaries who during the 1980s chose to blend into the mainstream corporate structure of our society, the staff at Harmony chose to remain in public service, where their social and ethical principles could serve as the cornerstone for their work. However, it is perhaps important to point out that either because of their own family background or through marriage, all but one of these individuals had some financial security that existed outside of their work at Harmony which made working for the "public good" easier. In contrast, Jo, one of the lower elementary teachers and a single parent in her thirties, expressed increasing concern over her financial position. During the year of our observations, the teachers at Harmony earned $18,000, and the school paid for 50 percent of their health insurance plan; however, teachers did not have any retirement program. Jo often talked of wanting to go back to school for an advanced degree, but she could not afford it. She worried about her retirement and her son's future educational opportunities. She once said, "I've even thought about teaching in a public school just to get the [health and retirement] benefits and increased salary, but I don't think I could handle what goes on [educational philosophy, instructional practices, human relationships] there."

As will be discussed in the third chapter, generally agreeing with the school ethos was seen as essential to obtaining a teaching position at Harmony. When asked to name significant books that had an initial influence on their educational thinking, the staff typically responded with books that clearly linked education to societal values, such as Kohl's *36 Children* (1968), Postman and Weingartner's *Teaching as a Subversive Activity* (1969), Kozol's *Death at an Early Age* (1967), and Wolf-Wasserman and Hutchinson's *Teaching Human Dignity: Social Change Lessons for Every Teacher* (1978). In addition, the teachers were quick to single out particular philosophical and social treatises that had exerted a significant influence on their approach to education. Dan, for example, cited Martin Buber's *I and Thou* as contributing the most to his worldview. Julie, an upper elementary teacher, saw a deep connection between her own educational philosophy and the thinking of Buckminster Fuller's concept of 'spaceship earth'.

Although democracy, empowerment, and liberation were all concepts that these teachers felt were important for their work, this value system was not narrowly or universally defined or acted upon. There were clear differences in the way teachers approached their teaching, the children, the purpose of schooling at Harmony, and the relationship between schooling and society. For example, Dan was the most theoretically knowledgeable (he holds an Ed.S. degree in curriculum studies) and socially active member of the staff. He not only promoted democratic ideals as the basis for the education within Harmony, but he also worked hard to establish democratic values and activities within the community. During 1987 and 1988 he created Youth Forums that got high school students throughout Bloomington and the surrounding county to join with community leaders (mayor, council members, police chief) to talk about the type of environment in which they want to live; he also organized Constitutional Issues forums that brought adults together to discuss current constitutional questions (such as freedom of speech) before our society; and he sits on the county's Youth Services board. Although a couple of other staff members became involved in community or political projects, there was no pressure from the school for staff members to engage in social activism, and several chose not to become involved in these activities. Disagreements between faculty members over school policies and procedures were common. In faculty meetings, Barb often emphasized more libertarian views of education and society than the other staff members. Her notion of emancipating students focused on giving individual children power to make decisions affecting their own time and actions. Relative to Barb, the other staff members' orientation was more focused on the students as a collective whole, and they emphasized the need for individual children to develop a greater sense of group responsibility. Although the teachers and administrators at Harmony reflected a variety of unique personalities and regularly disagreed on specific matters facing the school, they shared a clearly democratic orientation towards schools and society.

Whereas the process of selecting and interviewing those who sought work at Harmony resulted in a relatively homogeneous staff, there was a conscious effort to recruit students from diverse social, cultural, economic, gender, and racial backgrounds. Students came from all parts of the city and from the nearby rural areas. Although Harmony's annual tuition of $3,100 distinguished it from the public schools, only a few students came from upper-middle-class families. As stated in the Harmony brochure, "The school has maintained a student population made up of children with a diversity of interests and backgrounds. . . . [and] puts an emphasis on serving children most in need—often from low-income, single-parent families." In fact, only one elementary student paid full tuition. (If parents could not afford the total tuition, they were asked to pay 7.5 percent of their take-home salaries. Two-thirds of Harmony's operating costs are obtained through grants and local fund-raising efforts.) Students were not admitted to Harmony on a first-come-first-serve basis. Each parent and prospective student were interviewed by Dan and by the teachers from either the upper or lower program who would be teaching the child. Most reasons expressed by parents for wanting to send their child to Harmony fell into one or more of three categories: (1) they wanted a more intellectually stimulating education for their child than that found in the public schools; (2) they wanted a less authoritarian and more flexible education for their child than that found in the public schools; and/or (3) their child was having personal, interpersonal, or academic problems and needed more personalized attention than he or she could get in the public schools. In faculty meetings to decide on enrollments for a given year, several factors were taken into consideration.

> Because the new upper elementary teacher had not been hired yet, only Dan, Julie, and Barb met to decide on this year's upper elementary enrollments. Today they were considering the admission of three boys into the fifth-grade class. First, they analyzed the psycho-social makeup of the children already in this particular class. They had six girls and three boys. All agreed that this group was a challenging class [two boys in particular] for the teachers. They discussed these two boys at some length [family instability, past difficulties maintaining friendships, difficulty in getting them engaged in learning activities]. The teachers agreed that it was necessary to admit at least one boy in order to maintain the gender balance within the class, but they also felt it was important to find a child who [from their interview] seemed to have a stable family, to be interested in learning, and to be friendly and outgoing. They then turned their attention to the three recently interviewed children. Each staff member gave his or her impression of the three boys and their parents. Lee seemed like the most likely choice. He seemed warm and open, and his mother [a single parent] seemed

communicative and willing to work with the staff. Robert, on the other hand, had several severe difficulties [poor eyesight, poor gross and fine motor coordination, slurred speech, emotional withdrawal]. His parents said that he had been tested for learning disabilities but did not qualify for any special education programs in the public school. Yet they said that last year he really struggled and suffered both academically and emotionally [being the object of children's teasing, getting into physical altercations] in his class. Max seemed like an exceptionally bright child, and his parents were also articulate and looking for a substantive alternative to the "weak" education found in the public schools. Max's racial background [Afro-American] was seen as a desirable contribution to this group. However, technically he belonged in fourth, not fifth, grade [there were no openings in the fourth grade], and the staff was worried about whether he would fit socially into the fifth-grade class. [Since the curriculum is personalized for students, there was little concern about his academic ability.] In the end, they decided to admit all of the children even though this would push their enrollment over the desired number for this class. Lee seemed like he would have a stabilizing influence on this group of children. After much deliberation, they decided that Max, who was physically and intellectually mature for his age, would be able to fit into the fifth grade. While voicing concern about whether they would be able to respond effectively to Robert's problems, they decided to enroll him because they could "see" his pain, and they also felt that his presence would give the other children in the school an opportunity to accept and appreciate a wider diversity of people, including those with overt physical or emotional difficulties. (Summary of field notes)

This meeting was similar to others that were observed. In making admission decisions, the program teachers and curriculum coordinator would first assess the gender of the children needed to maintain a balance between boys and girls in each class. They would then discuss the psycho-social dynamics of the present grade-level group. If approximately 30 percent or more of the students in a given group already had significant personal or academic problems, then the staff would look to admit a child who seemed to be emotionally stable, academically capable, and self-motivated. If the group was already stable, then they would consciously select a child who seemed to be "in need," that is, who (because of the particular personal, family, or school-related problems she or he might be having) might especially benefit from the type of education provided at Harmony. Children also had a greater chance of admission if they had siblings already enrolled in the school or were members of an identifiable ethnic or racial group or economic class (since the school wished to enroll students from a mixture of backgrounds). Although an ability to pay full tuition helped a child's chances of being admitted, it was not considered as important as these other factors, and at no time did we observe any child being refused admission on the basis of an inability to pay the tuition. The student body was dominated by middle-income, white children, but approximately 25 percent had Afro-American, Native American, or Latino backgrounds, and a couple of children were from foreign countries (their parent or parents were associated with the university).

This brief overview presents Harmony as a school with a democratic tradition, broad support in the surrounding community, a stable faculty, and a secure enrollment. As previously mentioned, in 1986 Harmony's existence was affirmed with the acquisition of a former neighborhood school building.

SPENDING A YEAR AT HARMONY

As already discussed, it is impossible to separate the observer of social reality from that which is observed. Therefore, it seems appropriate for the reader to be introduced to who "we" are and what we did during our year at Harmony. Before obtaining my Ph.D. in curriculum studies from the University of Wisconsin, I taught in elementary, middle, and high school settings. My formal interest in democratic, emancipatory education began while I was in graduate school, although the roots of this interest can be easily traced back to my childhood and political activism during the late 1960s. Xiaoyang Wu, one of the research assistants for this project, is a doctoral student in curriculum studies at Indiana University. Raised in the People's Republic of China, she was forced to move away from her parents, who were intellectuals and thus held under suspicion, during the Cultural Revolution. She spent four years in a remote part of China as a "barefoot doctor" before being allowed to return to her studies in foreign languages. As a translator, she met a citizen from the United States, got married, and moved to the United States in 1982. Fluent in English, her experiences in Chinese schools and subsequent treatment during the Cultural Revolution brought a unique perspective to our observations of what was going on in Harmony's elementary school. Jeff Kuzmic, the other research assistant, taught science and math for several years in conventional middle and high schools before receiving his master's degree in comparative education. His work on this project coincided with his own progress towards receiving his doctorate in curriculum studies. Our backgrounds and interests brought a healthy variety of perceptions and perspectives to our team meetings.

Methodology

Our efforts to "learn from Harmony" resembled methods that one usually associates with interpretive research.[3] Observations and interviews (formal and informal) were the two main methods of collecting data. In addition, program literature, course outlines and announcements, and representative student-completed assignments were read. Although the bulk of the fieldwork was conducted between July of 1987 and June of 1988, we went back to Harmony on several occasions to discuss ideas and observations that were initially made with faculty members and, in a few instances, with children.

During the school year, each member of our team logged approximately fifteen to twenty hours per week observing the happenings at Harmony, reviewing field notes, or participating in team debriefing sessions. Observations of classroom activities occurred at different times during the day (mornings, afternoons, and entire days), in a variety of settings (whole group, small group, and individual instruction), and when different subjects were being taught. Various meetings, special events, and field trips were also observed. The initial purpose of these observations was to determine what actually happened in the course of the school year.

As mentioned in the previous chapter, we did not go into Harmony with a fully developed definition of *democracy*. Instead, we simply wanted to notice what type of educational issues and practices occurred in a school that overtly articulated democracy as a guiding principle for its educational programs. For example, our decision to focus on the dialectical tension between individuality and community was not determined beforehand, but arose as part of our examination of our field notes. Only towards the end of the school year at Harmony did I begin to scrutinize relevant literature in the fields of political theory, education, and sociology. Rather than predetermine specific items to look for, we used a number of general questions to guide our initial observations, such as, How are classrooms organized? What do teachers and students do in their classrooms? What types of interpersonal dynamics exist among the people associated with Harmony? and, What information, opinions, and feelings are formally and informally exchanged during class sessions, meetings, field trips, and at other times? As previously mentioned, we were particularly interested in observing any rituals found in the school. After we made our initial observations, we developed more specific questions from reviewing field notes, which we then used to guide future observations.

Each faculty member participated in several in-depth, formal interviews (see Bussis, Crittenden, & Amarel, 1976; Spradley, 1979) lasting from thirty to ninety minutes. The curriculum coordinator was formally interviewed twelve times during the school year. Using methods of theoretical sampling (Glaser & Strauss, 1975), we formally interviewed (one to three times) twenty students and their parent(s) during the middle of the school year (see Greenspan, 1983; Okolo, 1984). Care was taken to select a wide diversity of students. Grade level, gender, ethnic and racial backgrounds, level of self-motivated involvement in schoolwork and activities, stability of family life, and student "popularity" were factors taken into consideration. Using these same criteria, we conducted two group interviews (six students in each group) to cross-check findings we received from the previous student interviews. Although these formal interviews were informative, the vast majority of our verbal exchanges with faculty and students were informal. These informal interviews were usually short in duration and occurred "naturally," as would happen between any two individuals who were curious about each other. They more closely resembled dialogue between friends than the question asking and answer giving that one associates with "interviews." Most of the time, we "hung out" with these people in their classrooms, in hallways and bathrooms, in the parking lot, on field trips, and on the playground, and we would chat with them whenever the opportunity arose (before and after observations of specific events, during lunch, before and after school, during class breaks). By the end of the school year, we managed to chat with practically every elementary student and nearly every teacher associated with Harmony's three different schools. We also formally interviewed eighteen parents and informally interviewed an additional nineteen parents during the fieldwork.

Initially, interviews were structured around various areas of concern, such as the personal histories of the people associated with Harmony, the structure and goals of Harmony, the social and educational values of teachers and parents in relation to Harmony's goals, the faculty members' and students' perceptions of and feelings towards themselves and each other, and the faculty members', students', and parents' perspectives towards specific events that occurred and ideas that were expressed during the school year. As field notes were discussed and analyzed, more specific questions were asked during subsequent interviews or "chats" to gain deeper insight into situations and to clarify ambiguities. Interviews were designed to discover the way in which the people at Harmony interpreted the social world around them and the way these interpretations were used as the basis for their actions.

The "constant comparative" method of analysis was used as a guide for understanding what we observed at Harmony (Glaser & Strauss, 1975; Goetz & LaCompte, 1981). We reviewed our field notes daily and during weekly team debriefing sessions. Incidents and bits of information were coded into tentative categories. As these categories emerged, questions arose and were used to guide our investigations. Findings from these investigations were then compared to initial categories. Through this constant comparison of information, our analysis crystallized. As this process continued, special attention was given to events or ideas that seemed to challenge original conceptualizations, and the faculty (and in some cases students) at Harmony were asked to respond regularly to our ongoing analysis.

As will be evident in the following chapters, the purpose of this book is to analyze and develop concepts and visual impressions of elementary schooling for critical democracy. We have made a conscious effort to ground our project in the subjective lives of educators who share this general commitment to education and democracy. However, rather than project Harmony's elementary school as merely a model to follow, our goal is to use the images that emerged from this one setting to gain deeper insight into the issues, conflicts, constraints, and possibilities of developing a critically democratic pedagogy. This chapter has provided a cursory impression of the staff and students who work at Harmony. In the next chapter, we will extend this view and begin to look more closely at the power affiliations of staff members.

3

Power and Participation:
Teachers and Administrators

In the first chapter it was suggested that schools should be constructed in ways that foster a connectionist perspective among students and faculty in order to help establish critical democracy within the United States. Although exploring the power relationships between children and adults is central to any discourse regarding democratic education (which will be discussed in the next chapter), one cannot adequately examine democratic schooling for children and at the same time ignore the power relationships between the teachers and administrators. The dynamics of power and participation found among the adults that work within a given school reflect underlying values which in turn have an impact on the children who spend much of their time among these people. If, as in the vast majority of schools today, teachers work within a hierarchical, bureaucratic institution in which they have relatively limited power to participate in making the school what it is, then it stands to reason that most teachers will not think of and act in ways that will increase the power and participation of their students when it comes to organizing their classrooms. Institutions based upon instrumental and industrial rationalities make it extremely difficult for those who work within them to consider democratic values and practices, whereas institutions based upon a democratic ethos seem to encourage the expansion of power and participation among those who work within them (Pateman, 1970). In other words, it would be difficult to imagine a democratically operated school with teachers and administrators who have totalitarian classrooms. Similarly, it would be incongruous to create a democratic school for students and maintain a rigid, bureaucratic, and hierarchical power structure between administrators and teachers.

Harmony's history illustrates to some degree the way in which a democratic ethos can help expand the power and participation among people working together. Although Steve, the school's founder and director, had values which consistently reflected a democratic ethos, Harmony was not established initially as an experiment in teachers' democratic control over the workplace. Steve stated, "I never set out to create a workers' collective. My focus has always been on students." This lack of attention to power relationships between administrators and faculty is not particularly surprising. Many innovative schools (as well as other enterprises) have been established by dynamic individuals who had great vision and unending energy to "make things happen." Homer Lane's Commonwealth School (Bazeley, 1969), A. S. Neill's Summerhill (Hemming, 1972), John Dewey's school at the University of Chicago (Mayhew & Edwards, 1966), and Carmelita Hinton's Putney School (Lloyd, 1987) are just a few examples. As these accounts suggest, the type of personality needed to create innovative schools often is not the type of personality that one associates with collective decision making and egalitarian sharing of power.

During Harmony's initial years, Steve seemed distant to the elementary faculty. He was particularly concerned about who had the right to "speak" for and set the general direction for the school. He insisted that he be the person to set long-term policy goals and to represent Harmony to the community at large. At one point during the school's formative years, some members of the high school staff directly challenged Steve's authority as director and wanted to establish a workers' collective. These confrontations resulted in their leaving the school. As Steve stated, "The school was on such shaky ground in those years. Our funding sources were so tentative. Any offensive statement or activity by a teacher could have put us under, and there would be no Harmony today." After he was hired and for many years following, Dan, the curriculum coordinator, played a significant role as a go-between between the teachers and Steve. Dan brought to Harmony several valuable attributes: a strong commitment to the democratic process and democratic values, an ability to listen to and facilitate the ideas of others, a willingness to work hard and for long hours to help others succeed, and a belief in faculty (and other workers') control over their workplace. In addition, Steve and Dan developed a close personal friendship, as well as a working partnership which eventually resulted in joint ownership of the school. For many years, one aspect of Dan's role was to intercede and negotiate between Steve and the elementary teachers whenever necessary.

As the school moved into its second decade, the relations among Steve, Dan, and the other teachers have become more egalitarian. Jo, who has been working at Harmony for twelve years, put it this way: "Steve is a lot more open to the staff now than he used to be. The power in the school has spread out a lot since I first came here." Dan, Steve, and several teachers who had worked at Harmony for over five years mentioned the "mutual trust" that has evolved between the teachers and administrators, which they see as the reason why power has become more evenly allocated. Steve also pointed out that after fourteen years, Harmony is more established and secure within the community, and this has lessened his own need for control.

These events, along with a basic commitment to democratic values, slowly transformed the power dynamics among the adults who worked at Harmony.

In trying to understand the nature of, and potential for, democratic arrangements in the governance of schools, it can be helpful to consider symmetrical versus asymmetrical patterns of participation (Eckstein, 1973). Often drawing upon "classical" political thinkers, those advocating symmetrical patterns insist that the only organizations that are "really democratic" are those in which there is "*full participation* . . . a process where each individual member of a decision-making body has equal power to determine the outcome of decisions" (Pateman, 1970: 71). In symmetrical institutions there is an image of workers who are able to make institutional policies, oversee or determine management decisions, and exert real control over their immediate job environment (Rothschild & Whitt, 1986; Lindenfeld & Rothschild-Whitt, 1979). Those favoring asymmetrical patterns argue that institutions by nature will develop some form of hierarchical power structure. Within organizations one will always find that "abilities to produce intended effects and derive benefits are unequally distributed. . . . Someone affects more than he is affected, controls more than he is controlled, and/or gets more of what is allocated" (Eckstein, 1973: 1146). From this perspective, democratic participation reduces the asymmetrical nature of power within institutions, but it can never be completely eliminated. Although it appeals to our most egalitarian sentiments, merely calling for equal power and participation among teachers and administrators as some have suggested (e.g., Beyer, 1988) provides little actual guidance for those interested in establishing democratic schools or classrooms.

There are several practices and areas of concern that can be explored in understanding the relationships between teachers and administrators in democratic schools. For our purposes, it was helpful to draw out the "boundaries" of various individuals' manifestations of power within Harmony's elementary school. Although Harmony's structure provides a basis for the discussion of these practices and issues, it is important to stress that there is no one "right way" to structure democratic schools as work sites. Even a cursory overview of organizational literature indicates significant variety among democratically structured institutions (e.g., Rothschild & Whitt, 1988; Berman, 1982; Lindenfeld, 1982; Pearson & Baker, 1982; Zwerdling, 1982). Democracy can take several different forms, and in most cases will reflect aspects of both symmetrical and asymmetrical institutional relations. Harmony, perhaps like all institutions, does not perfectly reflect any one "model" of organizational structure.

DISTRIBUTION AND MANIFESTATION OF AUTHORITY

At the center of any democratic organization lies the issue of authority. On the surface, Harmony was structured in a pyramid similar to that of traditional bureaucracies (Weber, 1946: 196-244). On the top was Steve, the school founder, president of the governing board, and director. Just below him was Dan, the curriculum coordinator, secretary of the governing board, and middle school coordinator and math teacher. Finally, on the bottom of the pyramid were the teachers.

This differentiation of work roles reflects what is found in most asymmetrical organizations. In fact, a complex network of specialized jobs is a distinctive feature of most nondemocratic bureaucracies. Under the influence of scientific management (Taylor, 1911), the division of labor is maximized to its fullest extent. The notion of the Renaissance person who can accomplish numerous jobs is considered obsolete, inefficient, and impractical. This subdivision of work roles helps legitimate the authority of those on top over the labor force since they are the only ones who have access to information systems related to the operation as a whole and thus can exercise their power to direct the work of subordinates. In this way, work role differentiation is used to minimize the authority of most workers. In contrast, symmetrical institutions make a conscious effort to eradicate the distinction between bosses and laborers through such practices as work role rotation, universal distribution and demystification of specialized knowledge, and teamwork. In symmetrical organizations, everyone manages and everyone works. Administrative tasks are often done as part of a planned work circuit or on a voluntary basis. The elimination of labor differentiation gives everyone control over his or her immediate work station and an informed foundation for participating fully in organizational decision making (Rothschild & Whitt, 1986).

Although the absence of work role differentiation is ideal for democratic institutions, most organizations, even those the size of Harmony, are too complex to completely abolish it. Creating an intellectually and morally rich classroom experience is time consuming, mentally rigorous, and at times physically exhausting. Put simply, good teaching is labor intensive, and placing additional administrative expectations on teachers (and requiring administrators to teach) may not be in the best interest of the staff or students. Most individuals in Harmony did not want to participate in, or know how to do, everything necessary to make the school operate. In other words, minimizing the differentiation of labor would have been difficult, time consuming, and stressful.

Although Harmony's organizational structure and work role differentiation indicated a bureaucratic hierarchy, the actual way in which authority was distributed did not reflect a classical top-down flow of power. In fact, the differentiation of work roles within Harmony actually resulted in the disruption of "power from the top." The school did not simply set policy for teachers to implement; rather, each of Harmony's teachers and administrators had a "sphere of influence" or "realm of power" in which she or he maintained primary authority. Steve, as the school director, was in charge of the school's financial and legal status, the physical plant, long-term planning, hiring of staff, and relations with outside organizations (the city council, the neighborhood association, the Alternative Schools Coalition). Dan, as curriculum coordinator, participated (but to a lesser degree than Steve) in many of the above mentioned areas. However, the focus of Dan's authority was felt in his influence on class offerings, curriculum content, and instructional procedures. For example, he was instrumental in conceptualizing and establishing innovative courses entitled "Exploration," "Research and Discovery," "Creation," and "Recreation" for the elementary school (see Chapter 5). He also served as a consultant to all of the teachers: offering ideas for developing topics of study or instructional strategies, helping them find resources, and meeting with them regularly to keep informed on what they were doing and what they thought needed to be accomplished. Dan's authority was also strongly exerted both in hiring the staff and in selecting students for Harmony's high, middle, and elementary schools. The teachers exerted their authority primarily in their individual classrooms and within the elementary schoolwide activities. Whereas in "symmetrical organizations" authority (and hence responsibility for all aspects of the organization) resides in the body of workers as a whole, at Harmony these "realms of power" and the authority that flowed from them were based on the particular history or talents of the individual. As Jo, one of the lower elementary teachers, put it,

> I guess you'd say we have a "natural" hierarchy. By that I mean, people have the positions they have because there's a natural fit. It's natural that Steve is the director since he founded the school and does a great job of fund raising and overall leadership. I don't think the school would survive without him. In the same way, Dan's natural talents make him the best person as curriculum coordinator. He's like the heart or soul of the school.

Similarly, Steve once mentioned, "I don't think my best qualities would be useful in a classroom. You need really special talents to do a good job of teaching, and while I might be okay, there are a lot of people who are more capable than I."

These spheres of influence and authority disrupt the top-down flow of power found in most schools or other bureaucratic organizations. This disruption was clearly evident in that the curriculum (both what and how something should be taught) was classroom based. In contrast to most schools, at Harmony there were no official curriculum "objectives" distributed from the central office, no school-monitored timetable for reaching those objectives, no turning in of weekly lesson plans for approval, no school-approved textbooks, and no direct supervision of instruction. The teachers determined what content should be taught, what resources and experiences needed to be used for students to learn this content, and what criteria should be used to evaluate the students' as well as their own work. As Barb noted in her response to a question regarding the quality of her "work life,"

> All the teachers at Harmony should teach in a public school for at least a year or two before teaching here to find out how great it is here. In my old school [she taught in a large, metropolitan school district], the curriculum was rigid. Here I was trying to get these kids turned on to reading and writing by giving them a little control over what they wanted to read and write about, but every time I wanted to deviate from the set curriculum, I was told that I couldn't. I felt totally stifled as a teacher in that school. The only thing the administration really was interested in was keeping the kids under control. At this school I feel that I am encouraged to experiment as much as I want with the curriculum and how kids should learn. It's completely the opposite from my last teaching job. Dan is the ideal administrator. He allows you to be as creative as you want. He can be critical of what you are doing, but he's always supportive.

Unlike teachers in most schools, the Harmony teachers had control over what happened in their classrooms.

The commitment to maintain these "realms of power" as a functional policy reflected Dan and Steve's belief that the more control one has over one's own work space, the more fulfilled one is likely to be. In response to a question about his power over the curriculum, Dan stated,

> We want the teachers to be at the *center* of the curriculum. That's why it's best, praxeologically speaking, to let them determine what goes on in their classes. One reason for establishing Exploration and Creation courses [see Chapter 5] was to encourage our teachers to determine what they feel is worthwhile to teach these children. This idea came from the teachers, and all I did was figure out how to structure it into our program. Personally, I can see lots of things that I would like our teachers to do differently, and although I share my concerns or suggestions with them, I would never assert my authority over them. In fact, I do not have the power to do so even if I wanted, but I think this is a strength, not a weakness, in the way we run our school.

In some ways, the hierarchical pyramid could be seen as inverted at Harmony. Teachers were on the top, making the most important decisions related to what happened each day in the school, while Steve and, particularly, Dan provided the communication network, structural foundation, resources, and intellectual encouragement for the teachers to exercise their authority within their respective programs and activities. Perhaps

Schumacher's (1973: 231) image of an ideal type of administrative structure within complex institutions best illustrates the distribution of authority found within Harmony.

> The structure of the organization can then be symbolized by a man [administration] holding a large number of balloons in his hand. Each of the balloons has its own buoyancy and lift, and the man himself does not lord over the balloons, but stands beneath them, yet holding all the strings firmly in his hand. Every balloon is not only an administrative but also an *entrepreneurial* unit.

What this arrangement suggests is that the structure of a particular organization may not be as significant as the ethos (in this case a democratic ethos) which influences the power relationships among the people who work within it. On one hand, Harmony's differentiation of labor seemed similar to the structure found in traditional bureaucracies; however, in this particular setting it allowed for a significant distribution of authority. Given the time and energy it would take to eradicate work role differentiation in Harmony (or other similarly complex organizations) and still have the school operate effectively, and given the potential negative impact its elimination might have on teachers, administrators, and students, it would make sense to do so only as part of a conscious, ideological struggle against all forms of labor division.

Although Harmony's ethos created a meaningful distribution of authority, democratic organizations cannot comprise a collection of totally autonomous pursuits without succumbing to the individualism discussed in the first chapter. At Harmony the closer one was to one's own "sphere of influence," the more arbitrary one could be in making decisions; however, as within any organization, conflicts emerged that needed resolution, decisions affecting the group as a whole had to be reached, and some binding expectations on individual members by the organization as a whole did exist (for example, to provide quality instruction or to maintain the financial solvency of the school). In examining the distribution of authority, one must also investigate the way in which this authority results in organizational, non-"shop-floor"-level decisions: that is, how does authority get manifested among work role peers and across differentiated lines of labor?

As previously mentioned, symmetrical institutions are ideally established without hierarchy. Decisions that are binding on the group as a whole are legitimate only if all members have full and equal participation (Pateman, 1970). Decisions are not made through an elaborate system of protocol. Members do not offer or accept motions, there are no votes taken, and the majority doesn't rule. In the democratic ideal, decisions are reached through a "process of consensus" in which all members define the issues or problems needing to be addressed, negotiate possible resolutions, and then search for common agreement. If consensus cannot be reached about a given issue, then the status quo remains. In symmetrical organizations, all major issues (hiring of personnel, salaries, division of labor, job descriptions) are decided by consensus among the membership, and it is only these consensual decisions that have the moral legitimacy to be authoritative and binding on the group (Goodman, 1980; Rothschild & Whitt, 1986).

This form of power sharing could be seen within smaller working groups such as in administrative or elementary staff meetings. In these meetings there was full participation by the subgroup members, and there was usually an effort to reach consensus in making decisions. For example, neither Steve nor Dan would make any significant administrative decision without the input and consent of the other. Voting at staff meetings would occur only after extensive discussion failed to reach consensus and a decision needed to be made at the immediate meeting. The most noticeable aspect of these discussions was that the participants freely expressed their views. Teachers seemed to feel at ease challenging each other, as well as Steve or Dan, when moved to do so. Formal positions within these groups did not influence the final decisions reached. Rather, decisions were based upon the power of personal, logical, or moralistic appeals by given individuals. As a result, those members, such as Dan, who possessed particular group-processing skills (facilitating other members' ideas, defining problems and concerns, generating alternative solutions) and who could articulate their own ideas and the necessary actions that might flow from those ideas seemed to exert greater influence within this consensual arrangement than other individuals or than they might have under a simple voting procedure.

In addition to power being exerted through moralistic, logical, and personal appeals, the seniority of the individual also seemed to manifest power through this decision-making process. Under voting protocol, all members, including initiates, have "equal" voice through their vote on particular matters. However, within this consensual process, those teachers who had worked at Harmony for less than two years expressed feelings of powerlessness vis-à-vis the other staff members. Barb was particularly interested in having teachers assume more power over Steve's "sphere of influence," and she mentioned her desire for a school that was "more collectively run." The seniority of the teachers seemed to play a role in the power dynamics within the elementary staff. As Jim put it, "There's a horizontal hierarchy at this school. I just don't feel as if my ideas are heard like some of the other teachers'. I often hear things like, 'We don't do that at Harmony.'" When Jim raised this issue at a staff meeting towards the end of the year, the others conceded that perhaps the new teachers didn't have as much power as others because of seniority. But although power was not evenly manifested within this consensus process because of the seniority and/or communication skills of certain individuals, the key to successful decision making within these groups was found in the members' willingness to *negotiate* their individual interests with those of other members to create a unified solution.

As previously mentioned, organizations such as Harmony are too complex and labor intensive to rely solely on the full participation of all members in making decisions that affect the institution as a whole or even large segments of it. Because of the asymmetrical structure of Harmony, a variety of opportunities for democratic participation existed in decision making across differentiated lines of labor or between different "spheres of influence." In most "democratic" or "representative" bureaucracies (Gouldner, 1954; Lipset, Trow, & Coleman, 1962), one will find some form of "partial" participation (Pateman, 1970: 70) in which workers exert influence upon managerial decisions but superordinates determine the final outcome. This dynamic was common within Harmony. Because of Steve's "sphere of influence," he made many decisions (with full participation from Dan) that affected the school as a whole after obtaining "input" from the other members of the staff. For instance, when hiring an upper elementary math teacher, Steve and Dan prescreened several candidates before narrowing the choice to two. Then these candidates interviewed with the two upper elementary teachers, and eventually with the entire staff of Harmony. Before offering this position to one of the candidates, the staff had a lengthy meeting to discuss the candidates' values, intellectual qualifications, and personal attributes. In this case, the staff was evenly split between the two candidates, so Steve and Dan made the final decision. However, it was clear that if there had been strong objections to either candidate by either of the upper elementary faculty members (since this was within their "sphere of influence") or by some of the staff members at this meeting, neither Steve nor Dan would have offered this candidate a position. In fact, Dan verbalized this balance of power to the staff at a faculty retreat and later to us.

> Julie [the upper elementary natural/social science teacher] is leaving this year, and Jim [the lower elementary math teacher] wanted her position. Luckily Jordan, Julie's predecessor and probably the best teacher Harmony has ever had, wanted to come back [after living in Boston for six years] and teach. Naturally, Steve, I, and the other teachers who knew Jordan thought this was great. However, the teachers who didn't know him felt a loyalty to Jim. When we had our faculty retreat, they were upset that we [Steve and Dan] had already decided to hire Jordan over Jim, and we told them that we wouldn't hire anyone that they didn't want. And

we meant it. If we had tried to force our decision on them, the negative consequences would have been greater than the benefit of having Jordan teach here.

After a lengthy discussion by the staff, Jordan was offered the position.

Although this "input" was often sought prior to a given decision, it could also emerge as the result of a challenge by a member outside of a given "sphere of influence" about a decision that had "been made" by those within this sphere. In other words, the members of Harmony felt free to "cross" their differentiated lines of labor and "spheres of influence" to question and potentially alter decisions already made. For example, in an effort to ease stress on the school's budget, Steve made the decision to postpone the yearly staff salary raise (of $1,000) until the end of the year. Although this was not a problem for most faculty, Jo, one of the lower elementary school teachers and a single mother of a small child, became concerned.

> When I heard what was going to happen to our salary raise, I went in to talk to Steve. I told him I just couldn't afford to wait until the end of the year for my salary increase. I don't get any money from my ex-husband, so I need everything I make just to keep up. On the other hand, Steve didn't have the money to give all of us our raises in our monthly paychecks. So we called a staff meeting to talk about it, and came up with a workable solution. Basically, it was okay with everyone if I got my salary increase each month while the rest waited until the end of the year.

Another example of a member crossing into another sphere of influence occurred at the end of the school year when Steve became directly involved in a curricular decision by the elementary faculty. Jo and Jim (with the input and support of the other elementary faculty) wanted to alter their morning class schedule for the second and third graders from a departmentalized curriculum (math/science and language arts) in which they each taught "their subject" to both age groups, to self-contained classrooms similar to Michele's first-grade class. Steve and Dan opposed this change, and a couple of lengthy meetings were held (since each individual had compelling reasons for his or her position) until a mutual compromise could be achieved.

To summarize, the distribution and manifestation of authority is perhaps the most complex issue facing organizations based upon a democratic ethos. Although calls for total equalization of authority are appealing, for most institutions that have a complicated mission such as teaching young children, these calls are overly simplistic and ineffectual. As long as teaching children requires special talents and remains labor intensive, some form of work role differentiation will exist, and with it, to some degree, an asymmetrical manifestation of authority. However, the presence of an asymmetrical structure does not automatically result in the establishment of a bureaucratic organization. There is significant ground between a symmetrical organization and a tightly controlled bureaucratic structure that impedes all forms of democratic control. In Harmony, we observed authority moving in several directions: top-down, down-top, and sideways. Decisions were made with the full participation of the members, with partial participation, and with little participation within and across differential lines of labor and "spheres of influence."

What is perhaps most important is that democratic organizations avoid what Verba (1961) and later Pateman (1970) have referred to as "pseudo participation" among the work force. In this situation, subordinates are often informed and allowed to question and discuss decisions made by super-ordinates, but they are not given any real power within the institution. As Verba (1961) notes, the goal is to give workers a *feeling* of participation by employing a certain interpersonal style with employees. In actuality, the worker has a limited or no "sphere of influence," and superordinates' communications are designed to win "endorsements" from workers and increase their motivation to work. However, under "pseudo participation" these superordinates are not responsible to the members at large, nor can their decisions be directly challenged. As a result, this level of participation actually mystifies the democratic process, making it more difficult to alter the dynamics of power within institutions. Although we are not subscribing to the notion that the distribution and manifestation of authority need be totally equalized, what we are calling for are organizations committed to the reduction of domination so that individuals with authority have respon-sibility to the membership at large: that is, individual decisions may become known, challenged, altered, and overturned by the membership if necessary.

Perhaps the most illuminating insight from our observations of Har-mony's organizational structure concerns the potential power of a democratic ethos on an institution. It is important to remember that Harmony was not established as an experiment in workplace democracy. Yet when a school was created in which democratic values were openly discussed and seen as a foundation for pedagogical practices, these values filtered beyond adult-child relationships. Harmony's experience of work site democracy is partic-ularly powerful when seen in the light of other research findings that make the same observation (e.g., Lloyd, 1987).

WRITTEN POLICY

Another complex practice and issue regarding the power and participation of workers within organizations can be found in the area of written policy. Bureaucracies are formed on the premise that organizations should be governed by an elaborate and formal system of written regulations. In providing written rules, the organization minimizes the arbitrary nature of life in the institutional setting. Everyone knows what is expected of him or her, and decisions are then formulated, enacted upon, and petitioned in light of what is written down. Written policy within bureaucracies provides the opportunity for one's work life to be established and carried out in a predictable manner and if necessary reorganized in a systematic fashion. No one then can claim surprise or ignorance about what the organization expects. Rules cannot be whimsically altered to suit those individuals in power on a day-to-day or person-to-person basis. In this sense, written policies (or in the case of society, laws) are seen as the cornerstone of formal justice.

In symmetrical organizations there is a conscious effort to avoid written policy as a basis upon which to structure institutional life (Lindenfeld & Rothschild-Whitt, 1979; Rothschild & Whitt, 1986). This idea, of course, can be traced back to anarchist notions that within an ideal democratic society (or institution) there is no need for written policies, explicit rules, or governing bodies since the social order can be achieved through the cooperative, self-disciplined actions of its members (Guerin, 1970; Manicas, 1985). Although it would be impossible to have an organization completely devoid of policies, democratic institutions such as Harmony try to minimize explicit regulations governing worker participation as much as possible.

At Harmony, there were no written job descriptions, no written delegation of authority, no signed contract or staff manual listing organizational do's and do not's. Harmony's only explicit rule governing administrators and teachers (and even this was not written down anywhere) was that they must come to work. A spontaneous, ad hoc approach to operations took the place of written policy. When a situation arose that needed the attention of the group, a meeting was called and the appropriate policy emerged from this meeting. Rather than try to write policy for universalistic goals, these policy meetings focused on the peculiarities of individual situations.

The primary virtue of the lack of formalized and universalistic policies was that it provided greater flexibility in dealing with the daily life of the school. As Dan once stated,

> The thing I don't ever want to tell someone [a teacher] at this school is that we can't do something because there's some "rule" that says no. Schools should be run in order to facilitate the ideas of the teachers and students, not to prevent ideas from being turned into actions. If it's a good idea, and most of our teachers' ideas are good, then I see the role of the school as providing the support necessary to turn it into reality. We can almost always find a way to work around constraints. When you have lots of rules and regulations, it's almost impossible to "seize the moment" and act on a really good, spontaneous idea. At Harmony, I never want the "institution" to stand in the way of the people who work here, but that's exactly what most schools do to most teachers, not to mention students.

Although this flexibility was manifested mostly in curricular and instructional matters (see Chapter 5), it could also be seen at work in power relations across differentiated lines of labor. In fact, this issue was discussed at the previously mentioned faculty retreat (see pages 71–72).

> The teachers were asked for their input into the hiring of Jordan to replace Julie next year, and at first they were reluctant. Some questioned Dan and Steve's interest in their opinion since they felt the decision had already been made. One wanted to know exactly what power they had in making this decision: "I don't want to spend a lot of time talking about it if it's not going to make any difference one way or the other." Another teacher suggested that what should be done would be to determine exactly who, among the faculty and administration, had what power to do what within the school. He suggested that there be guidelines written that indicated this division of power. At first this seemed like a good idea to most faculty since everyone would know exactly what power he or she had within the school. However, Steve, Dan, and a few other faculty members argued against it. At one point Dan said, "Do you [the faculty] really want to give us [the administration] absolute power over various aspects of the school? Don't you always want to feel that you can get involved in the decisions that get made around here? Don't you always want to be able to challenge decisions that have been made by Steve or me? I think if we write down who can do what, we will grow to regret it. I think leaving things intentionally ambiguous allows for greater participation on the part of anyone who wants to get involved." After a lengthy discussion, the staff agreed with Dan's perspective and reached a consensus that it was better to avoid written guidelines that might formalize the exercise of power within Harmony. (Summary of field notes)

Although the absence of written policy provided a greater flexibility and flow of power within Harmony, potential dangers do exist in not having written rules and regulations. This potential was almost manifested during the confrontation that occurred when Jo and Jim wanted to move from a departmentalized to a self-contained classroom structure for their second- and third-grade morning curriculum (see page 72). As previously mentioned, Steve and Dan opposed this alteration, and Steve's initial response to the idea was extreme. After listing several pedagogical reasons for his position, he told us, "We've been doing it this way since the school started, and it's worked really well for our kids. Why fix things that aren't broken? The way I see it, if the teachers want to change this, they can find work at another school." When asked if he would really let teachers leave over this issue, his first reaction was clearly affirmative. When the elementary staff met with Steve and Dan for their end-of-the-year meeting, this topic was first on the agenda. Soon after the meeting began, several substantive pedagogical reasons for maintaining the current structure as well as for altering it were examined. After about an hour of discussion,

> Steve's strong feelings emerged and he mentioned that he did not think he would allow the teachers to change. Jo jumped in at this point and issued a strong objection. "I really don't like what I just heard. You can share your ideas and voice your objections, but I don't like hearing that somehow you can prevent us from doing this. We've always been in control of the curriculum. This should be our decision, not yours." At this point, Dan diffused the confrontation by stating that he was "sure we [the administrators and lower elementary program teachers] can find a solution to the problems that have been raised today," and they set up a special meeting to focus only on this issue. (Summary of field notes)

When asked what he would do if the teachers insisted on altering the morning schedule to self-contained classrooms and Steve asserted his intention to prevent that from happening, Dan told us,

> Even though I am in favor of keeping what we have, it should be the teachers' decision. So as curriculum coordinator, I would have to assert my authority over this area of the school, and would have to veto Steve's veto of the teachers' decision. However, I guarantee that this won't be necessary.

Dan's prediction was accurate. After some reflection, Steve no longer felt a need to assert his desires over those of the teachers, and a solution to the teachers' and administrators' concerns was worked out at the previously mentioned special meeting.

Although this situation was resolved in a manner that reinforced the mutual respect and commitment between the administrators and teachers at Harmony, it illustrates the primary danger of not having written policies or guidelines within such institutions. Without such formal policies, one can see how decisions that have tremendous impact on people's lives can be capriciously and undemocratically made by those in positions of power. Given a different set of people and circumstances, this episode could have destroyed Harmony's elementary school. Lindenfeld (1982) illustrates the dissolution of one democratically run free school simply because conflicts of policy could not be reasonably resolved within the organization. After all, most written contracts and job descriptions are the result of workers struggling for just and equitable treatment from administrators.

However, one should not assume that the resolution of this episode depended upon Harmony's "good luck." Policy decisions at Harmony and other well-run democratically organized institutions are not made arbitrarily. As Rothschild and Whitt (1986) note in their study of these organizations and as became apparent in the discussion that took place during the special meeting between Dan, Steve, and the lower elementary school teachers, policy decisions are based upon substantive values such as fairness, caring, equity, individual needs, and the common good. In this meeting, everyone made an effort to respond to the interests of Jo and Jim while addressing the concerns of Dan and Steve. Foremost in all of their minds were the pedagogical and psychological needs of the students who would be affected by any changes. It was the recognition and legitimacy of these substantive, democratic values that prevented whimsical or despotic policy decisions from occurring. Within organizations such as Harmony it is these values that provide consistency, if not universality, in policy decision making.

SOCIAL CONTROL

Practices and issues of social control are particularly perplexing for those who wish to establish democratic schools and other work sites. According to Weber (1946), organizations exist to enable people to accomplish particular tasks. In order to accomplish these tasks, bureaucratic organizations must have the cooperation (if not the goodwill) of those who work far from the center of power within them. As a result, social control becomes crucial as a means of ensuring that lower-level personnel efficiently implement the directives from those on top.

As bureaucratic organizations have grown and become more complex, different mechanisms for social control have emerged. Edwards (1979) identifies three types of control that organizations have employed in their efforts to ensure that individuals follow accepted procedures for maximum productivity. The first form of control is *personal*: a supervisor directly monitors workers' actions. The second form of control is *bureaucratic*: workers are governed by impersonal rules and regulations, and these are enforced through a system of sanctions and rewards. Bureaucratic control is less conspicuous than personal control, but no less constraining. As Gouldner (1954) notes, rules, regulations, rewards, and sanctions can easily substitute for more direct forms of social control. On the surface, this type of control can give the appearance of worker autonomy and participation within a relatively decentralized organization. However, what is not observable is that the premises of worker decisions and actions are carefully orchestrated from the top through the written policies of the organization (Blau, 1970; Bates, 1970). The final form of control identified by Edwards is *technical*: workers' tasks and the evaluation of their efforts are embedded in the physical structure of the workplace, the daily schedule, the types of tools required, and the nature of the product produced. Of all three forms of control, the most effective, undemocratic, and insidious is technical control. This is true because the means through which technical control is exerted are often in place when workers arrive and are thus taken for granted. As a result, few think of them as mechanisms of social control, and rarely do workers consider an alternative distribution of authority or work roles. Although unions and other labor organizations have been able to protect workers from unfair bureaucratic regulations or supervisors in many cases, it has been much more difficult to alter job descriptions, the physical structure of a building, the type of product produced, or the tools given to workers. Most workers and their unions have been willing to confine their interests to financial and physical safety concerns rather than focus on issues of participation and power (Montgomery, 1979; Urban, 1982).

As some educators note (Blumberg, 1980; Meyer & Rowan, 1978; Warren, 1973; Weick, 1976), most traditional schools have evolved as "loosely coupled systems"; that is, teachers' labor has been organized to minimize the need for direct supervision by administrators or bureaucratic rules. This organization often gives the appearance of teacher autonomy. Supposedly, when teachers "close their doors," they have significant control over what happens in their classrooms. However, a closer look reveals that traditional schools have adopted a highly sophisticated level of technical control through the use of standardized instructional programs and the proliferation of statewide achievement tests that determine school curriculum (Apple & Teitelbaum, 1986; Duffy, Roehler, & Putman, 1987; Frymier, 1987b; Goodman, 1988a; Woodward, 1986). Proponents of these instructional programs and standardized testing often argue that even though teachers are given these programs and even though these tests do determine the curricular content of a given grade, teachers can still determine "how" to use them and teach this curriculum. However, these instructional programs come complete with specified learning objectives (content), step-by-step instructional procedures (usually dominated by worksheets and drills), and quantitative exams to dictate what pupils learn. As a result, teachers' control over their classrooms often is restricted to merely coordinating the day's work (schedule time for each subject and ability group, plan seatwork to keep children busy, discipline pupils to keep them on task, maintain pupils' records) to guarantee that pupils "get through the material" on time. Because of the widespread use of these programs and tests and their embedded nature within the school, most teachers do not recognize them as forces of social control.

As previously discussed, democratic organizations attempt to minimize the legitimacy of centralized authority to achieve social control, whether it be by personal proclamation, written policy, or organizational structure (Rothschild & Whitt, 1986). However, it would be a mistake to think that organizations can exist, even symmetrical institutions, without some form of social control. In addition to personal and bureaucratic forms of social control, Perrow (1976) identifies *homogeneity* as a means of ensuring worker compliance. Selection for homogeneity is a common form of social control for upper-level management positions in bureaucratic organizations. Only people who have a particular worldview, who associate with particular types of people, who have similar life-styles, and, most important, who express a similar organizational philosophy are selected for positions of authority.

Since authority is more evenly distributed within democratic organizations such as Harmony, this selection of homogeneity is the primary means of socially controlling all workers, not just those in managerial positions. As previously mentioned, once hired, the teachers at Harmony had much greater authority over "shop-floor" (classroom) decisions and greater opportunity for participation across differentiated lines of labor than their public school counterparts. As a result, the process for hiring new faculty was much more extensive than that found in typical school systems. The two final candidates for the upper elementary position were each cumulatively interviewed for over twenty hours by various people in Harmony. Steve and Dan (individually and together) interviewed both candidates several times, and they made it a point to interview them in an informal setting outside of school (at either their homes or the candidates' homes) in an effort to, as Steve stated, "get to know them as people." Dan once told us that the "primary concern is to find a candidate who fits into the philosophy of the school." During the staff interviews and subsequent discussion of these candidates, the importance of faculty homogeneity was evident, both in terms of the talents needed to teach at Harmony and in terms of an understanding of the school's philosophy.

> After the two candidates were interviewed, the staff then discussed which one they wanted to hire. Each had obvious strengths and weaknesses. Bill clearly reflected the image of Harmony, or, as Michele stated, he was obviously a "Harmonite." Bill was twenty-eight years old, and a philosophy major from Princeton University. Since graduation, he had become interested in several "alternative" pursuits. He taught yoga, studied with a Native American medicine man, was involved in Quakerism and pacifism, played and composed folk music, and was learning about nutrition and health foods. During the interview, his responses to questions clearly indicated that he was attracted to Harmony's approach to education. Several faculty members mentioned that Bill seemed to be an extremely gentle and thoughtful person. The staff agreed that he seemed to have special interpersonal talents which would enable him to work effectively with the students. Most faculty felt that Bill would fit well into the community ethos of the school. As Francis stated, "Bill's the kind of person I'd like to work with and get to know. I liked his vibes." One drawback to Bill's hiring was that he had never taught before and had never worked with young children. Even though he had a strong math background (one of the job requirements was to teach math during the morning classes), a

number of faculty members expressed concern about his lack of teaching experience. Dan also mentioned that he was not sure of Bill's commitment to teaching and staying in Bloomington: "It's clear that Bill does not know if teaching is for him. As he said, he's interested in trying it out, but he has lots of interests, and I have doubts that teaching at Harmony will be his primary concern. Obviously, I want a teacher who puts Harmony above all other interests. In addition, Bill moved here in order to live with his girlfriend, who is in the School of Music. What happens when she gets her degree in a few years? Is Bill going to stay? As he said, he can't make any long-term commitments." Bart, on the other hand, was fully committed to teaching and living in this area. He had gotten his degree in 1982 from Indiana University in elementary education. After graduation, he taught for a year and then worked as a carpenter for six years. Although he was making "good money," he was "unfulfilled" and went back to teaching at a significant reduction in salary. He was recently laid off from his teaching position in a Montessori school, and during his interviews he expressed an intense desire to teach at Harmony. Bart also had numerous interests, including architecture, music composition, and science. What was particularly impressive was his demonstrated ability to develop original curricula (he brought in several examples of units he had developed over the last couple of years), which people felt would be exceptionally useful in teaching Exploration, Creation, and Research and Discovery classes [see Chapter 5]. In addition, it was suggested that his experience as a carpenter would be useful in his teaching of math. The primary concerns about Bart's candidacy were in the areas of philosophy and interpersonal relationships. During his interview he was not articulate about his own educational or social philosophy, and he didn't seem to fully understand Harmony's orientation to educating children. Dan stated, "What concerns me is that every time we asked him about what he would do with a kid who is in emotional turmoil, he always stated that it was necessary to deal with kids' personal problems in order to help them with their academics. In other words, it seemed as if the only reason for nurturing a child would be to help him or her be a better student. He didn't seem to understand that sometimes the affective needs of a child are more important than his or her academic needs." Alison wondered if Bart was interested in the complex discussions that often took place at faculty meetings: "Sometimes our meetings can get pretty abstract, and I wonder if Bart has an interest in this part of Harmony." There was general consensus that Bart lacked the proper philosophical orientation, although he possessed the unique instructional talents needed for Harmony. The mood seemed to be going in Bill's favor despite his lack of experience. However, Steve then stated, "You know, we pay a lot of lip service to diversity, but if we look at the staff we are not a very diverse group of people. Maybe the fact that Bart is different from most of us is actually something positive rather than negative. We could use more diversity on the staff." Alison then added,

"Bart definitely brings more diversity. He is a tinker, a Hoosier, someone who is just down to earth, a practical kind of guy. We have a lot of teachers who can be philosophical. I think that maybe we could use a teacher like Bart. I bet we have some kids who would be attracted to the type of person Bart is more than the rest of us." Michele cautioned, "Let's remember that whenever we've hired someone in the past who doesn't seem to flow with the philosophy of the school, that person usually ends up leaving." At this point, one teacher mentioned that they should consider that Bart isn't all that different. "Don't forget, he's good friends with _____ and _____. That whole group of people. He's not a yuppie. His life-style and basic values are clearly like ours." Jo asked Dan, "Do you think he would be willing to work with us on the philosophical level?" Dan added that when he talked to Bart's previous employer, it seemed that his educational philosophy would fit in well at Harmony. "The director praised Bart for his creativity and ability to relate well to his students and was critical of Bart for all the things we want in a teacher: that is, he didn't follow the Montessori method all the time and was 'too flexible' in his curriculum. I guess I think we could work with Bart. I think he has some real potential." Throughout this discussion, several straw votes were taken, and the tally was always about evenly split. Several teachers, like Alison, changed their vote more than once. One teacher stated that Barb and Julie, the two other upper elementary teachers, should decide, but they were also unsure. Steve then mentioned that there was a possibility that he might be able to hire one of them for the job training program. Consensus was soon reached that if this grant came through, Bart should be offered the elementary position and Bill should be offered the job training position. Otherwise, the decision would be left up to Steve and Dan. (Summary of field notes)

As mentioned in the second chapter, within Harmony it was possible to recognize significant differences among the faculty in terms of life-styles, educational philosophy, and social values. However, from the outside, the staff at Harmony, including Bart, appeared basically homogeneous. By using the selection of faculty for homogeneity as the method for social control, it is possible for workers to exercise significant power within the organization and at the same time not threaten the basic premises and practices upon which that organization is based.

Although selection for homogeneity was the primary means of social control within Harmony, there were also subtle ideological forces that restricted what one could conceivably do. As previously mentioned, Jim felt there was a "horizontal hierarchy" within Harmony that gave "senior" faculty members more power than "junior" members. At times Jim mentioned feeling that Harmony was too permissive in the way it treated students, and he felt restricted in his interpersonal relationships because they would not fit into this permissive orientation. On the other hand, Barb expressed feeling frustrated because she felt Harmony was too restrictive. She felt students should have more "freedom" and "choice," and felt somewhat inhibited by the school's structure and traditions. As previously discussed, in making group decisions (lower elementary program, elementary school, all three schools) some teachers were socially controlled by those, such as Dan, who could articulate personal, logical, or moralistic appeals better than others. Although the teachers universally recognized and expressed appreciation for the freedom and authority they had in making decisions, Harmony, like other democratic organizations, possessed various mechanisms for the social control of labor.

SOCIAL COSTS

The final issue to be discussed concerns the social costs of worker participation. Most individuals think of democracy as providing something to people; in fact, democratic living requires significant obligations from people. It is important to remember, as Rothschild & Whitt (1986) and others (Almond & Verba, 1963; White & Lippitt, 1960) point out, that greater worker participation carries with it a price. Within educational settings there is one "social cost" that is particularly worth noting: the labor intensiveness of teaching. As Apple (1986) and Densmore (1987) note, teachers (as well as other workers) are often socially controlled through the intensification of their work; that is, teachers are given large numbers of students, mounds of paperwork, and extra duties which keep them so busy that they have little time or energy to get involved in more substantive issues of education and schooling. However, even under much better working conditions, such as those found in Harmony, good teaching is labor intensive. As Alison, one of the high school teachers, noted during Bill's interview, the teachers at Harmony were expected to take on several responsibilities.

> Being a teacher here requires you to be comfortable without a job description. It simply isn't working X number of hours and teaching X number of courses and working with X number of students. You have to be on call twenty-four hours a day. It's not just teaching subjects, it's counseling with the children and their parents, participating in lots of long [staff] meetings, interviewing and selecting potential students, running errands for the school, planning curriculum, doing library work, helping out in fund-raising activities. In fact, only about half of our time is spent in the classroom. The other half is spent doing everything else that is necessary to make this school operate.

Although our observations indicated that teachers actually spent about two-thirds of their time preparing for and teaching classes, Alison's description of working at Harmony was accurate. Although getting involved in students' (as well as parents' and teachers') personal lives, confronting complex problems, actively engaging in substantive decision making with others, and having the freedom to generate and act upon their own ideas resulted in high levels of morale and a great deal of personal meaning among the teachers at Harmony, these same factors also took considerable time out of their lives and demanded a level of emotional intensity not found in most traditional schools. Jim and Jo stated that Steve and Dan set the pace and the quality of work in Harmony, and since they work "extra hard," they said, "we all do." Michele put it this way:

> What happens is this. We succumb to what I call the perfectionist syndrome. We constantly try to provide something really special, and as a result our normal workload is heavy. Then something comes up that demands just an ungodly amount of time and energy, like our midyear trips (three days), Holiday Follies (student talent show), or the Science Fair. Then when we get back to normal, it seems like a lull, so someone comes up with another idea that gets us going again. At times, it gets to be just too much.

In particular, staff meetings seemed to take significant energy and time. The elementary staff met once a week for two to three hours and had all-day retreats three times during the year. In addition, the teachers often met during lunch and before or after school to discuss particular children or situations that occurred during the day or to plan for a future event. The entire staff at Harmony would meet each month and have two day-long retreats at the beginning and end of the school year. However, what was unique about these meetings was that they rarely were limited to procedural or technical matters like those found at the "faculty meetings" of most traditional schools. To the contrary, because of the democratic ethos of Harmony and the fact that its purposes were not taken for granted, the staff often engaged in substantive philosophical discourses related to events that occurred or would occur at the school. Issues related to student power, teacher power, freedom (personal and academic), control, the meaningfulness of the subject matter taught, the quality of educational experiences, patriarchy, capitalism, or ecology were a regular part of the dialogue within formal and informal faculty meetings. For example, in planning the year-end trip to St. Louis, the only place that Dan could arrange for sleeping quarters was an army barracks. As a result, the staff had a lengthy discussion to decide if they should have the students stay there. Some voiced concern that they might be implicitly endorsing and legitimating United States militarism if they stayed there. Most felt that staying in the barracks would give them the opportunity to spontaneously discuss with the students the role of the military within a democratic society. In most traditional schools, the decision of "where to stay" would have been seen as strictly procedural and would not have been raised for faculty consideration; however, if it had been, the subsequent faculty discussion would probably not have included a discussion of militarism. It was clear that these teachers were engaged in creating not only the practices within the school but also the theories that generated these practices. Of course, all of these meetings and substantive discourses took significant amounts of time and energy.

Pateman (1970) and others have tried to argue that limited democratic participation breeds within people a desire to participate more fully. Therefore, symmetrical organizations are the ideal towards which we should strive (Beyer, 1988). Although Pateman's argument may be true for some people, there are boundaries as to how much one is willing "to give" in the name of democracy. Clearly, control over shop-floor decisions, such as within classrooms, is crucial to a democratic distribution of authority. However, what is more problematic is the extent to which people are willing to participate in matters requiring peer-group decision making and across differentiated lines of labor. As Crozier (1964: 204–206) noted in his study of workers' participation,

> Progress can always be made in the area of participation. However, the limits are narrower than one usually thinks. . . . People are ambivalent toward participation. On the one hand, people would like very much to participate in order to control their own environment. On the other hand, they fear that if and when they participate, their own behavior will be controlled by their coparticipants. . . . By refusing to be involved in policy determination, one remains much more free from outside pressure. . . . Retreatism [deciding not to participate] can be a very rational form of behavior whenever the individual concerned has good reason to believe that the rewards he is offered are not commensurate with his efforts, and feels that there is a good chance that he will be manipulated. The will to participate, finally, depends to a large extent on the degree of trust and openness in interpersonal relations characteristic of the cultural norms to which people [within the organization] adhere.

Within democratic organizations, if one is dissatisfied, either one must take responsibility for one's own dissatisfaction, or one must commit time and energy to altering the conditions. However, making this decision is potentially risky. For example, Jim was displeased with Harmony's curriculum and often complained that he couldn't do what he wanted. At the end of his first year at Harmony, he spoke to Dan about it, and Dan encouraged him to work to make the changes he desired (a more fully integrated and coordinated curriculum between classes and across grade levels based on ecological themes).

> Jim's response was that he didn't see himself as a "doer," that is, an activist who will work to make significant changes within a given organization. Dan suggested then that Harmony might not be the best school for Jim. "Around here if you don't make it happen, it won't happen." (Summary of field notes)

Within Harmony, subordinates or peer workers have the opportunity to alter the structure and substance of their work, but this opportunity, if assumed by an individual, exacts a price in time and effort, and it contains the real risk that these efforts may not be successful. Although full participation provides workers with significant rewards (Russell, 1982), it also has costs. In order to share power and the responsibility that comes with it, one must sacrifice in terms of other potential ways to spend one's time and energy. Expressing the desire to "create the world" in which we work is almost instinctive to most of us; however, assuming the sacrifices that are required for the full participation found in symmetrical organizations may be reasonable to only a few individuals. Most people may want more control among coworkers and across differentiated lines of labor, but the price necessary for this control may be too high.

Clearly, some individuals lack the interest and/or the talents necessary to work within democratic organizations. As pointed out in the first chapter, this is especially true in cultures such as ours, in which few people have opportunities to develop participatory attitudes and abilities. However, there is some evidence that experience in democratic organizations can alter individuals' values, the quality of their work, and their social identities (Perry, 1978; Russell, 1982; Schlesinger & Bart, 1982). Pateman (1970: 105) suggests

> that we do learn to participate by participating and that feelings of political efficacy are more likely to be developed in a participatory environment.
> . . . The evidence indicates that experience of a participatory authority structure might also be effective in diminishing tendencies toward non-democratic attitudes.

There was some support for this contention at Harmony. As the year progressed, we observed that Bart, the new upper elementary teacher, became slowly more involved in the workings of the school. During his midyear review with Steve and Dan, he expressed dissatisfaction with his own teaching and questioned the disciplinary approach taken towards the students. He felt that the staff spent too much time telling students what not to do, and that they should spend more time telling them initially how they want them to behave. Dan and Steve encouraged Bart to "get more involved." Nevertheless, it took nearly the entire year before Bart began to feel comfortable enough to assert his ideas. According to Dan, upon his return the following fall, Bart participated to a much greater degree than in his first year. "Bart has really come through this year. He's much more committed to the school, and has taken some real leadership in the upper elementary program. I had my doubts about him after last year, but I'm really happy with the way he's working now."

To summarize, it may not be in our best interest to look at symmetrical organizations as the ideal form of democratic participation within school settings. To do so might only invite potential burnout or decreased effectiveness on the part of the teachers. Advocating full participation may in fact obscure the type of discourse necessary to increase the democratic participation of teachers in the running of their schools. As mentioned at the beginning of this chapter, symmetrical schools are probably impossible to achieve, and it is unlikely that most teachers would want the responsibility of full participation on top of their classroom demands. If our only model of democratic participation is found in symmetrical organizations, then our sensibilities are being artificially narrowed. Calling for fully democratic organizations may appeal to our most cherished ideals, but it does little to actually foster democratic actions. What would be more helpful and realistic is to struggle to create democratic organizations within an asymmetrical structure. Perhaps for this reason, Harmony provides some useful illustrations of teachers' democratic control over their own shop-floor labor and participation in the management of the organization in which they work.

REFLECTIONS: TEACHER EMPOWERMENT

In recent years there has been a growing call for teachers to become more "empowered." However, as this notion has become more popularized, its meaning has become increasingly vague, to the point that one can question its usefulness for altering the working lives of teachers. Initially, the concept of empowering teachers emerged from an analysis of teachers' work as part of labor and gender studies within education (Apple, 1986; Densmore, 1987; Giroux, 1988b; Goodman 1988a). Drawing, in part, upon the work of several labor sociologists (e.g., Braverman, 1975; Burawoy, 1979; Edwards, 1979; Gordon, Edwards, & Reich, 1982; Wood, 1982), teachers, like other workers (both industrial and professional) under twentieth-century capitalism, have lost significant control over their own work processes. Through an overly rationalized organization of the workplace (as reflected in the use of the previously mentioned prepackaged curriculum programs used in traditional schools) which results in the fragmentation, isolation, and mechanization of labor, workers are becoming "deskilled," "disenfranchised," or "degraded"; that is, the conceptualization of how a particular job should be accomplished is largely separated from those who actually do the work. As a result, workers eventually have little ownership over their craft. As new employees are brought into these rationalized work sites, they are often unaware of the special talents and thoughtfulness that were historically required of given occupations. Under these conditions, any initial talent and craftsmanship eventually atrophy, and skilled industrial workers and professionals become mere technicians that efficiently follow the directives of the organization.

In addition to these labor studies, gender analyses of occupations have also contributed to the call for teachers' empowerment. The basic thrust of these studies has been to illustrate the role that patriarchy has played in the oppression of women workers. As Barrett (1979) notes, women's work has been *vertically* separated from men's occupations. As a group, women have been tracked into particular types of occupations (teachers, secretaries, nurses, waitresses, salesclerks, domestic cleaners) rather than others (doctors, lawyers, managers, executives), and then these occupations are rationalized by men as being insignificant. As Mead (1949: 159) states,

> In every known society, the male's need for achievement can be recognized. Men may cook or weave or dress dolls or hunt hummingbirds, but if such activities are appropriate occupations for men, then the whole of society, men and women alike, votes them as important. When the same occupations are performed by women, they are regarded as less important. In a great number of human societies, men's sureness of their own sex roles is tied up with their right, or ability, to practice some activity that women are not allowed to practice.

The impact of this patriarchal tracking can be seen most clearly in occupations that have been "feminized," such as clerical work and teaching, or "masculinized," such as medicine (transformed from male to female staffing patterns or vice versa). Because of patriarchy, as women filled the classrooms, teachers' status and autonomy diminished. Men who stayed in education became building administrators, curriculum writers, and educational researchers. The "work" of educating our children was thus divided into two camps. One group engaged in empirical and conceptual research, wrote textbooks and other types of instructional programs, and supervised how education was implemented. This group was almost completely dominated by men. The second group, dominated by women, became the recipient of the former group's efforts and was expected to implement its plans. The gender composition and relationship between these two groups has essentially remained unchanged, serving to keep women relatively powerless and "in their place." Efforts to challenge these patriarchal circumstances have been directed primarily at helping women gain access to traditional male occupations rather than at upgrading work that has been labeled "women's work."

Given this background, the call to empower teachers was a direct response to particular historical and social conditions. The empowerment of teachers was initially an effort to directly challenge the "deskilling" of teachers by substantively rethinking the relations of power within schools. In addition, the empowerment of teachers was rooted in a political, cultural vision. Ideally, teachers become empowered in order to help themselves and their students participate in the creation of a more socially just and compassionate society; that is, empowerment is a means to a social as well as educational ideal.

Recently, however, the notion of empowering teachers has been effectively expropriated by neoconservative educators. The result is a call for empowering teachers that in fact maintains current power relationships. Perhaps the best illustration of this phenomenon can be found in Gene Maeroff's (1988) popular book, *The Empowerment of Teachers: Overcoming the Crisis of Confidence*. From Maeroff's perspective, "empowerment . . . is a term somewhat synonymous with professionalization. It does not necessarily mean being in charge . . . more than anything else it means working in an environment in which a teacher acts as a professional and is treated as a professional." The goal of empowering teachers is to "enhance the teaching profession by giving teachers more respectability, authority, and status" (1988: 6,15).

Although Maeroff notes the value of collegiality and teachers working together, his view of empowerment is primarily individualistic. For example, throughout his book he glamorizes the individual recognition given to teachers who were selected for participation in CHART, the in-service program set up to empower various teachers, as well as advocates competition among teachers through programs such as "teacher-of-the-year" contests. Maeroff's notion of empowering teachers is clearly possible within traditional schools because it is restricted to particular individual teachers who have earned the right to exert more power. He suggests that to become empowered, teachers should prove that they are willing to intensify their labor by working after hours and during the summers. Once shown to be worthy, they can receive certain "empowering rewards" for such activity: "the greater freedom to choose textbooks, a place on a curriculum-writing team, an assurance of being called upon to mentor a younger colleague, the promise of released time to attend seminars regularly" (Maeroff, 1988: 46). Within this concept of empowerment, the basic dynamics of power in schools are left unchanged. Although Maeroff mentions the need to give teachers access to power, his emphasis is on simply developing greater communication between teachers and administrators. There is no mention of directly challenging the type of hierarchy found in traditional schools. Even if teachers are given greater control over their own work, Maeroff

(1988: 55) is quick to point out that this work needs "to be carefully monitored." In this sense, Maeroff's notion of change reflects an "instrumentalist" perspective (Fay, 1977); that is, those currently in authority should define the way in which teachers should be empowered and are the ones to "give" teachers whatever power they obtain.

Most important, Maeroff's analysis is stripped of any historical or social context. It seems that teachers lack power because of their own inadequacies. For example, one reason for teachers' lack of power is that they are basically ignorant. "Part of the reason why teachers have not exerted more authority is because they are not sufficiently well informed to do so." In addition, teachers' lack of status is due to their "self-imposed shackles of low esteem" (Maeroff, 1988: 6). Nowhere in Maeroff's book is patriarchy or the degradation of labor under twentieth-century corporate capitalism mentioned as a contributing factor behind teachers' lack of autonomy and power. The answer to the "crisis" in education is empowering teachers so that they can more effectively implement the goals of those in authority. In fact, he suggests that teachers' empowerment rests on their ability to "rub elbows" with those in society (industrialists, intellectuals, scientists) who currently occupy positions of power. "If teachers think of themselves as having such connections and if, eventually, they are perceived by others as being tied into a collegial network that extends into higher education and business, then surely this will be a boost toward empowerment" (Maeroff, 1988: 7, 59). Given Maeroff's limited analysis, it comes as no surprise that his "empowerment of teachers" is devoid of any substantive social, moral, or educational agenda. Rather, there is only a vague reference to making teachers' teaching and children's learning better.

> Empowerment, of course, is not an end in itself. If teachers who gain more power over their work situation do not end up doing their jobs better, then empowerment will mean little or nothing so far as the education of children is concerned. Of what value is greater power in the hands of teachers if it is not used in behalf of the learning of their students? The improvement of learning should be the goal of empowerment. (Maeroff, 1988: 106)

By removing the political and cultural context from which this term emerged, neoconservative educators have effectively crippled it as an effective expression for critical, democratic change. Neutralizing critical concepts that gain popularity by separating them from their political content, as is illustrated in Maeroff's book, is a more potent, and thus dangerous, strategy than proposing different concepts based upon conservative ideologies and visions of schools and society.

At the macro level, one cannot comprehensively discuss democratic schools and the empowerment of teachers without referring to patriarchy and the industrial rationality that has shaped this occupation (as well as others) within our society: that is, substantive changes in the way teachers work will not occur unless there are basic alterations in the quality of labor in our society. However, this relationship between schools and society does not mean that strategies for empowering teachers cannot be attempted at the micro level of a given school. Although Harmony should not be seen as a model for empowering teachers, on the basis of the issues previously discussed, there are a couple of practices worth emphasizing.

Perhaps most important, within schools there needs to be a significant and meaningful distribution of authority. Given the current structure of schools, building administrators can play an important role in providing teachers with authentic spheres of influence or realms of power and in creating an atmosphere in which teachers are free to participate and challenge decisions that are made across lines of differentiated labor (Brady, 1985; Lightfoot, 1986; Nathan, 1983). Like Dan, administrators need to see themselves as the person, using Schumacher's (1973) image, underneath and holding on to the balloons, rather than as the "father figure" who protects his weak and obedient "charges," the "coach" who cheers and gives pep talks to his "team," or the "ship captain" who welcomes his teachers "on board" and who protects his ship and its cargo from rough waters and pirates. Building administrators consciously need to eschew the paternalistic authority coveted by most of those in positions of power. What was most impressive about Dan's leadership was his own theoretical knowledge base, which helped him develop a critical, democratic perspective of schooling and society, and his recognition of the value of the "feminine" side to his personality. His honest caring for Harmony's teachers as people and his talent for listening, reflecting, and actively nurturing teachers' points of view played a significant role in facilitating these teachers' efficacy and power. Several of the faculty referred to Dan as an "ideal" administrator simply because he, as Barb noted, "doesn't act like an administrator." Dan's administrative style was similar to Fay's (1977: 204) concept of an "educative" model for change.

> According to the educative model, theoretical knowledge is useful to the extent that it informs people what their needs are and how a particular way of living is frustrating these needs, thereby causing them to suffer; its goal is to enlighten people about how they can change their lives so that, having arrived at a new self-understanding, they may reduce their suffering by creating another way of life that is more fulfilling. . . . The educationist obviously believes that his analysis can be effective insofar as it leads to a new self-understanding by the audience to which it is directed.

Rather than use his talents and theoretical knowledge to manipulate situations, Dan emphasized helping teachers better recognize and therefore address their concerns and the concerns of their students.

Even though building administrators are in a position to facilitate the power of teachers, teachers must be the primary agents in their own empowerment. In particular, opportunities for substantive communication are essential to this process. Although Maeroff and other neoconservative educators mention the need for teachers to communicate with each other, what is often missing, and yet crucial, is the substance of these communications. Perhaps our most noteworthy observation of Harmony teachers' work was the content of faculty discourse. As previously mentioned, almost without exception and even in the discussion of many procedural issues, faculty dialogue was grounded in ideological and ethical considerations because the educational and societal goals and principles at Harmony were not taken for granted by the faculty. Questions of educational and social purpose were always seen as problematic and open to questioning and review. Talking by itself does little to empower people. To the contrary, it was the questioning, the listening to and working through different points of view, and the generation of ideas that occurred within Harmony's faculty meetings (both formal and informal) that fostered the empowerment of these individuals. As previously mentioned, the teachers at Harmony were continually in the process of creating and refining not only their craft through these discussions, but also the theories upon which they based their craft. If attention is not given to the substance of communication, then empowerment could conceivably mean having everyone sit in a circle, with a guarantee that each person has an opportunity to speak.

In establishing schooling for critical democracy, it is necessary that teachers exercise significantly greater power than that which is currently found in traditional schools. Although a symmetrical organizational structure would reflect a truly democratic association, in most schools it is not a realistic alternative. Most schools are too large, and even in small schools such as Harmony, educating children is too complex and requires a level of intensity that makes the complete elimination of differentiated lines of labor difficult to imagine. To suggest that a symmetrical organization is the only structure worthy of democratic principles can undermine our efforts by keeping educators from examining important issues as they struggle to create institutions based on a democratic ethos. Trying to establish a democratic, asymmetrical organization presents critical educators with several problematic practices and issues. This chapter has examined four that were clearly reflected in the work of teachers and administrators at Harmony. Proposing simple prototypes and step-by-step guidelines for creating the democratic organization of schools is not in the best interest of those who educate our children. Rather, it is better for teachers and administrators to struggle through these issues for themselves, to create institutional structures that grow out of their unique situations. Perhaps the most important element in this effort is to overtly situate schooling within a democratic rationality and then let teachers and administrators work through and develop the organizational structure over time. In this way, structural form will most likely reflect the existential experiences and needs of the participants within a given school. As Gorz (1982) notes, the call for teachers or other workers to exercise greater democratic control over their workplace should not be seen as an end in itself. To the contrary, the democratic participation of workers needs to be seen within a context of basic social and economic change within society, that is, as a strategy for promoting critical democracy.

When most people think of democratic education, they often ignore the power dynamics between the adults who work in such schools. Greatest attention is given to relations that exist between adults and children, as well as between the children themselves. This chapter has attempted to rectify this oversight. Although the power dynamics between adults is crucial to establishing schooling for critical democracy, it is only one piece of the puzzle. As a result, in the next chapter, we will turn our attention to power relations between adults and children.

4

Power and Participation:
Adults and Children

Interpersonal relationships within schools have been the focus of more research and the topic of discussion at more educational meetings than perhaps any other pedagogical issue. There is a plethora of articles and books that deal with "structural arrangements," "student discipline," or "classroom management." One reason there is so much attention devoted to this topic is that nearly everyone recognizes that children covertly learn many significant things about themselves, their fellow students, adults, and the society in which we live through the interpersonal dynamics that exist in schools. In fact, one might question whether it is possible to add to this enormous body of literature. However, it is also difficult to consider not devoting some attention to the dynamics of power between adults and children and between the children themselves in order to establish elementary schooling for critical democracy. In fact, educators interested in promoting more democratic forms of educating our young people often emphasize the need to alter the current authoritarian relations of power and the limited participation of students that exist in most traditional schools. Unfortunately, vaguely worded calls for "more humane relationships" or "greater participation on the part of students" do little to help those of us interested in democratic schooling. What is needed is an examination of the way relations of power and control are played out in democratic settings.

Over the last two decades, numerous approaches to teacher-student relationships have been developed. For example, one progressive model, *Teacher Effectiveness Training* (Gordon, 1974), describes a variety of interpersonal communication skills for teachers that are aimed at providing a more humanistic atmosphere within classrooms. The primary focus of this approach is to help teachers respond effectively to each student's concerns and to avoid win/lose power confrontations. During the conservative restoration in the 1980s (Shor, 1986), Canter and Canter's (1976) "assertive discipline" approach gained tremendous popularity. This model of human relationships is based on behavior modification principles according to which rules are clearly stipulated by the teachers (or in many cases on a schoolwide basis through the principal's office) for students to follow. Subsequent punishments for breaking these rules are also predesignated so that students know the exact consequences of not acting properly. Even though these two approaches and many others like them (Wolfgang and Glickman, 1986) are antithetical to each other, they do have a few things in common. Most of these models focus almost exclusively on relationships between teachers and their students. The emphasis is on ways that teachers and administrators should "treat children" in a given school or classroom to prevent them from misbehaving. Rarely do these models devote much attention to relationships between students as an important aspect of a school's interpersonal dynamics; nor do they give much consideration to the underlying issues of student power and participation as part of their programs. Finally, and perhaps most important, the social purposes of establishing one style of interpersonal dynamics versus another are often totally ignored. The stated goal of many of these models is limited to managing children's behavior for effective classroom or school operations. The vast majority of these various human relations models fail to ground their suggestions within a thoughtful analysis of schooling or within a particular socio-historical context.

However, to adequately discuss relationships between teachers and children or between children and their peers in schools, it is necessary to place this discourse within our particular societal context, that is, within a society dominated by an ideology of individualism. As mentioned in the first chapter, schools for critical democracy need to deliberately foster a connectionist perspective among our children. One of the most important means of instilling this perspective is through the interpersonal relationships of the people within a given school building. Because of the power of individualism, elementary educators need to consciously create a connectionist power structure in their schools and classrooms if they are to effectively nurture critical democracy in our society. In this regard, several practices and issues related to students' power and participation within democratic schools can be discussed in light of our observations at Harmony.

SOCIAL BONDING

All institutions by their very nature create an atmosphere which in turn regulates the attitudes and behavior of those who work within them. As discussed in the first chapter, the atmosphere in most public elementary schools results in feelings of estrangement, not only between staff and students, but also between the students themselves. Although teachers and students spend a considerable amount of time with each other, their relationships and communications remain formal and superficial, creating within schools what some (Gee, 1989a; Givon, 1979; Heath, 1983; Lesko, 1988) have referred to as a "society of strangers." In societies or institutions of strangers, literate styles of communication are legitimated against other forms

of interaction. There is also rigid stratification between super- and subordinates. This stratification is often reinforced by imposing psychological
sanctions on those who violate this separation. As Goffman (1961: 93) notes
in his study of "total institutions" (conventional schools share many of their
characteristics),

> When unusual intimacies and relationships do occur across the staff-inmate
> line, we know that involvement cycles may follow and all kinds of awkward
> reverberations are likely to occur, with a subversion of authority and social
> distance that again gives one the impression of an incest taboo.

When examined, the language associated with interpersonal dynamics in
traditional schools is dominated by notions of management, control, and
discipline, that is, concepts common to groups of strangers rather than to
people who are working together as a community. Obviously, it would be
impossible to develop a connectionist power structure in a school that
operated as a society of strangers.

Establishing a connectionist power structure in schools can be seen as
an effort to create a "society of intimates" among the staff and students.
Drawing upon animal studies, Givon (1979: 287) states the following:

> In terms of personal character, social status, probable motivation intent-
> goals-needs, as well as the likely sequence of daily activities, each individual
> member knows all other members intimately and accurately. It is a society
> . . . where the size of the social unit within which interaction and
> communication takes [sic] place is relatively small. . . . It is thus a society
> with a largely *shared* model of the universe.

Perhaps the most important strategy used to develop this power structure
within Harmony was an emphasis on the social bonds among the students
and between students and teachers and administrators. This social bonding
was fostered through several different means: establishing a collective identity
among the children, teaching students the value of collective responsibility,
and consciously reducing the stratification between teachers and students.

Over the years, the teachers at Harmony established various structures,
activities, and rituals that provided opportunities for students to develop a
collective identity. First, the school was consciously kept small. There were
approximately eleven students per class, and the lower (grades 1-3) and
upper (grades 4-6) elementary programs acted as semiautonomous units
so that the diverse concerns of the students and teachers could be more
sensitively addressed. As will be discussed, this size allowed both students
and teachers to communicate enough to know and understand each other's
personalities, temperaments, and life situations (joys, points of stress). Within
this small circle of people, it did not take long for an individual student or

teacher to begin feeling that he or she was a member of some special grouping. Among both teachers and students there was a merging between their "private lives" and their "school lives."

Specific rituals also promoted the students' collective identity. At the beginning, middle, and end of the year, the entire school would go on an extended trip. The school year always began with a three-day camping trip to a nearby state park.

> The first hour of the school year started with tremendous noise and commotion. Students (and their parents) were loading their suitcases and bicycles into the waiting vans, trucks and cars, eagerly catching up on the happenings of their summer vacations, and spreading excitement through the parking lot. Just before leaving for the park, Julie called everyone together to discuss where the cabins were located in the park and the cabin assignments for the children. Except for the first graders, who would all sleep in the same cabin with their teacher, Michele, the children could choose their own cabin. At one point Julie said, "I know you are all anxious to spend time with your friends from last year, but you'll notice that we have a few new students this year." She then introduced them and said, "I would like it if you would make a special effort to locate these kids and invite them into your cabin." Throughout the three days of hiking, bike riding, swimming, playing, cooking, cleaning, singing, and working through conflicts together, a family atmosphere began to develop. In fact, several of the students we spoke to referred to Harmony as "our family." (Summary of field notes)

During January the school spent three days in Indianapolis, and in May the students traveled to North Carolina and visited (among other places) a museum devoted to the Native American life-style. Although these trips had academic goals, the primary purpose seemed to be the development of school cohesiveness. Harmony's annual Art Fair, Talent Show, Science Fair, and Spring Festival, as well as several fund-raising activities, all contributed to the students' collective identity. In addition, the school established several regularly scheduled student-teacher "meetings," as described below:

All-Campus Meetings	Met first Friday morning of each month for 30 to 90 minutes to discuss issues concerning the high, middle, and elementary schools.
Family Meetings	Met Monday mornings for 30 minutes. Lower and upper elementary programs met together to discuss school-related issues.
Program Meetings	Met Tuesday, Thursday, and Friday mornings for 30 minutes. Each pro-

gram met separately to discuss program-related issues. On the first and third Fridays of each month, classes were postponed and Program Meetings lasted 60 to 90 minutes if needed to facilitate extended discussion of relevant issues.

Peer Group Meetings   Met Wednesday and Friday mornings for 30 minutes. At the beginning of the year, the children formed themselves into ongoing, multi-aged small groups to discuss school and interpersonal issues. Each Peer Group was facilitated by a teacher.

Although these meetings had multiple purposes that (as will be discussed) included giving students a voice in policy making, they also contributed to the students' sense of a collective identity. In particular, Peer Group Meetings were specifically designed to help students "work through" interpersonal difficulties and promote good fellowship. The teachers occasionally took their Peer Groups on special afternoon trips during the year, and a couple of them had Peer Group slumber parties at the school. Because of these various meetings, the collective identity that was formed among Harmony's elementary students was significantly different from what one might find in the name of "school spirit," in which students are encouraged to mindlessly develop patriotic feelings for "our school." As previously mentioned, the social bonding that existed at Harmony emerged from students and teachers getting to know and understand each other as human beings, supporting each other during times of difficulty, working through conflicts with each other, and becoming involved in activities that reflected schoolwide or programwide purposes.

Another particularly important aspect of the social bonding at Harmony was the conscious effort made to help children develop a degree of collective concern and caring for the well-being of their fellow students and society at large. Staub (1971) notes that American children often ignore calls of distress from others and suggests that the reason lies in subtle, isolating messages that are given to them through our popular culture and in schools.

Individuals in our culture seem to learn . . . not to interfere with another's affairs, to "mind their own business," to respect the privacy of others. . . . Obedience to such rules of appropriate social conduct may be generally thought of as less obligatory than obedience to norms that prescribe "morally" relevant behavior, for example, that one ought to help others in distress. Nevertheless, the former may have greater force in guiding children's behavior because they are taught extensively and are enforced across a variety of situations. (1971: 137-138)

This lack of concern for others was especially noticeable during the "Reagan Revolution." As the United States Department of Education (1989: 1) recently noted, "In the annual UCLA/ACE survey of [college] freshman attitudes, the proportion of freshmen who classified helping others in difficulty as either an essential or a very important life goal . . . [hit] the lowest level in 17 years."

In contrast, efforts to increase students' awareness of their responsibility to help others were routinely made in Harmony's elementary school. For example, as mentioned in the second chapter, one reason for admitting Robert into the fifth-grade class despite several serious problems (very poor gross and fine motor coordination, poor eyesight, significant speech impediment, emotional withdrawal) was, as Dan stated during the staff meeting that decided on the year's new admissions, "to help students learn to value differences among people." During the first half of the year, Robert had difficulty making friends. Finally, he asked Julie, one of his teachers, for help, and they decided to bring it up at a Program Meeting.

> Julie started this meeting by saying that Robert had asked her to discuss his problem of making friends with the group. Several students suggested that he stop teasing, hitting, making faces, poking, and "bugging" other kids. Julie suggested that perhaps Robert didn't know how to make friends and his "bugging" was a poor attempt to get their attention. A few students said that it wasn't always Robert's fault. Emily said, "Sometimes he's the one that gets picked on and teased." Nathan suggested that these conflicts might have become "a habit." Julie asked what could be done. Several students suggested just stopping. Julie said that was a good idea, but it might be hard to stop since it's a "habit." After some more discussion, Julie suggested that the students tell Robert, "Remember, we want to make friends," when he "bugs" people. Everyone agreed that was a good idea, and also agreed to make a conscious effort not to tease Robert anymore. (Summary of field notes)

As the year continued, Robert and the other students were observed falling into old patterns. However, each time it came to a teacher's attention, the emphasis was on helping students care for each other rather than on simply having them follow predetermined rules of "proper school behavior." It is important to stress that, from the faculty's perspective, situations like those involving Robert often take significant time to resolve, which was one of the reasons given to us for having students spend several years with the same group of three teachers (lower and upper elementary) rather than being "passed on" to a new teacher each year. Since the problem is defined in much more complex terms (that is, as developing social bonds) than simply changing "children's inappropriate behavior at school," there was no "rush" for a quick solution (to keep Robert from "bugging" the other children). There seemed to be among the faculty a sense of patience when dealing with problems of social bonding, and in Robert's case this patience seemed to work out. As his mother told us at the end of the school year, "Robert is like a completely new kid now. He's become a much happier person since going to Harmony. He's learning to make friends, and he communicates much more. He's not nearly as withdrawn or angry as he used to be."

Discussions at Family and Program meetings often centered on "bonding" issues (teasing, fighting, exclusion of students from peer activities) among students. For instance, at one lower elementary Program Meeting there was a lengthy discussion of a game that had spontaneously developed over the last several weeks.

> The next agenda item for the meeting was to talk about the "contamo" game being played at school. Several children didn't like the game and wanted it stopped. Jo, the faculty leader for this meeting, first asked for a full description of the game. It was similar to many children's games such as "cooties" in that one student was chosen as having "cooties," or in this game she or he was "contaminated" ("She or he is contamo!"), and all the other kids ran away in disgust while calling this person names. Jo then asked kids how they felt when they played this game. Several students shared particular stories related to this game in which various feelings were expressed. For most, the game was fun as long as you weren't the one declared as "contamo." When "chosen," students talked about their hurt and angry feelings. Several students mentioned that they didn't ever like being "teased." Jo asked why teasing hurts people, and the students tried to answer her, but none were very articulate. Jo then asked if there were times when one enjoyed being teased. Some kids responded with stories about when it didn't hurt to be teased (when they were able to laugh at themselves). Jo asked them how they could tell if someone was enjoying being teased or not, and several students made suggestions related to body language (smiling, laughing, crying, hitting, holding one's head down). Jo then asked if there were other things that students could do to let people know they didn't like being teased, and several students mentioned Harmony's policy that any child could ask other children "to stop" teasing or whatever and the children should respect that wish. Finally, Jo asked how many children wanted to play "contamo" anymore. Four boys said they did. Jo then said, "Okay, except for you guys [the four boys] 'contamo' will not be played anymore at Harmony. You guys understand that you are the only ones who want to play this game?" They said yes, and the meeting moved on to the next agenda item. (Summary of field notes)

The value of social bonding at Harmony was underscored by the fact that it was one of the graduation requirements; that is, in order to graduate from sixth grade students had to demonstrate that they, as Dan and other teachers often told them, "were part of the solution, not part of the problem." Expressed in a variety of statements, the "problem" was "how to create a caring, mutually respectful, and supportive community within the school." Towards the end of the school year (March), the graduation of two students was called into question because for several years, they had often initiated discord and disturbances among students and between teachers and students. These boys had to sign contracts (drawn up by themselves, their parents, and their teachers) spelling out the behavior and attitudes they were expected to manifest during the rest of the school year in order to graduate. For example, Tommy's contract read as follows:

1. Refrain from belligerently arguing with others in group settings. Wait for an appropriate amount of time before responding to other people's ideas.
2. Take responsibility for your own actions. Admit mistakes and your part in what happens in school.
3. Understand that contracts must be taken seriously. Signing this contract means you will honor it; only negotiations can change it.
4. Control your anger in class so that it will not be disruptive. Discuss with teachers how to express your anger in more appropriate ways.
5. Develop a clear understanding of what we mean by "disrespectful behavior" by talking to each teacher in the elementary school.
6. Participate in a meeting between you, Sam, and Jim [lower elementary teacher] to work through feelings which prevent positive interactions.
7. Follow the schedule agreed upon to complete your graduation project. Check with a member of your committee to show progress towards agreed-upon goals each day.

Each student (and his parents) met with his teacher several times prior to graduation to monitor his compliance. Although both boys graduated, Tommy failed to fully live up to the spirit of all the conditions in his contract. As a result, a meeting that included the upper elementary school teachers, Tommy, his parents, and Dan was held, and everyone (including Tommy) agreed that he should not go to Harmony's middle school in the fall.

Perhaps the most important way in which students at Harmony were taught the value of creating a community in the school was through the modeling that the teachers did for them. Throughout the year, we were struck by the consistent warmth and concern that the teachers showed their pupils and the attachment that took place between them as a result. As one might expect to see in progressive schools, teachers and students called each other by their first names, and they were often observed hugging, sweet-talking, and holding hands with each other. It was common to observe students asking teachers to help them solve interpersonal disputes. The teachers' abilities to nurture students in distress were noteworthy. Teachers became fully involved in their students' academic, social, and family lives. Take, for example, the interchange that took place in this parent-teacher conference.

> Julie, Barb, and Bart expressed their deep concern regarding Lee's (a fifth grader) withdrawn behavior. As they discussed his life history with his mother (a single parent), she told them that he was angry about not having a father. The last couple of months it had gotten worse because she hadn't been able to spend much time with him. She was in graduate school most of the day, and she had to work from five until ten or eleven several nights in order to pay the bills. They discussed Lee's fears of being abandoned. As part of a short-term solution, both Barb and Julie offered to take Lee home with them on the nights that his mother had to work late. (Summary of field notes)

Numerous students mentioned their teachers' caring and alluded to them as surrogate parents: "She (or he) has been like a mother (or father) to me." Even when students and teachers had conflicts, because time was taken to fully resolve the issues involved, these altercations usually ended with the participants feeling closer and more bonded to each other. When students' insensitivity and lack of responsibility were confronted by teachers, there always existed an atmosphere of forgiveness and rewards (usually verbal) when the students altered their antisocial posturing.

However, this intimacy occasionally would contribute to a libertarian atmosphere in the school. Because of the reduced stratification between students and teachers, a legacy of "free schooling" seemed to pervade Harmony from time to time. This legacy seemed to make some teachers hesitant to assert their authority over children's behavior. During any given day some students would act in self-indulgent ways (disrupting class discussions and activities, causing loud disturbances in the hall, throwing trash, marking up lockers) without teacher intervention. Some teachers, especially at the beginning of the school year, ignored rather than directly engaged students when they disrupted what was happening during meetings and class sessions. In some instances, the friendship that existed between teachers and students seemed to give students greater license to act in egocentric ways. Jim, one of the lower elementary teachers, told us, "Too often our students think that because we are their 'friends,' they can do whatever they want, and we will always back off, and too often we do." Reducing the stratification between students and teachers is necessary in building a connectionist power structure; however, as will be discussed in the next section of this chapter, one should not make the mistake of thinking that teachers and students need to be "equals" in order to promote critical democracy.

As previously indicated, traditional power structures in schools often foster children's isolation and alienation. Researchers suggest that the formal, institutionalized relationships that are common in schools seriously erode children's sense of compassion (Bryan, 1975). Unless children are deliberately provided with experiences that provide for more caring relationships, they reproduce these destructive interpersonal dynamics and structures as adults (Johnson & Johnson, 1974). Bryan (1975) notes that children who are encouraged to express themselves and who feel comfortable seeking help when needed are more likely to offer assistance to others when needed. Developing the social bonds among students and their teachers is crucial for establishing a connectionist power structure in schools. In this sense, social bonding implies intentional efforts to promote a collective identity and responsibility among students and a reduction in the stratification between teachers and students.

TEACHER AUTHORITY

One of the most significant dilemmas facing those interested in democratic education is the question of teacher authority. As mentioned in the first chapter, challenging the legitimacy of teachers' authority was perhaps the major goal for most of the radical alternative schools that mushroomed in the late 1960s and early 1970s. The assumption was that the way to "free" children was to rid them of the autocratic dominance of adult control. However, the notion that children do not need conscious adult intervention regarding social values and interaction stems from the sentimental and problematic assumption that children will (if only left alone) "naturally" become concerned with the well-being of the world around them.

One does not have to be a sociologist to see that children in our society have difficulty putting the common good in front of their own immediate desires. As illustrated in the first chapter, given our cultural values, putting emphasis on increasing the "personal freedom" of students will probably result in antisocial, egotistical posturing among children rather than the "free child" so often lauded in the radical school literature. Children's true individuality (rather than their self-indulgence) can grow only within a community structure in which there are restrictions and expectations placed upon the individual by that community. Dewey (1922) argues that human beings are not "naturally" good or bad, intelligent or foolish, or ethical or amoral. Each person throughout his or her life has contradictory impulses to act and feel in an infinite number of ways, and it is largely through our interactions with others that we come to value our self-interests or the common interests of a community. As conceptualized here, the radical reform of schooling for critical democracy projects an authoritative role for teachers to actively construct the educational environment required. Teachers need to consciously create rituals and structures and act with reasoned authority in order to nourish a connectionist perspective within children.

Like most children in our society, Harmony's students did not come to school with a particular interest in democracy or community values. In addition, a few students in each class were admitted because they were in some type of "emotional pain" resulting from unstable family dynamics or negative experiences in public schools. Initially, these students had a particularly difficult time showing an interest in or concern for others around them. However, without a clear understanding of the relationship between the values of individuality and of community in our society, teachers at Harmony had difficulty exercising the authority needed to promote a connectionist consciousness. For example, Barb, who had been at Harmony just one year prior to our observations, often expressed community values in group meetings; however, she also had strong libertarian views when it came to her educational and interpersonal philosophy. To her, "emancipating" children meant giving them power to make decisions affecting their own time and actions. She once questioned whether "adults should have authority over children." Rather than use her authority to promote a connectionist consciousness among the students, Barb would in some instances act in ways that promoted her individualistic values. Take, for example, a typical situation that occurred in one of the Family Meetings.

> Sam and Tommy, two sixth-grade boys, were constantly disrupting the discussion by talking to each other and playing with some small objects. Barb, the faculty leader for this meeting, finally asked the two boys to leave. However, she did not direct them where to go or what to do. A few minutes later Michele, the first-grade teacher, heard them yelling in the gym, and confronted them on their behavior. In her discussion of this situation with Michele, Barb's rationale for limiting her concern to simply ejecting Tommy and Sam from the meeting was rooted in her libertarian philosophy. She felt that there should be no negative consequences for being ejected from Family or Program meetings, and that students should have the right to spend this time as they pleased. "If kids don't want to be at a meeting then we shouldn't force them. Our goal should be to get them to *want* to be here." Later, we asked Barb if individual children such as Tommy or Sam had a responsibility [to seriously participate] to the other students and faculty members who take part in group meetings and the democratic process represented in these meetings. She responded by saying that she had never thought about the rights of the group in relation to the rights of individual children in this type of situation. (Summary of field notes)

Teachers who wish to promote critical democracy in our society need to recognize that they must assume authority over children in order to teach them how to live according to community values. Assuming this authority is particularly important given the individualistic, cultural context in which these children live.

As mentioned in the previous section of this chapter, the teachers at Harmony generally exercised their authority without harshness or insensitivity. Feelings of love and friendship pervaded the power relationships between most teachers and students. It is a common belief among radical educators that caring and acceptance are incompatible between super- and subordinates. However, although the stratification between teachers and students was significantly reduced at Harmony as a way of establishing social bonds, on a daily basis the teachers demonstrated ways in which adult authority could be manifested within an atmosphere of caring. Jo, one of the lower elementary teachers, was particularly adept at exerting her authority over students without resorting to personal denunciations. Take, for instance, the nonpunitive response that Jo demonstrated as she dealt with a number of situations (such as students' misbehavior) that are commonly seen in elementary classrooms in our society.

Jo began the class by saying she had a number of "concerns" to discuss with the students. First, she mentioned that when she came in the room that morning there was paper on the game- and bookshelves. She said, "You know I don't mind if you use materials before school begins, but when you're finished what should we do with them and why?" Several students answered that the materials need to be put away because paper will be abused if left out and thus be unavailable to other students, paper costs money and people have to work hard for the money it takes to support the school, and paper comes from trees and thus it is important not to waste it. She asked for volunteers to clean up the mess during break. She then pointed to several beanbag chairs around the room and said, "You'll notice that I've put the beanbag chairs back. [They had been removed two weeks earlier.] Does anyone remember why I removed them?" Several children told stories about fighting each other to sit in them. Jo then asked if they felt they were ready to have them replaced, that is, if they could share them and not fight over them anymore. The students unanimously said they would be able to share them, and Jo agreed with their assessment. Finally, she said, "This morning I noticed a couple of sentences and drawings on the blackboard that disturbed me. I don't mind if you use the blackboard. Wonderful things can happen when you feel free to write and draw on it, but these sentences can hurt people's feelings. What's the most important rule at Harmony?" The students stated Harmony's "golden rule," "Harmony is a place where people's bodies and feelings are safe." Jo then asked the class why they thought someone might write something on the blackboard that would hurt other children's feelings. Several students suggested that the person might have written it to "be funny," or the person might have been angry with someone. Jo asked what they should do when they were upset with someone, and the students answered that they should talk to that person or ask for help from a teacher. Jo ended the discussion by saying that she hoped whoever wrote it would think about how words can hurt other people, and would think about alternative ways of expressing his or her feelings. (Summary of field notes)

Jo's response to these typical types of "misbehavior" reflected a belief among Harmony's teachers that all children have the capacity for goodness. Rather than express their authority in ways that emphasized the reprimanding and punishment of children, they grounded their authority in an affirmation of children's abilities to learn from mistakes.

In addition to using adult authority within an atmosphere of caring, teachers at Harmony also used their authority to help children become aware of their responsibilities to the collective well-being of the group of students among whom they worked. One illustration came during the fall camping trip.

A new student was seen groveling around in the dirt while the other children were seated at a picnic table. Dan, the curriculum coordinator, started going over to him, when Peter, a fourth-grade student, called out, "Kick him once for me!" and the other students laughed. Dan whirled around to face Peter and told him to "find a stick and sit on it." After checking to see that the student on the ground was all right, he returned to the table and said, "You people really have to help Peter. All of you have been hurt by things he has said at some point or another, but if we laugh when he says mean things to others, he will continue to do it. You have to let him know that you don't like it when he says insensitive things to people, or he won't stop. It's not just Peter's problem, it's a problem that we all must take responsibility for." (Summary of field notes)

The emphasis on teaching children about the connection between their actions and their social responsibility to others cannot be stressed enough. If students' antisocial actions are not confronted within a context of community values, then teachers' actions can easily reflect a conformist rather than connectionist perspective. Although the teachers at Harmony often helped students understand their social responsibility, there were several moments when this did not happen. For example, when Michele confronted Sam and Tommy about their behavior once they were ejected from the Family Meeting (see page 103) she did not address their responsibility to the group as a whole. Instead she merely emphasized that they shouldn't be allowed to "play" after being removed from these meetings. From her perspective at that time, Tommy and Sam needed to be reprimanded for misbehaving in Family Meeting. As a result, there was no attempt to engage them in a dialogue regarding their actions and their responsibility to the other students and faculty members in the school. However, not participating in meetings, disrupting class discussions, and other forms of misconduct by individual students need to be seen not only as a singular problem but also as a collective concern of the group. Given the individualistic ethos found in our society, it is unrealistic to expect this collectivist orientation to emerge naturally from most elementary school children. The effectiveness of any given educational strategy depends upon the ideological underpinnings of the teacher employing it. If teachers do not understand the way in which they need to use their authority to create a connectionist power structure within schools, then they will have difficulty promoting critical democracy.

POWER SHARING

No discussion of democracy and education can take place without addressing the issue of student power. As previously mentioned, if there is one element that separates traditional schooling from democratic schooling, it is a commitment to involve students in substantive decision making (Wood, 1988). Although recognizing the legitimate authority of teachers is crucial for establishing a connectionist power structure in schools, it is also necessary to provide avenues for students to engage in the responsible exercise of power. We contend that teachers and students should not be "equals" within elementary schools. However, a connectionist power structure does suggest that students will be involved in power-sharing experiences. Setting the limits of this power and making arrangements for students to engage in deliberations over real school policy (in contrast to the "power" typically allocated to student councils) is a central concern for educators interested in democratic education.

As in most institutions, there was a distinction (although unstated) between "rules" and "privileges" at Harmony. In traditionally structured institutions, both rules and privileges are predetermined by superordinates. Rules set policy, and privileges are given to subordinates as a form of social control (Goffman, 1961). At Harmony, a conscious effort was made to keep the number of teacher-defined, predetermined rules to a minimum. In fact, the only universal elementary school rules were that students had to attend class and complete agreed-upon academic assignments, that students could not play in the parking lot, and that students could not leave campus without permission during school hours. As previously mentioned, Harmony had one broadly stated rule that was used as a criterion for regulating the interpersonal behavior of teachers and students. Referred to as "Harmony's Golden Rule," it stated, "Harmony is a *safe* place [free from being hurt or abused] for teachers' and students' bodies and feelings." Rather than having lists of "do's and don't's," the elementary school established most rules *retroactively* with students' participation as a result of their becoming aware of the negative consequences of specific situations. For example, specific rules governing such behavior as students' running in the halls, teasing each other, eating during meetings, interrupting each other during discussions, and climbing on lofts were decided during classroom discussions or Program or Family meetings as a result of specific instances which occurred during the school year. Take, for instance, the following example of rule making.

> The next item to be discussed at the lower elementary Program Meeting was introduced by Hannah. She complained that some kids were throwing stones at her and her friends this morning. Jim, one of the lower elementary teachers and the leader for today's meeting, asked how this type of behavior got started. It seems that the kids were playing with leaves, first throwing them in the air and then at each other. However, in the pile of leaves there were some rocks and sticks, and a few times kids were hit by these objects. Jim then asked what should be done about this situation. Several kids suggested that there should be a rule against throwing things at each other. Jim said that he thought this might be a good idea, but added, "Aren't there some things that it might be fun and also *safe* to throw at each other?" The kids then started naming objects that it might be fun to throw at each other, such as water, feathers, or confetti. Jim suggested that maybe the rule should state that kids should not throw anything that could possibly hurt other people. The kids agreed, and Jim asked, "But what if someone doesn't want anything thrown at them even if it's safe?" Nearly every child unanimously called out that "he [the victim] should tell him [the thrower] to *stop*, and then he [the thrower] should." So the "stop" rule was reinforced. Jim then summarized what the students had decided. (Summary of field notes)

The rationale for this "retroactive rule making" was expressed by Dan at a faculty meeting.

> Bart, a new teacher in the school, suggested that the students needed to be given more clearly defined rules at the beginning of the year. He felt that in this way a lot of trouble that the children get into could be avoided. After a minute or so Dan responded, "Up until now, we have consciously avoided setting up rules at the beginning of the year because we have wanted the kids to understand that rules are tied to concrete situations of living. We haven't wanted students to simply 'follow rules' that they have no history in making and no idea of why they are needed in the first place. We have wanted them to help make rules that are necessary in order to live in our school." These points of view were then discussed by the other faculty members for some time. In the end it was decided that the number of rules given to the children at the beginning of the year should be kept

> to a minimum, but that they [the teachers] need to reevaluate the predetermined rules at the school at a later date, and perhaps a few more rules could be added to those that already exist. (Summary of field notes)

As Sarason (1971) notes, this retroactive rule making is extremely rare in most of our society's schools. Teachers and administrators, even those who "pride themselves on their adherence to democratic principles" (Sarason, 1971: 178), often establish rules in their schools and classrooms that suggest that "children cannot participate constructively in the development of a classroom constitution [rule making]" (Sarason, 1971: 176). However, if students are not given an opportunity to engage in making rules that emerge from their concrete experiences, then they are reduced to passive, uninterested members of school life, and this situation undermines efforts to promote critical democracy in our society.

In addition to having students involved in establishing school rules, Harmony's Family, Program, and Peer Group meetings gave students the opportunity to establish school privileges. During the year we observed, the students voted to give themselves several privileges, such as unsupervised use of the gym, an open campus lunch hour for sixth graders and freedom to eat lunch anywhere on campus for the rest of the students, and use of the office telephone. One third-grade student had an older brother in the high school, and during the first semester proposed and had passed a privilege allowing young students (grades 1–5) to go to lunch off campus with high school students.

Although having children participate in establishing privileges for themselves is significant, in order to promote a connectionist perspective, this process needs to accomplish more than just give students the power to do what they want through "voting." The primary focus of the collective deliberation that we witnessed at Harmony was to help students understand the relationship between freedom, the exercise of power, and social responsibility. Through Family, Program, and Peer Group meetings, the teachers made a conscious effort to teach students that they must consider the "collective good" in making decisions. The privileges voted on by the students were preceded by discussions that explored the conditions and limitations of the particular freedom being granted. In each case, the possible abuse of privilege was considered and then included in the final proposal. For example, to enjoy the freedom of open campus during lunch hour, the sixth graders had to have their parents' permission, could go only within a specified distance of school, could go only to those places open to the public, and had to be back ten minutes before classes started. Students could eat lunch anywhere on campus, but they could not leave trash on campus grounds. Younger students could leave campus with high school students only if the parents of both provided written permission for the specific day. The rationale for each condition was thoroughly discussed in an effort to help students understand that their actions were interconnected to the concerns, feelings, and actions of other people who cared about them.

When students did not live up to the conditions of a particular privilege, the emphasis was on teaching them to take responsibility for their actions rather than on punishment. This concern for responsibility at Harmony was perhaps best illustrated by what happened to the students' privilege of using the gym when unsupervised by a teacher or administrator.

> In most cases, the abuse of a given privilege was handled on a person-by-person basis. However, so many students failed to adhere to the stipulated conditions of having access to the gym (engaging in destruction of equipment and other property, reckless play that resulted in numerous injuries [young children were afraid to go into the gym], playing on the stage, screaming and other unnecessary noise) that this privilege was temporarily rescinded by Steve [who as school director had control over the physical school building]. After approximately five weeks, students began to ask their teachers when the gym was going to be reopened. To this question the teachers replied that reopening the gym was not their responsibility. Instead, they were waiting for the students to come up with a plan to reopen it. This began a series of discussions that were held in several Peer Group, Program, and Family meetings in all three of Harmony's schools. In these meetings, teachers shared their skepticism about the students' desire to use rather than abuse the gym. At first, students suggested that the staff simply begin to supervise the gym. This solution was unacceptable because the teachers did not want to spend the little time they had before and after school and during lunch supervising the gym. At an All-Campus Meeting, a student committee (composed of students from the high, middle, and elementary schools) was formed to develop a plan to reopen the gym. After a couple of weeks, the committee established rules of behavior for students in the gym, created a student committee to police the gym, instituted penalties for those individuals who failed to meet the conditions for using the gym, and formulated an appeals procedure for those who felt unjustly accused of breaking gym rules. This plan was acceptable to both the staff and students, and as a result, the gym was reopened. (Summary of field notes)

Developing a connectionist power structure in schools does not suggest that students will be given absolute power to determine what happens in their school. Rather than focus on the "freedom" that power sharing provides students, a connectionist structure emphasizes the social responsibility that comes with individual freedom and power. This concentration on teaching students about the relationship between social responsibility and personal freedom is the most distinctive difference between a connectionist power structure and the hierarchical structure found in traditional schools and the libertarian power structure found in most "free" schools.

DISCIPLINE

Discipline is a topic that many radical and critical educators would rather not discuss. When people are primarily concerned with "liberating" or "emancipating" children, they often do not like to think about strategies for responding to children who are acting in antisocial ways and thus need to be constrained. However, as mentioned in previous chapters, whenever groups of people interact in complex living situations, there is a need for some type of social control (Berger & Luckmann, 1967). No responsible discussion of elementary schooling and democracy can long avoid the issue of student discipline. How groups of students are controlled during daily events and what response is given to students who "misbehave" are questions asked by all teachers despite their political, social, or educational ideologies. Although those educators interested in democratic schooling have noted that traditional education is dominated by a language of "management and control" (Apple, 1979; Giroux, 1988b), this does not mean that elementary schools could exist devoid of any social control.

As mentioned in the previous chapter, Edwards (1979) identifies three mechanisms (personal, bureaucratic, and technical) of control that institutions have employed in their efforts to ensure that individuals follow accepted procedures. It is not difficult to find all three forms of control being used in today's schools. However, bureaucratic and technical forms of control increasingly are seen as the most effective and efficient. These forms of social control are seen as valuable because they potentially remove the teacher and student from engaging directly in conflict by preventing students from acting in an inappropriate fashion. For example, bureaucratic control systems such as the "assertive discipline" model emphasize the need for rules and punishments for noncompliance to be clearly spelled out to students at the beginning of the school year. All the teacher has to do is identify those students who are not following a given rule and the "system" takes over. Likewise, technical control of students attempts to isolate children from one another, thereby greatly reducing their interactions and hence potential discipline problems. Technical control mechanisms are typically manifested through such things as seating arrangements that place children in assigned desks in rows to prevent them from talking to each other (Sarason, 1982) and "individualized" instructional systems which require students to spend most of their time in their seats answering questions in workbooks (Carlson, 1982). The value of these forms of social control is that they are relatively easy to administer and are considered "just" in that everyone is treated the same by standardizing procedures. However, as Edwards (1979) implies, bureaucratic and technical forms of social control are inherently antidemocratic because they rob people of opportunities to have a voice in rule making or in stipulating the consequences of antisocial behavior.

A connectionist power structure would encourage a personal form of social control that recognizes the dialectical relationship between teachers and students. In Harmony, forms of bureaucratic or technical control were difficult to locate. There were no single desks in rows. Students worked at tables, in beanbag chairs, and in lofts. As will be discussed in the fifth chapter, over half the instructional activities called for students to work together in small or large groups, and assignments often had students involved in observations, discussions, role plays, art and music activities, and social action projects. As a result, there was significant interaction between students, and teachers had to rely on their personal intervention when the class dynamics (loud talking, students' altercations, horseplay) prevented the continuation of normal class operations. This orientation towards personal control was stated by Jo, a lower elementary teacher, during Bart's job interview with the staff.

> For example, if a kid swears at a teacher, it won't be dealt with in an institutional way. We don't have a "rule" against swearing. You have to deal with it in a personal way by finding out why the child is angry, frustrated, or what. Is it an ongoing problem? Why is he manifesting his feelings in this particular negative manner? At Harmony we get the whole child, the whole range of emotions.

Harmony's willingness to personally engage students who are involved in antisocial activities reflects a commitment to avoid standardized social control responses. As Dan, the curriculum coordinator, stated,

> In one of our Family Meetings, we asked the kids if they wanted us [the staff] to treat everyone the same. At first, they felt that this was the only fair way to deal with misbehavior. However, we then pointed out that each one of them is unique; that each one has special problems, talents, and capabilities. We asked if being "fair" as they defined it allowed us to respond to this uniqueness. After a long discussion, they realized that setting up uniform rules and punishments for everyone is not really fair. Eventually, they agreed that each person and incident should be responded to as a unique case.

This personal engagement and lack of standardization at Harmony clearly reflect a connectionist orientation towards discipline; however, by themselves these practices are not sufficient. Personal control can be used by teachers much like bureaucratic and technical forms of control, that is, to merely ensure student compliance with standardized rules and punishments. As discussed in the first chapter, personal forms of social control as typically reflected in most radical schools can also emphasize the individual freedom of students to "do their own thing." Within a connectionist power structure, disciplining students has a fundamentally different purpose from either of these forms of social control.

Instead of emphasizing the compliance of preestablished behavior or extreme forms of individual freedom, discipline efforts at Harmony were seen as opportunities to teach children to be responsible for themselves and to their fellow human beings. This effort to teach children about being responsible was perhaps best illustrated in the establishment of Harmony's "crisis meetings." When students were accused of actions that "put themselves, other children, or the school in jeopardy," a crisis meeting was called. At this meeting, each student was confronted by two teachers (one of whom was chosen by the student to act as an advocate if needed). The focus of this meeting was to find out exactly what happened, why it happened, what the potential or actual consequences of the student's actions were, and what responsibility the student would take for his or her own behavior. Once these were determined, the teachers and student collectively decided what appropriate measures the student needed to take to reestablish himself or herself as a responsible member of the school. Take, for example, a situation that involved a fourth-grade boy named Bruce:

> One day after school a number of children were playing "war" [which is against school policy but in itself does not warrant a "crisis meeting"] in Jo's third-grade classroom. [Jo had already gone for the day.] Jo's classroom is connected to a mini "lower elementary library" by a classroom divider that is usually kept open. Along one wall in each room is a loft that is approximately eight to ten feet above the ground and is used as a "reading space." As part of the war game, Bruce and several boys in his group climbed up into the library loft to get away from the "enemy" [another group of boys]. Bruce then climbed from the library loft to the loft in Jo's room by stretching across the opened divider and encouraged the others to follow. Ralph, one of the boys who were playing, casually told Jo, who was his mother as well as his teacher, about the incident that night at home. The next morning Jo called a crisis meeting for Bruce because she felt he had put himself and other students at significant physical risk. When confronted by Jo, Bruce denied climbing across the room divider and encouraging others to follow his lead. Jo calmly put her hand on his knee and said, "Now Bruce, I want you to think real hard and remember that it is very important for you to be honest when we ask you these questions. Did you climb up in the loft, walk on the outside of the railing, hang on to the divider, step on the bookshelves, climb over to the loft in the other room, and strongly encourage other boys to do the same as you?" Once again, Bruce denied he had done these acts. At this point,

three of the children who were playing with Bruce came in and told their story, and Bruce finally acknowledged what he had done. Jo then asked Bruce why he thought the teachers might think this act necessitated the calling of a "crisis meeting," and he mentioned the physical danger involved for himself and the other children with whom he was playing [some as young as eight years old]. Jo, Julie, and Bruce also discussed the potential destruction of property and the negative image of Harmony his type of behavior might create in the minds of people who live in the community if one of the children had followed Bruce's lead but ended up getting hurt. At one point, Jo and Julie emphasized the need for Bruce to recognize that he was a model for other children to follow; that is, he needed to understand that his actions had an impact on other people besides himself and that he needed to take some (although not total) responsibility for the way his actions influenced his peers. Then Jo mentioned that, in addition to coming up with an appropriate response to his dangerous behavior, they would also have to deal with the fact that he had lied about doing it. She then discussed with him why it was important that he take responsibility for his actions rather than deny them. They briefly discussed issues of trust and the need for "ownership" of one's actions. Finally, they discussed what should be done regarding his dangerous behavior after school. After several options were reviewed, it was decided that Bruce would have to be supervised [remain in sight at all times] after school by the weekly "after school" teacher for one month, and for the next two weeks he would be expected to keep the library [the site of his transgression] clean and put books away after school. In addition, he was to address the students at a Family Meeting to discuss what had happened. At the next Family Meeting Julie, the discussion leader for that day's meeting, introduced Bruce as a "man on a mission for peace." Bruce then mentioned that during the last couple of weeks there had been several "war games" played at school and that there is a policy against this type of playing on school grounds. Julie asked him why, and he said the policy was created because war games often lead to the type of playing in which children can get hurt, and they tend to desensitize children to the fact that people kill and are killed in war: that is, war is not a "game" and shouldn't be treated as if it is. Julie then asked the other students and teachers present what they thought. Tommy, a sixth grader, didn't agree. He thought it was "okay to play war." Sam, his close friend, agreed and said that "no one can be forced to fight in a war." Max disagreed and mentioned the draft, but Sam said, "You could go to jail or another country if you didn't want to fight." Hannah mentioned that even "playing war" can cause people to get hurt. She told a story of how several years ago [before they had the current policy] a number of children were playing war with squirt guns. One of the children playing put dish detergent in his gun, and it got into the eyes of several students. A number of children jumped in at this moment to tell "war stories" of their own. Finally, Julie asked if the

> policy on not allowing war games to be played on school grounds should
> be continued. A vote was taken, and all but four students voted to keep
> Harmony's antiwar policy. (Summary of field notes)

One of the most notable characteristics of the teachers at Harmony was
the attention they gave to students' taking responsibility for their own actions.
They were quick to affirm to students the value of taking responsibility when
students would assume it on their own, and they would point out any
"growth" in this direction to us if we happened to be near an appropriate
situation. This attention was illustrated during a class period in an Exploration
course (see Chapter 5) on stamp collecting.

> Lee and Meg (two fifth-grade students) were placed together in a group
> sorting through stamps, and after about ten minutes, Meg complained to
> Barb that Lee was taking all of the interesting stamps while leaving almost
> none for her to examine. Barb came over to the table, but Lee quickly
> apologized and then they resorted the stamps in a more equitable manner.
> Later Barb told us, "I'm really proud of Lee today. Usually when he has
> been accused of something he gets extremely defensive. But you saw what
> he did today. It's the first time he has taken responsibility for what he has
> done. It's a big step, a real sign of growth on his part." (Summary of field
> notes)

Rather than being used as merely a means of restricting the behavior of
students through technical or bureaucratic prevention and punishments, a
connectionist power structure suggests that discipline be used to help students
become more aware of the impact their antisocial behavior has on the
community within which they live.

Finally, discipline within a democratic framework must make it possible
for students to feel that they are free to express themselves regarding any
disciplinary matters concerning them. Perhaps the most oppressive aspect
of the discipline conducted in most traditional schools is that students are
often silenced by the process. In fact, students who question the actions
of superordinates often find themselves in more trouble. Children who voice
their protests over disciplinary treatment or regulations are often viewed as
insolent.

Discipline from a connectionist perspective is based largely on the ethics
of caring (Gilligan, 1982; Noddings, 1984), in which the superordinate has
greater concern for disciplining in ways that promote feelings of mutual
affection, respect, and comfort than for deciding whether or not a subor-
dinate is receiving "just treatment": that is, as an act of caring, teachers and
administrators face the problem of creating an environment in which students
feel affirmed and cared for while at the same time their behavior is being
evaluated and often restricted. At Harmony, this affirmation often was

manifested through feelings of affection that the teachers felt for the students, but it was also manifested most noticeably in situations where subordinates were free to voice their ideas and if necessary challenge the power of superordinates. For instance, Barb was disturbed by the behavior of the students in some of the places they had visited during the midyear three-day school trip, and she brought the subject up at the first upper elementary Program Meeting after returning to campus.

> Barb began the meeting by sharing some of her feelings about the trip to Indianapolis. She mentioned several things that she liked about the trip, but said she also wanted to discuss with the students something that "disturbed" her a great deal. She went on to point out several instances (visits to specific places) in which she "felt embarrassed" because of the way students were behaving. In particular, she felt many students were discourteous when being taken on guided tours to various places: students were doing such things as not paying attention, talking while a guide was trying to explain things, and wandering off from the group. Several students responded by saying that the guides were "boring," and it would be "dishonest" of them if they pretended to be interested when they were not. Barb tried to explain her conception of courtesy and the need for it in society: that is, even if one is not particularly interested in something that someone says, one should recognize that this person (in this case the guide) was giving of himself or herself (in this case making an effort to teach them something) and this effort on the guide's part deserved the students' respect (attention). Most students came to see Barb's point of view, but a few refused to go along and remained unconvinced. The discussion lasted about 45 minutes, with Barb giving the last word to one of the students who said she wasn't clear when it was appropriate to be "honest" and when it was appropriate to be "courteous" if the two notions were in conflict with each other. (Summary of field notes)

Another manifestation of giving students a voice came at various times throughout the year when they were explicitly told that if they felt they were being treated unfairly by a teacher or administrator, then they should go to another teacher or administrator to help rectify the situation. Dan, the curriculum coordinator, often was asked to help mediate conflicts that might arise between students and teachers, and he saw these conflicts as an opportunity for developing more caring relationships between children and adults. During the year we spent at Harmony, several instances arose when students asked Dan or another teacher to help resolve a conflict between them and a teacher. Take, for instance, an incident that occurred between Jim, who was teaching an Exploration course (see Chapter 5) in journalism, and some of the students who had signed up to take this course.

During today's class four or five students were not paying attention. They talked among themselves and did not accomplish the activities that were planned for this day. Finally, with about 15 or 20 minutes left in the day, Jim told these students that if they did not want to participate, they could leave and go across the hall to the multipurpose room. However, at 2:45, when the day ended, Jim found these students and told them that they would have to remain at school for the 20 minutes that they had missed in class. The students thought this was unfair and asked Dan to intervene. Dan started the meeting by asking Jim what had happened. He talked about their inattention and disruption in the class. Dan asked the students if they could see how their behavior had caused disruption of Jim's teaching. At first they were defensive and wanted to talk only about the "unfair" treatment that they were getting from Jim, but Dan told them that they would have an opportunity to discuss their concerns later. Now he wanted to know if they understood "where Jim was coming from." Eventually, they began to see how their disruptive behavior was not the best way of responding to any complaints that they might have about the course or Jim. Then Dan asked them to share their concerns. Most immediately, they felt it was unfair of Jim to ask them to stay after school since he had "invited" them to leave in the first place; that is, Jim's tone was such that they did not think there would be any repercussions if they left. Otherwise they would not have left the class. However, they also complained that Jim didn't seem very responsive to their input into the class. Jim responded that he was not paying attention to them because they seemed resistant to "putting any positive energy into the class." After these issues were discussed in more detail, Dan said that he thought both the students and Jim could find a way of better meeting each other's needs than by getting into power confrontations. Everyone agreed. The students said that they could be more cooperative and attentive in class, and Jim said he could be more sensitive to their interests. Dan mentioned to Jim that the meeting had gone on well past the 15 or 20 minutes the students were supposed to stay after school and asked him if he felt it would be okay if the students left now. Jim said that would be fine. Everyone seemed to leave the meeting feeling better about each other and about the class. After the meeting, Dan mentioned to us, "At Harmony we want to know *why* a child might insult a teacher [as one of the students had done with Jim] rather than just *if* a teacher was insulted. By focusing on 'why' rather than just 'if,' we can help a child grow and become more responsive to those around him." (Summary of field notes)

Sarason (1982) suggests that schools almost never involve students in discipline matters. There seems to be an implicit assumption on the part of teachers and administrators that young people are either uninterested in or incapable of directly addressing situations that call for disciplinary action. Many critical educators totally ignore the problem of discipline and schooling because it seems inimical to their ideological goals. This reluctance, however, cannot be justified. It is impossible to conceive of teaching even relatively small groups of children such as those found in Harmony's classrooms and not be confronted with dilemmas of discipline. Unfortunately, this reluctance to adequately confront the issue of discipline has greatly reduced the credibility of critical educators and their ideas about educating children in our society. Instead of viewing discipline as a natural outgrowth of an authoritarian system, critical educators need to conceptualize the way in which the disciplining of children can be practiced to foster a connectionist perspective within children: that is, discipline practices need to arise from an image of the type of "character development" of children that we hope to encourage within schools. Although this is perhaps a more difficult task than simply condemning all efforts to discipline children as oppressive, it is essential if we wish to offer meaningful alternatives to the current power relationships that exist in most of our schools.

REFLECTIONS:
TOWARDS CONNECTIONIST POWER DYNAMICS IN ELEMENTARY SCHOOLS

Issues and practices of student participation, power, and control are among the most difficult and complex problems facing educators interested in democratic schooling. As previously mentioned, some educators who are critical of traditional schooling seem to imply that it might be possible to have schools without some form of adult authority over students. Although this notion appeals to our liberatory values, it is in fact irresponsible. As Shaheen (1988) notes, many children come to school sad, angry, confused, and hard "to reach." As discussed in the first chapter, most young people in our society come to school with a strong individualistic orientation towards life. Bureaucratic, technical, or laissez-faire approaches to the dynamics of power among students and between students and teachers cannot provide our children with the community values and guidance needed to promote critical democracy. Rather, it takes teachers and administrators who through the dynamics of power between themselves and their students cultivate children's self-esteem, help children realize that they are not alone in this world (demonstrate that people do sincerely care for them), and teach children that caring for others is as important as caring about oneself.

In advocating the creation of a connectionist power structure in elementary schools, it is important to avoid setting up school arrangements and practices that result in valuing social conformism rather than community. As discussed in the first chapter, some schools that place a strong emphasis on values of community (such as those found in the Soviet Union, China, or fundamentalist religions) have, in fact, established practices that promote social conformism (Bronfenbrenner, 1970; Kessen, 1975; Peshkin, 1986;

Rose, 1988). Requiring unquestioned obedience and passive acquiescence to adult authority at all times, stressing "correct" answers to interpersonal and moral dilemmas, and placing so much value on group solidarity that the individual who disagrees becomes "silenced" through intimidation are some of the practices found in these schools that result in a social conformist rather than community ethos. To be genuinely effective and critically democratic, the effort to influence children's perspectives in the direction of a connectionist orientation must be made in an atmosphere in which children can freely examine and express their convictions without fear of intimidation.

As previously discussed, one of the central notions of democratic schooling is to provide young people with opportunities to exercise greater power than that found in conventional classrooms. During the last decade there have been several calls for "empowering students." However, in itself, giving students opportunities to exercise power says little about democratic living. As Foucault argues, power has no value outside of the social context within which it is manifested (Dreyfus & Rabinow, 1982). One does not have to be a historian to know that power can be used for good or evil purposes, and often the most vile exercise of power occurs in situations when groups of people form a narcissistic identity and then use their collective power against others, such as during our country's involvement in Vietnam (Peck, 1983). The key to understanding power lies in the purpose to which it is directed. For example, several neoconservative educators equate empowering students with giving them the skills necessary to take advantage of the opportunities provided within a competitive marketplace (McLaren, 1988). In this sense students are taught how to gain power for their own advantage. Similarly, libertarian educators equate student power with providing students with as many choices as possible concerning how they (as individuals) want to spend their time and energy. Although providing students with choices and power over their own time and energy is important, a connectionist perspective towards student power goes beyond this to include students' responsibility to the community of people (peers, teachers, administrators, parents) with whom they live. From a connectionist perspective, power and freedom for young people are directly tied to increasing their sense of social responsibility and to teaching them an ethic of caring (Noddings, 1984). In this regard, perhaps the most impressive aspect of Harmony's elementary school was that students seemed to learn to take responsibility not only *for* their actions (keeping the building clean, their own interpersonal behavior), but also *to* people. In particular, students learned to be responsible to themselves, to each other, to teachers, to administrators, to parents, to the school as a whole, to the local community, and to society. The purpose of gaining power within a connectionist framework is to care for (be responsive to the needs of) others as much as to care for oneself.

Facilitating young people's power is, of course, central to democratic education. Because of Harmony's independent status, it is free to establish rituals and structures that may be difficult in most public schools. For instance, the teacher-pupil ratio helps tremendously in facilitating the social bonds between adults and children. The amount of time devoted to addressing interpersonal dynamics through Family, Program, Peer Group, and crisis meetings would be difficult to schedule given the "back-to-the-basics" mentality that dominates the daily routine in our public schools today. However, in spite of these constraints, public school teachers and administrators interested in democratic schooling can draw from the experiences observed in Harmony's elementary school. First, as Wood (1988) notes, students have few or no decision-making opportunities within traditional schools. Classroom and school rules, punishments, routines, and rituals, along with hundreds of other aspects of daily life within schools, have been established long before students ever arrive on their first day. Yet Wood (1988) goes on to point out that whenever a teacher has an opportunity to make a decision, she or he also has the option of using this moment to facilitate student involvement in decision making. Even such simple issues as how desks or other work space should be arranged in the class or the manner in which classrooms are decorated can give young children the opportunity to participate in decisions that directly affect their lives and hence provide them with a sense of power. On a more substantive level, most new teachers are warned to "start the year out tough, because you can always loosen up later on." The implication is that teachers should make it a point to establish a clear set of rules and punishments for children, and teachers should "be hard" on kids at the beginning of the school year to make sure students don't "take advantage" of a teacher's "good nature." Our observations at Harmony suggest that teachers interested in democratic education should seriously consider doing the opposite: that is, allow classroom rules to be established *retroactively* as the need for them arises and provide opportunities for students to participate in the establishment of necessary rules and privileges. Perhaps the most apparent observation that we made at Harmony was that the students had a deep interest in matters of discipline, control, and freedom. With proper guidance from the teachers, these young people were able to seriously consider the tensions that exist between individual freedom and the common good of the school community. More important than the question of whether children should have greater power within educational settings is the question of for what purpose (self-advancement or the common good) they are going to exercise this increase of power.

As previously stated, issues and practices of power and participation between adults and children are discussed and written about more often than perhaps any other topic within education. These practices and issues are especially important within a discourse on democratic education because we recognize that democratic attitudes, values, and behavior are more likely to emerge among people when they have opportunities to participate in democratic experiences (Pateman, 1970). However, most children's social settings in our society (family, church, school, scouting, and other youth clubs) rarely offer these experiences. Often educators who are interested in viewing education as a vehicle for democracy limit their vision to giving children opportunities to "vote" on various issues or "choices" about how they want to spend their time. However, if we are to move towards critical democracy in our society, then our notion of democratic experience must be significantly expanded beyond these simplistic rituals. The kinds of issues and practices that we observed being manifested in Harmony (social bonding, teacher authority, power sharing, and discipline) are necessary to provide young people with occasions to directly confront the tension between their freedom to act in accordance with their own desires and their social and moral responsibility to others who share their world. From our perspective, it seemed that the way in which teachers and administrators at Harmony approached the problem of power and participation reflected a fairly good balance between the values of individuality and community. However, it must be remembered that Harmony exists within a society dominated by an ethos of individualism. The vast majority of students come to school with this ethos firmly embedded within their consciousness. For this reason, educators interested in critical democracy need to emphasize those aspects of power and participation that will increase students' sense of, and commitment to, values of caring and social responsibility. This emphasis, we argue, is necessary to counterbalance the individualistic values that are promoted in our popular culture, to which children are particularly sensitive. Schools, as primary institutions in society, are ideal settings in which to establish interpersonal dynamics, specific time periods, environments, rituals, myths, and organizational structures to give young people the democratic experiences they need. When these opportunities are provided within a caring milieu, children will develop the confidence to actively participate in society for the common good and the trust that their participation will be valued.

Although issues and practices of power and participation are central to fostering a connectionist perspective among children, they are not the only avenue through which this perspective can be cultivated. In fact, many democratic educators make a mistake in thinking that democratic education refers solely to issues and practices related to the power dynamics between adults and children. Just as important are issues and practices concerning the curriculum that is taught to children and the instructional strategies used to teach this content. The overt content within elementary classrooms, as well as the more subtle lessons that emerge from the instruction used in a given setting, teaches children a great deal about the type of society in which we live, the kind of life we hope to lead, and our place in that society. In the next chapter we turn our attention to curricular and instructional matters in an effort to illuminate the possibilities for a connectionist elementary curriculum.

5

Curriculum and Instruction

As mentioned in the previous chapter, many educators think of democratic schooling solely in terms of interpersonal relationships between adults and children. Although these relationships are central to any effort to educate young people, it is our contention that the key element in establishing elementary education for critical democracy is the curriculum within a particular school. The term *curriculum* as used here refers to what is learned through the content, form, and learning experiences that exist within classrooms and schools.

As several educators have illustrated, the curricular practices and content that exist in schools reflect at any given historical moment the competing social, political, and psychological interests that exist in the broader culture within which schools exist. Wexler (1987) notes that since the emergence of what has been referred to as the "technical" or "information" age, the concentration of power in society has shifted from those who control the production of material goods to those who control the means of knowledge production in our society. Systems of knowledge, of the language that we use to articulate how life should be lived and how society should be structured, have increasingly become systems of power. As a result, those institutions that have a significant influence on the ideas that are socially popularized, such as schools and the media, play a particularly powerful role in modern industrialized societies. Because of this focus, much of the scholarly work, what Giroux (1986) refers to as a "language of critique," within the field of curriculum studies during the last twenty years has been directed at decoding whose interests are being served through the content, instruction, and learning experiences found in our schools.

As discussed in the first chapter, the curriculum found in the vast majority of our schools (both public and "alternative") reflects those interests that are best served in a society dominated by an individualistic ideology. Although the language of critique has provided significant insight into the nature of schooling in our society, it has failed to provide us with visions of what can be done to counterbalance the individualistic ideology that dominates schools and society. As previously argued, if elementary schooling is to play a significant role in the creation of critical democracy in our society,

123

then the curriculum in such schools needs to cultivate a "connectionist" perspective among students, teachers, and administrators.

In a society that takes the values of self-interest and individual achievement for granted, an elementary curriculum that fosters a connectionist perspective reflects a radical departure from the status quo. However, merely calling for a curriculum that will move our children towards a more balanced consciousness does not address the necessity for discourse on what form and substance this curriculum needs to take. Most efforts to portray events that illuminate critical approaches to curriculum have been the result of self-reflective reports located at the university or high school level (Berlak, 1988; Ellsworth, 1988; Giroux, 1978; Lewis & Simon, 1986). Weiler (1988) and Belenky and her colleagues (1986) portray the work of "feminist" teaching in high schools and colleges, respectively. Critical practices portrayed within elementary schools are particularly rare and when found are usually chronological descriptions of events without careful articulation of those issues and practices that will guide others interested in critical curriculum alternatives (e.g., Dennison, 1969; Kohl, 1968). By locating our discussion within the lived experiences of the educators and students in Harmony's elementary school, we are able to project images of practice that lend insight into creating the type of elementary curriculum needed for critical democracy.

As discussed in Chapter 2, coursework within Harmony's elementary school was divided into lower (grades 1–3) and upper (grades 4–6) programs. The morning classes were departmentalized by subjects, with the exception of the first grade, which was self-contained. The afternoons were reserved for a variety of special topic classes developed and taught by teachers and/or visiting instructors. The weekly classes were scheduled into the following time periods, each with a specific curricular title and function.

Quiet Hours	Met Monday through Friday mornings. There were two 70-minute Quiet Hours (language arts and math/science) in the lower elementary program, and three 45-minute Quiet Hours (social/natural science, language arts, and math) in the upper elementary program.
Research & Discovery	Met Monday, Tuesday, and Thursday afternoons for 50 minutes. Students worked on independent study projects under the direction of a teacher.
Exploration Hour	Met Monday, Tuesday, and Thursday afternoons for 45 minutes. Teacher-created, topical, multigraded courses that emphasized informal student investigation and exploration

	into subject matter. Students selected a new course each month.
Creation Hour	Met Wednesday afternoons for 105 minutes. Teacher-created, topical, multigraded courses that emphasized student participation in fine arts, performing arts, handicrafts, or community service. Students selected a new course each month.
Recreation Hour	Met Friday afternoons for 105 minutes. Field trips and/or activities that involved physical activity.

As we spent time observing Harmony's elementary curriculum being manifested on a day-to-day basis, we were provided with an opportunity to identify curricular practices and issues that could be used to counterbalance the dominance of individualism in our society. In some respects, these practices are not that different from those found in any number of schools with a "progressive" educational tradition. In other respects, there are subtle but important differences. It is important to emphasize that the usefulness of any curricular content, practice, or idea actually lies in the ideological foundation of those who are teaching and learning. A particular activity (such as small-group work) within a school may look the same in two classrooms, but the impact of this activity will vary significantly between teachers and students with a connectionist perspective and teachers and students with a social conformist or libertarian perspective.

BUILDING A CONNECTIONIST RATIONALE

As children grow up in a given society, they are exposed to numerous and at times conflicting messages about why they should learn or attend school. As discussed in the first chapter, the dominant message in the United States is that schools provide children with the learning necessary for them to participate, *as individuals*, within society as presently constructed. Although often spoken of as a virtue in our society, the notion of working (or in this case going to school) to help others is not one that is widely promoted. As previously mentioned, most students did not enter Harmony's elementary school with much interest in democracy or in establishing a more just and caring community. Our mass culture and economic system does not emphasize community values and actions among the general population, and the children who attended Harmony were not impervious to the influences of societal values. In Harmony, as in most schools, there were moments throughout the year when the rationale for going to school was directly or indirectly discussed with students (for example, as an introduction to the new school year, in response to students' questioning why they had to learn some particular content). Because of the strong individualistic messages children in our culture receive, it is important, whenever the opportunity arises, that children be asked to consider a connectionist rationale for learning and going to school. This rationale emphasizes the view that children need to learn to achieve not just some individual goal but a form of social responsibility. Children need to be exposed to the view that the reason for learning is to nurture their intellectual talents for constructing our society into a more democratic, just, and caring place to live. Students need to hear that democratic societies cannot grow and develop (let alone survive) unless their citizens are well informed and have the educational abilities and sensitivities needed to critically examine the world in which we live. Students need to be repeatedly asked to consider the viewpoint that their learning is not just for their own benefit, but for the democratic well-being of our society (and the world) as a whole.

On several occasions Harmony's teachers expressed to us that education should be seen as a means of making the world a better place in which to live. However, when we specifically asked teachers about their goals for having students learn particular classroom content, their answers often reflected an individualistic orientation. Illustrative of this perspective is Jo's statement:

> I want kids to have the education they will need to live whatever kind of life they want. The most important thing is that they are happy in what they do. If they want to be some type of professional, we want to give them the education that will provide that opportunity for them. On the other hand, if they want to be a stablehand, that's fine too, if that's what gives them the most meaning in their lives. Hopefully, we provide them with the education that makes it possible for them to make intelligent decisions about their own lives.

The teachers at Harmony spoke of their concern that in our society children are pressured to conform to an overly narrow set of values and life-styles. Several mentioned that they believed schooling should be designed to help their students live "the life they want to live" rather than merely fulfill the labor and consumer needs of our corporate economy. This rationale was observed being expressed (in one form or another) to students at various times throughout the year. When asked why going to school was important, the vast majority of Harmony's students responded in individualistic terms, such as to get a job, make money, or obtain a personal goal (college education, travel).

An understanding among children of the relationship between personal freedom or opportunity and social responsibility is extremely difficult to obtain given our individualistic society. Most schools in our society fail to offer students any comprehensive reasons for attending school and learning. In place of a well-articulated rationale, a marketplace explanation for learning seems to be taken for granted by the vast majority of our public. Yet even this rationale is rarely discussed at length with the children who attend our schools. The assumption seems to be that children aren't interested in knowing why they should attend school, or that even if they are interested it is really none of their business. In either case, children are seen as passive functionaries rather than active participants in their own lives and the life of society. In order to promote critical democracy through education, children need to be routinely engaged in dialogue that helps them seriously explore why they should go to school and learn as much as possible. Given the dominance of individualism in our society, children need to be exposed to a connectionist rationale for learning whenever these discussions arise.

TEACHER-CENTERED CURRICULUM

As illustrated in Chapter 3, the teachers at Harmony have the ultimate power to decide the curricular content, instructional strategies, and learning experiences in their own classrooms. Aside from their ability to understand and relate to children, the most important characteristic that Dan, the curriculum coordinator, looks for in prospective teacher candidates is their intellectual ability to decide what should be taught to children and their talent for developing a curriculum in order to teach it.

This orientation is, of course, in direct opposition to what many believe to be the core of radical education, that is, a "student-centered" curriculum. In the minds of many, a "teacher-centered" curriculum reflects the authoritarianism that dominates educational practice within most of our schools. In the minds of many radical educators, a major problem in traditional schools is that teachers, not students, make curricular decisions. This teacher domination, it is argued, suppresses the natural instincts within children to learn and grow. From this perspective, democratic education implies that children should be free to learn what they want to learn, how they want to learn, and when they want to learn. Until children are allowed to take responsibility for their own learning, education will continue to be coercive and thus oppressive. The idea that the curriculum can be democratic and teacher centered seems to be fundamentally contradictory in the minds of many critical educators. However, this perception is based on a faulty image of, first, the teacher's control of curriculum within traditionally structured schools, and second, the benefits of student-centered schooling.

Many radical educators equate "traditional" education with teacher-centered education. However, when teaching in conventional classrooms is carefully examined, one actually finds teachers, not at the center of the elementary curriculum, but on its edge along with the children. During the last decade, concern over teachers' accountability has increased dramatically, and in response, schools have adopted the use of prepackaged instructional programs as the basis for classroom curriculum. As mentioned in Chapter 3, these programs are specifically designed to raise pupils' scores on state and/or national standardized tests, and they come complete with specified objectives (that is, content), step-by-step instructional procedures (dominated by workbooks and drills), and quantitative exams to measure exactly what pupils "learn." Instead of establishing relevant and meaningful curricular goals, developing original and stimulating content, and designing thoughtful learning experiences based on an intimate knowledge of their own and their pupils' interests and talents, teachers are relegated by these prepackaged curricular programs to a managerial rather than educative role. Today, teachers in most schools are encouraged to become "educational technicians" who merely coordinate the day's work (schedule time for each subject, organize children into ability groups, distribute seatwork to keep children busy when not in small groups, maintain paperwork on students' completed work, administer programmatic tests, and discipline pupils to keep them on task when necessary) rather than actually teach children content. Getting the children through these programs on time in a smooth, quiet, and orderly fashion becomes the main criterion upon which teachers are evaluated (Apple & Teitelbaum, 1986; Gitlin, 1983; Goodman, 1985; Woodward, 1986). As Duffy (1987: 358) and his colleagues state, "Because teachers know that they must teach to the test, that they must follow the basal textbook sequence, and that they must adhere to procedures established by superiors, they conclude that they are not supposed to be decision makers." In their review of research, Lanier and Little (1986) conclude that opportunities for teachers in schools to exercise informed judgment, engage in thoughtful discourse, and participate in reflective decision making regarding curricular matters are practically nonexistent. Zeichner (1986: 88) notes that

> numerous analyses, conducted from a variety of ideological and political perspectives, have concluded that the effect of many of the recent policies affecting teachers has been to promote greater external control over the content, processes, and outcomes of teachers' work and to encourage teachers to adopt conformist orientations to self and society as well as technical orientations to the role of teacher.

Increasingly teachers are becoming disenfranchised from their work; that is, the conceptualization of curriculum and learning is separated from those who actually teach. Although many (Frymier, 1987a; Myers, 1986; Wise, 1979) point to the accountability movement and state-mandated testing as the source of this phenomenon of disenfranchising elementary teachers from their occupations, other scholars (Apple, 1986; Goodman, 1988a; Grumet,

1988; Medler, 1972; Wirth, 1983) have illuminated broader ideological, social, and political factors which are rooted in industrial and patriarchal rationalities.

Suggesting that the curriculum be teacher centered is in fact a departure from conventional schooling. Putting teachers at the core of the curriculum implies that they have substantive ideas upon which to base their curriculum (are thoughtful, knowledgeable, and curious people in their own right) and that they have the talents to stimulate children's thinking and desire to learn, given proper support. Teachers, from this perspective, have what Eisner (1979) refers to as "educational connoisseurship," the ability to discover "what is educationally significant." As previously mentioned, this perspective is clearly manifested in the power that teachers at Harmony have to decide curricular goals, resources, experiences, and content.

Although "children's interests" is an often expressed ideal in establishing elementary curriculum, its benefits are problematic. On the surface, this notion of children taking control over their own learning appeals to many of our most cherished notions of freedom and liberty, but it can, in fact, be a paralyzing form of pedagogy that has oppressive rather than liberating consequences for teachers and students. For example, Barb, who (as mentioned in the previous chapter) had been at Harmony just one year prior to our observations, expressed strong libertarian views when it came to her educational philosophy. She questioned, during numerous interactions with her colleagues, if teachers should be "directive" in teaching children, and often argued that children should have ultimate control over their own education. During the year she would vacillate in her approach to teaching. At times, she gave students nearly total freedom to "do [learn] what they want." During these periods, there were almost no controls over students' actions. Take, for example, the following interaction:

> Barb was reading a novel to her fifth-grade class. After about five minutes, Max got out of his seat with the usual amount of noise associated with such actions, walked in between Barb and the rest of the students to the "library shelf," looked for and picked out a book, walked in front of Barb on his way back to his seat, sat down, and opened his book. Barb stopped her reading while Max was involved with his task, and after he sat down she asked him, with a touch of chagrin in her voice, what he was doing. He replied nonchalantly, "I want to read this book." Barb asked if he felt he could read the book and listen to her read at the same time [a physical impossibility]. However, she accepted his answer when he told her he could, and merely continued reading without bringing to Max's attention how his actions disrupted the flow of the class. (Summary of field notes)

These periods of "student-controlled learning" would last until Barb would become frustrated that the students weren't engaged in any meaningful learning and would often disrupt those few students who were seriously working. Then she would go through a period in which she was more directive, and she would require students to work together and complete expected assignments. However, often her efforts were met with resistance from a small minority of students, and she would spend considerable time and energy dealing with this resistance.

> For several days now Barb has tried to get Tommy and Sam to complete their language arts assignments in class and cease disrupting others from doing their assignments. However, when confronted by Barb, they strongly denied that they were "doing anything" [me thinks they protest too much]. Today, Barb brought in a video camera to tape these boys in an effort to "prove" to them that they were not completing their assignments and were disrupting other members of the class. Unfortunately, whenever Barb got out the camera, Tommy and Sam immediately stopped their disruptive activities (talking, poking at each other or other students, walking around and bumping into other students' chairs) and started working on their assignment. As a result, she was not able to "catch them in the act," and her efforts to do so only caused additional commotion during times when other students were trying to work on their assignments. (Summary of field notes)

Eventually, Barb would have to exercise strong force to get these few students to complete their assignments and to keep them from disrupting other students. However, after some time would pass, she would feel guilty about exercising this control and reassert her beliefs that "children should be in charge of their own learning" and that "children should not be forced to learn." Once again, she would give students their "freedom to learn" until enough students would choose to do nothing that it became difficult to teach them anything. As might be expected, Barb spent considerable time dealing with her students' anti-intellectual attitudes. Throughout the year, she expressed her inner turmoil to us as she struggled to understand how "directive" she should be. She believed that if students were allowed total control over the curriculum they would eventually get bored with "doing nothing" or "disrupting." They would then "want to learn," and she "would be ready for them." However, Barb did not think the parents or other teachers at Harmony would wait until this period of boredom (which she felt could take months) was over, and she felt that their cooperation would be necessary for her ideas to work. As a result, she was caught in a difficult, and at times oppressive, pattern of pedagogy for both herself and her students.

Although an image of children actively pursuing their own intellectual interests is appealing, based on our observations at Harmony, the most intellectually inspiring aspect of this school's elementary curriculum was that the teachers were intellectually engaged in their professional fields of study (language arts, science, math), the theory and practice of pedagogy, the "human condition," and the "world" in which we live. They were active readers of literature (in their content fields, popular intellectual and/or aesthetic magazines), attended workshops, seminars, or lectures dealing with educational, psychological, aesthetic, religious, social, and political themes, and regularly discussed their ideas with colleagues.

At Harmony, the teachers were encouraged to use their evolving questions and ideas related to the above areas of concern as the basis for the elementary curriculum. In other words, as the teachers learned about this life we, as human beings, lead and the world in which we live, they would translate their own contemplations into curriculum for children to explore. Take for example, Jo's, the lower elementary language arts teacher's, first "writing unit" of the year. During the summer she had studied more about the "whole language" approach to language arts and thought it important to focus on children's imagination. She had always enjoyed studying and teaching about animals, and from past experience knew that second and third graders usually love this topic as well. So she developed a unit entitled "Magical Animals" as the initial major writing project of the year.

> Jo gathered the class together on the floor and told them about their first writing assignment. She said, "A lot of you know that I have always liked learning about animals, and I thought it might be interesting to write some stories about different kinds of animals and then make a book of your stories that other people could read. As I thought more about it, I wondered if we might not want to write stories about animals that don't really exist: that is, I thought it might be interesting to write stories about animals that we invent ourselves. We could call our book of stories 'Magical Animals.' What do you think?" At this question, the children unanimously agreed that this assignment was a "neat" idea. She then said, "One way to start thinking about writing stories is to hear how other people have written about a similar topic." At this point, she took out a book called *Kartusch* by Steven Kosgrove, and read them the story about imaginary animals named "Furry Eyeballs." She ended the lesson by showing them where she was keeping several other books that had stories about "make-believe" animals, and she asked them to read these stories as they thought about creating their own "animal." The next day, she began an art project in which the children learned how to make "animal masks." She started this project by brain-storming with the children about different types of and uses for masks (sports, medicine, construction, parties, religious ceremonies). She then mentioned some cultures, such as the American Indians, who had a special feeling of connection to the animals that lived near them. She said that for many of their spiritual ceremonies they created animal masks. Jo went

on to explain that in some cultures masks were used as symbols for making a statement, and she gave several examples (to show appreciation to their gods, to ward off evil spirits, to show respect for various animals, to bring good fortune) from an American Indian anthropology book she had with her. She asked the students if they wanted their masks to "make a statement" about their beliefs. She then said that it might be a good idea to look at some American Indian masks in order to get ideas for their own masks. They did, and she showed them a book about masks used by American Indians during their precolonial history, pointing out that some of the masks were of "make-believe" animals and some were of animals known to exist. As she showed and discussed each mask, the children responded by saying "neat," "cool," "ah," and "ooh." After finishing the book, she showed them where other books would be kept for them to examine. Eventually, the children would be making three-dimensional papier-mâché masks, but today's task was for them to draw a mask that would resemble their "magical animal." During the next few weeks, the children finished their masks while they wrote rough drafts of their stories, discussed these with Jo and other students in "authors' circles," and finally "published" their class book. (Summary of field notes)

As will be discussed in the next section of this chapter, the result of putting teachers at the center of the curriculum seemed to be a never-ending array of stimulating units of study. For example, Julie developed an Exploration class entitled *Underground* after reading David Macaulay's (1976) book of the same name. Bart taught a Creation class on architectural drawing and model making based on his own study of this field and his previous work experience as a carpenter. Barb taught an Exploration class on rockets after meeting someone whose hobby was making model rockets. Some of the most powerful educational experiences we observed occurred when the teachers developed curricular ideas and experiences that students would probably not have listed as one of their interests. For example, we were extremely surprised at the beginning of the year when Julie (in her upper elementary social/natural science classes) asked students what kind of "things" they would like to learn, and several students mentioned "chemistry." We shared our surprise with Julie, and she said, "Last year I thought it might be interesting to teach some chemistry, and for some reason the kids really liked it." After we observed her "experiment-based" chemistry lessons later that year, it was easy to understand the reason for the children's enthusiasm for this unusual elementary school topic. From our vantage point, the most profound educational experiences at Harmony occurred when teachers decided what to study, stimulated interest in this topic, found and made available a variety of resources from which students could learn, and then carefully planned and implemented experiences through which this topic became meaningful to students. When these experiences occurred, children's consciousness and interest in learning seemed to genuinely expand.

Although Barb might be correct and eventually some students might become "bored" with their choice not to engage in intellectual matters, thus creating an opportunity for a student-centered curriculum, from a connectionist perspective this orientation is fundamentally flawed. First, the notion that a student-centered curriculum is the ideal foundation upon which to develop a democratic education stems from the sentimental and problematic assumption that children will (if only allowed to pursue their own interests) "naturally" become invested in learning about and concerned with the well-being of the world around them. Second, a student-centered curriculum is based on the individualistic assumption that schooling is designed for the benefit of children as isolated beings rather than needed for the creation of a compassionate, thoughtful, and interdependent society and planet. The radical reform of schooling for critical democracy projects an active role for teachers to construct the type of education required.

In advocating that teachers be at the center of the curriculum, we are not naively suggesting that this focus of control, by itself, will result in an elementary curriculum for critical democracy. To the contrary, teachers need to consciously create rituals and structures, develop curriculum content and instructional activities, and act with reasoned authority in order to nourish a connectionist perspective within children. As will be discussed below, a curriculum for critical democracy will have several characteristics in addition to being teacher centered.

COLLABORATIVE LEARNING

From a connectionist perspective, it is important that teachers use their autonomy to promote students' collective sense of efficacy and control over the educational experiences found in their class. As Vygotsky (1978) argues, student learning should be seen not as an individualistic phenomenon but as part of a social process. Cognitive growth is more substantively enhanced when it moves back and forth from a social or interpsychological context to an individual or intrapsychological context. From Vygotsky's perspective, cognitive development is inhibited when conceived as an isolated process of gradually accumulating knowledge and skills rather than as a dialectical transformation that takes place between two or more people as well as within one's own mind. In most instances, learning should be viewed not as an isolated event but as a result of arbitration and a joining of consciousness with others. This collaborative concept of learning is central to a connectionist concept of curriculum and was manifested in several ways at Harmony.

One noticeable way in which learning was seen as a collective experience was in the manner teachers and students negotiated what was learned. As previously illustrated, teachers at Harmony had the final word on what happened in their classes. However, as mentioned earlier, teachers at this school were carefully screened prior to employment to ensure as much as possible that they would be sensitive to the composite needs, interests, and efficacy of students. Students at Harmony were required to attend class and complete assignments; however, they also had numerous opportunities to make academic decisions. It is important to remember that students selected the Exploration and Creation courses they wanted each month, and the topics for their Research and Discovery projects were, with teacher input, self-chosen. The majority of Quiet Hour assignments were broad enough for students to have some choice in what they wanted to study within structured parameters. For example, during the spring, Julie's upper elementary natural/social science classes studied "ancient cultures." The children formed themselves into small study groups (two to four people) and chose a culture to research (Greek, Chinese, Russian, Japanese, Indian, medieval English, Egyptian). Julie then gave each group the following assignments:

1. Each group will collect ten to fifteen important dates from its culture's history for the class timeline [which was posted on the room wall].
2. Each group must make a map showing the extent of the civilization studied and its main sites and features.
3. Each of you must write a "Back in Time" story pretending you are a person living back in the ancient civilization your group is studying. Two people may write a dialogue, etc.
4. Each group must make a poster showing the writing system your culture used.
5. Each group must try to find answers to questions which classmates ask about the group's culture during class discussions.
6. Each person must do some reading about the group's culture. What and how much will be worked out with me. Your reading should include a book that is historical and at least one folktale. You are encouraged to look at as many pictures of paintings or other artifacts from the culture you study as possible. View any filmstrips on your culture that we have on file.
7. Your group should decide and then complete other types of projects, such as making models, investigating further some aspect of the culture (food, religion, tools, clothing, famous people), or reproducing artwork. For these projects creativity is especially encouraged! See me for other possible ideas and before you start work on these projects.
8. Final projects will be displayed in the room, and perhaps at the Spring Festival.

Once assignments were given, teachers were open to negotiating with students around specific demands. On each day of school, at least one or two students would ask if they could skip a particular math problem, a story in their reading books, or a writing task. Teachers would or would not give them permission, or they would offer a substitute assignment depending upon the circumstances of each situation. It was evident that the students at Harmony felt completely comfortable initiating discussions with their teachers regarding what they should study. Likewise, teachers would also initiate this negotiating process. Take, for example, the following incident that occurred during one Research and Discovery class session:

> Barb went over to a small group of boys who had chosen to make a claymation movie on dinosaurs. They had been looking at photographs and making some initial clay models. Barb noticed that one student's figure looked much more like a bird than a dinosaur. She asked him about it and said, "We don't really know what dinosaurs looked like because no human beings were alive then, but we have found skeletons, so we have some ideas. What you have here is fine, but you have to show me that your view of dinosaurs has some support based on what information we do have." After she left, this student began to look more closely at the photographs and altered his figure. (Summary of field notes)

The dynamic of allowing students some choice within parameters set by the teacher was central to Harmony's view of using education to prepare children for democratic participation in society. During a group discussion at an Alternative Schools Conference, Harmony's curriculum was criticized by several participants as being "too coercive" (not child centered enough). Dan, Harmony's curriculum coordinator, responded by saying,

> Letting kids "do what they want" is not empowering. In life no one can always do what he or she wants. Kids need to learn how to arbitrate in order to come to mutual respect and understanding. We don't see conflict between teachers and students as a bad thing. Conflict can be very empowering. We provide kids with the opportunity to successfully negotiate what they and their teachers feel is important to learn. This helps them become more empowered because they have to articulate their reasoning for exploring something other than what was originally planned.

The process of negotiating curriculum within Harmony did not seem to result in repressive educational conditions. When asked by us, teachers, or parents what they liked about Harmony, students unanimously mentioned their power to make choices about what and how they wanted to learn.

Perhaps even more important than viewing student choice and negotiation as central aspects of a connectionist curriculum is the need to have learning encountered as a collective rather than isolated experience among the children. This goal is, however, a particularly difficult one to address in our society. Research on the social cognition of children in the United States related to their notions of achievement suggests that most children move increasingly from a "temporal" to a "comparative" framework just prior to and in their early years of school. When children use a temporal framework to examine their own achievements (and the feelings of self-worth that are attached to these achievements), they contrast their ability to accomplish something now with their previous inability to accomplish it. As children reach the age of three or more, they develop a sense of history, and they realize that what they could not do yesterday they can do today, and what they cannot do today they will be able to do tomorrow. When children's understanding of their achievements is supported by those close to them, these comparisons become satisfying and pleasurable (Suls, 1986; Suls & Mullen, 1982; Suls & Sanders, 1982). This historical understanding gives children an enduring sense of self-worth (Albert, 1977). However, this temporal notion of achievement begins to weaken just as children enter school age (Suls, 1986; Veroff, 1969). Whereas a preschool child in the United States might ask, "Can I do it better than I did before?" a child during the early school years begins to ask, "Can I do it better than the other children in my group?" One does not have to be a psychologist to recognize the competitive nature of this orientation. Unless elementary schools consciously attempt to balance this "comparative" framework and offer more collaborative notions of self-achievement, it will be difficult for most children to develop attitudes and values consistent with critical democracy. Unfortunately, as Chafel (1988) notes, it is widely acknowledged that the conventional elementary curriculum promulgates this comparative orientation through, for example, the establishment of tracking, reward systems for individual achievement over others, and standardized testing. As indicated in the first chapter, traditional curricular practices emphasize these isolated and competitive learning experiences. Postman and Weingartner (1969: 20) suggest that traditional curricula in most schools teach students a subconscious but powerful message that one's "own ideas and those of one's classmates are inconsequential." One group of researchers suggests that, in part because of the way education is conceptualized, American children are "not only irrationally competitive, they are almost sadistically rivalrous" (Nelson & Kagan, 1972: 91).

Whereas this comparative orientation among children regarding their sense of achievement is usually ignored or even encouraged in most conventional schools, it was directly confronted by Harmony's teachers. Take, for instance, Jo's interaction with her third-grade class after returning the results of the only standardized exam they took during the school year.

"Now that you guys know how well you did on this test, I'm asking you not to compare your score with the other kids' scores in the class." At this point, one student mentioned that he and a few of the students had already compared their scores. Jo responded by saying, "Well, what's done is done, but maybe you'll decide not to compare your scores with anyone else. Does anyone know why I am asking you to keep your scores to yourself?" At this point, a number of students called out, "So you won't hurt someone's feelings if they scored lower than you." Jo said, "Right, that's part of it. What other reason might there be for not sharing your scores?" Two children then talked about how tests are given only "so that teachers can help us better" rather than as a final judgment of how smart someone is at a given time. Jo then added, "Each of you is special. What you get on a given test doesn't mean you're smarter or better than anyone else. What's really important is that you try hard, help each other, and learn as much as you can." (Summary of field notes)

When students engaged in comparative "one-upmanship," their actions were challenged. For example, Max, a bright fifth-grade student, often called attention to his classmates' academic weaknesses. On several occasions, the upper elementary teachers talked to him about his need to "put other kids down." As in many discussions of this nature, the goal was to explore his feelings and help him become more sensitive to the feelings of other students. Although he often agreed with his teachers, he continued to verbally express to other children that their work and academic abilities were not as good as his own. One day, however, his behavior in this regard prompted Barb to become more forceful.

The students were told they could go to the bookshelves and pick out a book to read for the rest of the class period. When Max noticed that Jack (who was not a very good reader and had a poor concept of himself as someone who could learn) had chosen a particularly easy book to read, he laughed and said in a mocking tone to no one in particular, "He always picks out the easiest books to read. I could read dozens of those kinds of books." Immediately, Barb broke in and expressed a rare ultimatum: "Max, we've talked about this before, and I'm tired of it! I don't want to hear you saying this kind of stuff again. If you do, I'll just have to separate you from the class until you learn to be more sensitive." (Summary of field notes)

In our society, it seems as if social comparisons among groups of children are inevitable. What is important is to use these opportunities to help students examine their own behavior and attitudes in light of promoting a collective sense of learning. Ignoring this common dynamic among our young people will only lead to feelings of insecurity, competition, and eventually hostility. Although confronting this type of social comparison is important in efforts to develop a connectionist curriculum, other, more active measures are also needed.

In opposition to competitive learning, many educators think in terms of "cooperative learning" strategies (Slavin, 1990), and on any given day the teachers at Harmony were consciously incorporating cooperative learning experiences into their curriculum. Take, for instance, one of Barb's language arts lessons:

> Barb had the students work in pairs today. Each group created a "story board" that reflected the plot of a traditional ethnic folktale. When asked about the rationale for this arrangement, Barb responded, "Lately I've felt I needed to do more activities that would demonstrate to the children how learning can be more rewarding when done as a cooperative venture. So I paired students who do not read very well, but are perhaps good artists or visual thinkers, with those who are good readers to show them that they can learn from each other and build upon each other's talents to create something." (Summary of field notes)

Although these types of cooperative activities are important, alone they do not adequately reflect the essence of a connectionist curriculum.

More important than the cooperative nature of a given activity are the values and ideology that underlie such practices. As Dewey (1933: 215) noted, in determining the significance of a given phenomenon the important thing is "not the thing done, but the quality of mind that goes into the doing." From a connectionist perspective, what is most important is demonstrating to children that each individual's learning is intimately connected to the learning of those who share a given pedagogical experience. What was particularly impressive about student learning at Harmony was that, in most cases, the students felt they learned *together* rather than as isolated beings. Many assignments called for students to work in study groups. During those periods when assignments were "individualized" (children using unique materials and studying different content), students were often directed by teachers to other students to give and/or receive assistance, not as a special or unusual circumstance, but as a normal course of events. Take, for instance, the following interaction between Jim, the lower elementary math teacher, and one of his students:

> Jim was helping Bill understand place values and how to carry numbers when adding. First, Jim asked Bill to explain how he had arrived at the answers in his book. When he finished, Jim said, "I'm not saying the way you are doing this is wrong, but here is another way you might work these types of problems." After describing his strategy, he said, "Try that and see if it works for you. If it doesn't, come back and we'll take another crack at it, or maybe you could ask Jason how he does it. He seems to under-

stand how to do these problems; maybe he can offer some ideas I haven't thought of." (Summary of field notes)

Students in Jo's lower elementary language arts and Jim's math classes were often grouped so that they could work together and help each other on a given task.

At Harmony, there seemed to be a prevailing sense that students' education was a shared experience. Curricular practices were almost always designed to give groups and individuals numerous opportunities to exchange what they were learning and their work with other students and teachers. We were consistently impressed by the serious manner in which the teachers responded to students' input during class discussions, thus setting a model for the students that their "personal" knowledge was as important as "school" knowledge. This type of shared learning seemed so well integrated into various class assignments that one could easily overlook it. Take, for example, the following first-grade lesson on the "senses of ants":

> Michele asked the children to review the human senses from a previous topic they had studied, and they contrasted these with the senses of ants. As the lesson continued, Michele was particularly good at getting these young children thoughtfully involved. For example, when they discussed taste, she asked, "What kind of experiments could we do to test if ants taste?" After several suggestions, she synthesized their ideas into an experiment (setting different kinds of food in front of some of the ants from their ant farm and seeing what they chose to eat). She then asked the children to hypothesize which type of food the ants would eat by asking them to think about the foods that attract ants in their own homes. The children eagerly shared their "ant stories," and as is often the case with young children, their stories wandered significantly from the question that was asked. However, Michele listened to each child carefully and verbalized those points from their stories that were germane to the topic being discussed. The lesson ended with a trip outside to hunt for ant trails or hills. Throughout this lesson, Michele responded to students' comments with real interest. A half-hour after school, several children came rushing into Michele's room saying they had discovered an ant trail. Michele willingly went out with them as they excitedly showed her the rotten apple on the ground and the ant trail leading away from it. (Summary of field notes)

The school hallways were filled with students' projects. Teachers were often observed using terms such as *we* or *our* to describe the work that was being done in class, and the class as a whole would be rewarded (usually verbally) for work well done. There were no single desks in rows; students worked together at tables, in beanbag chairs, clustered on the floor, and in lofts.

Collective learning at Harmony was evident even in what initially appeared to be a highly individualized assignment—the final graduation Research and Discovery project.

As the spring semester began, the graduating students (sixth graders) were told that this semester's Research and Discovery class time would be devoted to their graduation projects. These projects included (1) a ten- to twenty-page term paper on a topic of their choice, (2) a visual display (e.g., a poster board, slide show) of their topic highlighting the information they had learned about this topic, and (3) an oral presentation of their topic at the graduation ceremony. The paper assignment included writing a proposal, an initial thesis statement, a list of potential resources, at least twenty note cards, an outline, a rough draft, and a proofread final draft. The visual assignment also required a proposal and final product, and the oral presentation had to be a rehearsed and polished speech. At first this seemed like an overwhelming assignment for most of these twelve-year-olds; however, it soon became obvious that this process was to be a collective effort. Each student chose a two-person faculty committee made up of at least one of the three upper elementary teachers (Julie, Bart, and Barb) and one other teacher from the elementary, middle, or high school. The student and the committee members developed a time schedule of due dates for the different parts of the graduation assignment (proposal, outline, final draft), and the teachers worked closely with each student to help her or him with each task. Extra time was set aside during the day for graduates to work with their committee members. As the end of the semester approached, students spent time on the phone and at the homes of their committee members working on their graduation projects. In addition, an unexpected interpersonal dynamic occurred. At first, each student we talked to felt overwhelmed and secluded by this assignment. Some students procrastinated, and others complained about the amount of work. It seemed to be an isolating burden. However, this sense of isolation was soon transformed into strong bonds of camaraderie. As the weeks passed, students began to help each other complete various parts of their assignments. It soon became clear to the other students in the school that the "graduates," as they were called, were involved in something "big." From our perspective it seemed that we were observing, as Dan stated at the end of the year, a "rite-of-passage" ritual. Like other rituals involving sacrifice or hard work, it brought those individuals who participated in it a deep sense of bonding. Although each student created his or her own project, they went through "it" (as the graduate assignment was called) together. On graduation day, when their visual projects and term papers were put on display for the families, teachers, and students of Harmony to examine, and after their oral presentations, the "graduates" shared in a collective sense of accomplishment and "glory." (Summary of field notes)

Whether it was the graduation project or any number of other school assignments, more often than not there was a feeling among the students (even when they were working alone) that they were studying topics together, as a collective body, rather than as isolated individuals.

What is particularly noteworthy was that this sense of collective learning did not seem to undermine the value that Harmony placed on individual creativity. Perhaps Barb's observation at the spring Science Fair best expressed this dualistic set of values.

> The children were putting the final touches on their displays prior to opening the doors in the gym for the spring Science Fair. As we stood in the middle of numerous displays of children's inventions, science experiments, and mechanical contraptions, Barb said, "Look around you at all these projects. Can't you just feel the creative energy in this room? This fair might be the best representation of what Harmony is all about to me. When my children went to school at _____ [a local elementary school], probably less than half the students participated in the Science Fair, and the emphasis was totally on winning a ribbon for the 'best' project. Here I think every child but one or two has some kind of display. Preparation for this Science Fair has been a schoolwide celebration of individual creativity. Yet there has been none of the competition that is always at the heart of these kinds of activities in the public schools." (Summary of field notes)

This dichotomy was also observed during the previously discussed graduation project. At the same time that the students developed a deep sense of group pride in the result of their collective work, their presentations gave each of them an opportunity to have his or her moment in the "limelight"; each received applause for his or her unique ideas; and through the display of the projects each student's intellectual and creative abilities were recognized and valued.

Collective learning is an essential characteristic of a connectionist curriculum. Resisting and offering alternatives to the competitiveness in our schools and society is crucial for establishing critical democracy. Although it is essential that students' sense of uniqueness and creativity are preserved, engaging children in cooperative activities and, more important, providing them with a genuine sense of shared learning are a necessary foundation for the type of education envisioned.

EXPANSIVE KNOWLEDGE BASE

As discussed in the first chapter, one of the more ironic aspects of the individualism that dominates our society is that it often has created institutions that promote social conformity. While extolling the virtues of "individualized instruction," the conservative push within education has been to "canonize" a narrow body of knowledge against the wide expanse of knowledge available as legitimate. First, the "back-to-basics" movement created an atmosphere in which the elementary curriculum became dominated by "skills" content such as reading, writing, and math. As Goodlad (1984) notes in his extensive examination of schools in the United States, subject matter found within the humanities, social studies, and natural sciences, that is, subject matter with the opportunity to examine more substantive content, has been relegated to minor status, especially in the primary grades. The "basic skills" are taught as separate subjects and are seen as the "content" of school rather than as the means by which one explores content. In other words, children learn to read (answer fill-in-the-blank and multiple-choice questions on worksheets and tests, give short verbal responses to regurgitation-type questions, and read short passages when called upon), but they rarely read to learn (Goodlad, 1984). This "skills development" curriculum has in part been consecrated through the use of the previously mentioned instructional programs that have been adopted as *the source* of curriculum in nearly *every* school in our society. In addition, it has been further "sanctified" through the widespread adoption of state-mandated, standardized tests. As Darling-Hammond's (1985: 209) study suggests, the impact of this "canonization" of curriculum has been dramatic.

> We learned from teachers that . . . they spend less time on untested subjects, such as science and social studies; they use less writing in the classrooms in order to gear assignments to the format of standardized tests; they resort to lectures rather than classroom discussion in order to cover the prescribed behavioral objectives without getting "off the track;" they are precluded from using teaching materials that are not on prescribed textbook lists, even when they think these materials are essential to meet the needs of some of their students; and they feel constrained from following up on expressed student interests that lie outside of the bounds of mandated curricula.

A number of critics (Apple, 1979; Carlson, 1982; Shannon, 1987; Wise, 1979) have pointed out that this "skills development" criterion for determining what is seen as "proper school knowledge" has largely prevented our elementary schools from being places where young people learn to question, to critically observe and explore, and to develop a sense of curiosity about the world in which we live; nor does this curriculum give voice to students' experiences and ideas. To the contrary, this "officially sanctified" elementary curriculum has, in effect, reduced most of our schools to vocational training centers geared to meet only the most fundamental mechanical needs of an advanced industrial economy.

As Aronowitz and Giroux (1988) note, beginning with Reagan's second term, the push to "canonize" the curriculum in the schools took on a new dimension. In addition to viewing elementary (as well as secondary and postsecondary) schools as sites for industrial training, this new force pressed for schools to be locations for narrowly defined cultural production. This recent push has had the goal of establishing a national language and knowledge base in order to preserve the "essence" of Western civilization (Bennett, 1984; Bloom, 1987; Hirsch, 1987; Ravitch & Finn, 1988). These educators bemoan the "cultural relativism" that influenced the school curriculum starting in the late 1960s. In particular, they scorn the notion that popular culture or ethnic-, racial-, and gender-based knowledge should be placed on a par with the "Great Thinkers" of the European (and later Euro-American) heritage.[1]

Although these criticisms are somewhat accurate about the state of education (the anti-intellectualism among young people in our society, the lack of substance in the curriculum of many schools), the "cure" does not address the central problem. For example, Ravitch (1988: 39) is correct in pointing out that the social studies curriculum in the primary grades is void of substance and meaning: "Imagine the plight of the typical first grader: She has seen television programs about space flight, wars, terrorism, foreign countries, and national elections, but her social studies textbook is about neighborhood helpers and family roles." However, her solution is to merely replace this "tot sociology," as she calls it, with a curriculum based on stories of "[European] explorers, pioneer life, American heroes (especially Washington and Lincoln), and famous events in American history." By third grade she suggests that students should study the accomplishments of such people as "Joseph; Moses; David; Ulysses; Alexander; Horatius; Cincinnatus; Siegfried; Arthur; Roland; Alfred the Great; Richard the Lion Hearted; Robert Bruce; William Tell; Joan of Arc; Peter the Great; Florence Nightingale" (Ravitch, 1988: 38). Her solution is to replace one narrow curriculum with another.

It is not that knowledge rooted in Western civilization is unworthy of study in elementary schools; the problem is that this body of knowledge is seen as superior to other bodies of knowledge that could potentially be taught. The belief, as Bloom (1987) argues, that the Euro-American heritage (or any one culture) somehow contains "universal" value is a position that should be highly suspect in a society based on democratic principles. What is more disturbing is that, rather than critically examine Western civilization, this new push calls for the simple memorization of its most basic content. As Scholes (1988: 323) states in his synthesis of Bloom's (1987) and Hirsch's (1987) educational agenda,

> Together, they set the conservative agenda for American education. Hirsch will make sure that everyone knows what the classics are and respects them,

> while Bloom will see to it that an elite can be defined by actually knowing
> these classics. In this way, the masses will be sufficiently educated to respect
> the superior knowledge of their betters, who have studied in a few major
> universities.

With the exception of those students from the most powerful and privileged backgrounds who would one day attend our "most prestigious" universities, the goal is for students to superficially know the names, dates, and locations of "important" people, events, and cultural artifacts.

From a connectionist perspective and as Aronowitz and Giroux (1988) illuminate, these efforts to "canonize" the school curriculum are fundamentally antidemocratic. At Harmony there was a conscious desire not to officially sanction certain knowledge as "consecrated information." As Dan once said to a visitor who asked why Harmony didn't have an easily identifiable curriculum,

> Kids . . . should learn that there are an endless number of things to learn
> about and get involved with in this world. In stating what should be taught
> in a given class, you automatically restrict what a class could potentially
> study. The whole purpose of education is to broaden, not limit, what people
> can learn.

There were no "official" lists of objectives for the courses taught at Harmony. The classroom-based nature of the curriculum encouraged a wide diversity of topics to be taught during the morning Quiet Hour classes (magical animals, literary humor, literary "classics," human values as expressed through literature, pacifism, American slavery, endangered species, pioneer women, democratic government and the U.S. constitution, insect anatomy, chemical versus physical change). In addition to these morning classes, Harmony created the Research and Discovery class that met three afternoons (for 50 minutes) each week, in part to emphasize to students that their learning could go along an infinite number of paths. Each month students would conduct an independent study on their chosen topic. In the lower elementary program, students would primarily keep journals in which they recorded what they learned about their topic. This work in the upper elementary program would usually result in a written paper and some form of visual and/or oral presentation (speech, dramatic reading, role play). As one might speculate, since Harmony's elementary school contained over sixty children, a wide range of topics was represented in any given month. For example, in March some of the Research and Discovery topics included South Africa, Holland, Stevie Wonder, wasps, cheetahs, calendars, octopi, astrology, the Holocaust, American Indian clothing, motorcycles, photography, model rockets, planets, and seashells. As previously mentioned, these Research and Discovery classes prepared students for their graduation projects, which also reflected Harmony's belief in not restricting the knowledge that students and teachers wished to explore. Some of the graduation projects we read explored the Amish, caves, penguins, gymnastics, seals, and modern architecture.

Quiet Hour and Research and Discovery classes clearly reflected teachers' belief in an expansive curriculum, and organizationally this commitment was most forcefully exemplified by the establishment of Exploration classes, which met three afternoons for 45 minutes each session, and Creation classes, which were scheduled for Wednesday afternoons. As previously mentioned (see pages 124–125), every month each teacher would develop a unit of study for both Exploration and Creation classes. Students across grade levels would sign up for their preferences. (Dan would deal with the administrative problems of making sure that students got into at least one of the three choices they made for each class and that no one class was overcrowded.) Popular classes were often offered twice or occasionally three times during the school year. The emphasis in Exploration and Creation courses was on exposing students to an extensive range of topics in a relaxed, informal atmosphere. No homework or major reading or writing assignments were given, and students' work was not rigorously evaluated. Most assignments focused on student involvement in activities such as art and/or music projects, creative drama, community action projects, crafts, field trips, and experiments. For example, a course on "architecture" taught students how to create architectural drawings and make model buildings; a course on "rocketry" focused on students making their own model rockets; and in a course entitled "Underground" students visited several locations, such as a new building site (to study how buildings are supported underground), the city sewers, a stream that ran under the local shopping mall, the steam tunnels that connected the buildings at the local university, Harmony School's boiler room, an area where a telephone worker was laying underground cable, and a cave. As the following course descriptions (used to inform students of their options for a given month) suggest, the emphasis of these classes was on stimulating students' sense of joy in the exploration and creation of knowledge.

Blood and Guts	Come learn about your body and how it works. We'll do experiments and some dissection of animal parts. (Lower elementary)
Make Your Own Video	Write your own story, play, rap, or song, or find somebody else's. Add props, music, lighting, scenery. The sky's the limit. Be your own producer, director, and star. (Upper elementary, middle, and high school)

The Magic of Flight	Bring your kite, radio-controlled airplane, hot air balloon, or paper airplane, and we'll sail on the wind of March. Activities will include studying how birds and planes fly, flying your favorite creation, and a field trip to the airport. (All grades)
The Science of Advertising	We'll explore propaganda techniques used in advertising. Projects may entail product testing and development. (Upper elementary, middle, and high school)

Each month students had between ten and fourteen different "courses" which provided them with a vast assortment of topics from which to choose (Recycling, Endangered Species, Radio Plays, Slide Show Production, American Sign Language, Music Composition, Human Sexuality, Physics, Zoology, Ecology, Star Mapping, History of Science, Inventions of the Past and Future, Photography, Journalism, Bird Sanctuaries, Ceramics, French). To us as observers, these Exploration and Creation classes were exciting alternatives to what we and other researchers typically see in classrooms. By emphasizing a relaxed exposure to and engagement with knowledge, Harmony seemed to develop a thirst for inquiry in the children that spilled over into those classes with more rigorous academic expectations. In interviews with parents, we often heard comments similar to those reported by one mother:

> My kids have gotten a more comprehensive education at Harmony than they would have gotten in the public schools. For example, my daughter came home one day and told me I was a witch. She explained that there had been a guest speaker in her [Exploration] class that day who defined a witch as someone who is spiritually close to the land, protects the earth, and is devoted to learning about the earth's resources. As a result of this class, she decided to study herbal medicine for one of her Research and Discovery projects. (Summary of field notes)

In critical democracy, schools and teachers need to be encouraged to reach out to the broad expanse of knowledge that potentially will stimulate a child's desire to learn about the world in which she or he lives. The goal should be to connect young people in a fundamental way to the diverse fields of knowledge available to human beings. By "officially" legitimating a narrow band of knowledge as "school knowledge," educators cut off children from a meaningful understanding of themselves, other peoples, and the planet upon which we reside.

SOCIAL VALUES

The curriculum found in a given school can be seen, as stated in Foucault's (1979) terms, as a "discourse" or "regime of truth." What happens and what is taught in classrooms represents a story that is told to children. Since the storyteller cannot be separated from the story itself, the curriculum in schools always reflects points of contestation between storytellers with competing social, political, and psychological values. As previously discussed, in spite of their "public position" as value neutral, conventional schools teach children values consistent with a society dominated by an ideology of individualism. It is a society that on one level declares a commitment to equality and justice for all its citizens, and yet largely ignores the inequality promoted along economic, racial, ethnic, gender, sexual preference, nationalistic, and other lines. Although most upper elementary school children in the United States can tell a visitor that they live in a "democratic" and "free" society with "equal opportunity for all citizens," few are given opportunities to explore the meanings, the degree of accuracy, or the social values behind these words.

Education in schools and other settings is an innately value-laden enterprise. However, as mentioned in the first chapter, one should not consciously emphasize certain social values over others unless one has compelling reasons to do so. The impact that individualism has had (and continues to have) on our children and society provides educators who are interested in critical democracy with such a reason. In the last chapter, it was suggested that the development of children's responsibility to themselves, their peers, and those adults who care for them (parents, teachers, relatives) needs to be at the core of issues and practices related to the power dynamics within schools. Although this localized sense of social responsibility is crucial for critical democracy, young people also need clear instruction to help them visualize democratic values within a broader societal and global context. Given the above perspective and the fact that children in the United States live in perhaps the most industrialized and powerful nation in the modern world, a connectionist curriculum at this time in history would ideally sensitize students to issues such as classism, sexism, racism, ethnocentrism, environmental destruction, and other concerns facing people who hope to live democratically.

Encouraging children to embrace connectionist social values frequently was observed being spontaneously integrated into the curriculum at Harmony. The following two incidents are representative of numerous interactions that occurred on a weekly basis at Harmony.

> In today's Program Meeting, Jim, the faculty leader, showed a UNICEF
> filmstrip in preparation for students' (who had unanimously volunteered)

fund-raising activities. Jim was reading the text of the filmstrip and read the word *brotherhood* as *personhood*. Pam, a second grader, corrected his reading of this word. Jim thanked her and mentioned that while masculine words have historically been used to represent humanity in general, their use excludes women and is thus not very accurate in his opinion, which is why he changed the word *brotherhood* to *personhood*. He then asked these young children to share their opinions. (Summary of field notes)

Since today is "Presidents' Day" (February 15), like many teachers around the country, Julie diverged from her normal curriculum. She had received in the mail 5 x 7 pictures of each president, which she put on one of the walls in her classroom. However, instead of merely glorifying these men, as was being done in the vast majority of American classrooms on this day, she engaged her students in a discussion by initially asking them how many presidents on the wall were women, members of minority groups, or poor. The students also investigated on this day such questions as which presidents owned slaves, which ones were responsible for taking land away from American Indians, and which ones did the most (and least) to promote human and civil rights. (Summary of field notes)

Many of the social science and humanities topics examined during Quiet Hour, Research and Discovery, Creation, and Exploration classes directly addressed issues of race, gender, and social justice. During February (Black History Month) in Julie's Quiet Hour classes, Afro-American studies became the focus of the upper elementary curriculum, and in March (Women's History Month) this focus shifted to women's studies. For example, in the year we observed, the upper elementary classes studied "American slavery and its aftermath" (the failure of Reconstruction, the establishment of institutional racism, civil rights movements). In March, these classes shifted their attention to the "Western expansion of the United States" and focused on the lives of "women pioneers" (as well as the conflict between Euro-Americans and American Indians). Central to Barb's teaching of literature was an examination of the moral and ethical values reflected in an author's work. One of the units in the lower elementary language arts Quiet Hours during this year was on "pacifism and peace makers."

In both social science and humanities, there was a particularly strong emphasis on developing within students a "global awareness" to counter the ethnocentrism found in our broader society. As Julie once said,

We don't want our students to look at different types of people with suspicion and fear. We want them to appreciate the diversity of cultures on our planet. We want our students to understand that if we [human beings] are to survive, we have to learn how to live with respect for and in peace with all kinds of people.

In the year we observed, the school's theme for the annual Spring Festival was "International Day." During the month prior to this event, each Exploration class studied a different culture or related issue (Soviet Union, Pueblo Indians, Switzerland, Japan, West Africa, International Peace, Japanese Drama, Indian Cooking). Julie's Quiet Hour classes studied a unit entitled "Ancient Cultures" during this month, and Research and Discovery projects asked students to study, write reports, and make a presentation on a culture of their choice. During this same time period, Barb arranged for campuswide presentations (choir singing, slide shows, games, dancing, candy making, lectures, jewelry making) by adults and children from Malaysia, Mexico, Nigeria, Japan, Brazil, China, Egypt, Turkey, Israel, Saudi Arabia, and South Africa. As Barb said to a local reporter, "I (and the other faculty) really think a part of the education system here should be international understanding."

Perhaps the most significant aspect of these cultural studies was the effort made to help students understand the values and perspectives of people from other ethnic and cultural backgrounds as a way of helping children "work through" preconceived societal views. For example, when Jo announced that she was going to study the Soviet Union in her Exploration class, some students responded with boos and hisses. (There had been a recent incident between the Soviet Union and the United States, and Reagan was once again calling that country an "evil empire.") Jo responded by saying, "This is exactly why I wanted to study this country. How are we ever going to learn to live in peace unless we try to understand how these people live and in what they believe?" In one class session, Dan role-played being the Soviet ambassador to the United States and the children (mostly lower elementary) played reporters at a news conference. Dan did his best to respond to these children, not as an "American," but as a person committed to Soviet values and life-style.

> One boy asked, "If the Soviet Union is such a good place to live, why do the people have to stand in lines to get food and clothes?" Dan responded (in his best imitation of a Russian accent) by saying, "This is a very important question. To you these lines mean that our system does not work. However, to us these lines represent our commitment to social justice. You see, we are a poor country. We do not have the vast resources that a country like yours has. For example, we are capable of producing only a certain amount of beef for our citizens. If we allowed it to be sold at the highest price as is done in your country, there would be no lines of people standing to get some because only a few people could ever afford to buy it. In our country we control how much beef can be sold for so that everyone can afford to have some. However, since there is only so much, we must ration how much each person can buy and limit the number

of stores that sell it. This causes long lines for those popular products such as beef, but it reflects our view that it's better for all people to have some meat than for a few people to have as much meat as they want while the majority of people get none." (Summary of field notes)

In several of the classes, students were asked to write or speak as if they were a member of another cultural or ethnic group. Take, for instance, the following Quiet Hour lesson:

> Julie read several excerpts from chapters in *Touch the Earth* [McLuhan, 1971] that explored American Indian reaction to the "Western expansion" of the United States. For example, she read the following quote from Chief Luther Standing Bear: "We did not think of the great open plains, the beautiful rolling hills, and winding streams with tangled growth, as 'wild.' Only to the white man was nature a 'wilderness' and only to him was the land 'infested' with 'wild' animals and 'savage' people. To us it was tame. The earth was bountiful, and we were surrounded with the blessings of the Great Mystery. Not until the hairy man from the east came and with brutal frenzy heaped injustices upon us and the families we loved was it 'wild' for us. When the very animals of the forest began fleeing from his approach, then it was for us that the 'Wild West' began." After listening to several of these quotes, the students discussed their impressions of what American Indians must have experienced during this time in our country's history, and Julie talked about the living conditions on some of the reservations she had visited. After this discussion, she asked the students to assume the identity of an American Indian during the latter part of the 1800s and write one or two quotations like those found in *Touch the Earth*. Afterwards, she edited these quotations into a book for each student. (Summary of field notes)

When asked about these types of assignments, several of the teachers mentioned that they felt they helped the students at Harmony "get beyond themselves" and increase their understanding, compassion, and empathy for other people (especially those that have been historically oppressed and marginalized) and for other species. (Several of these assignments asked students to "speak for" endangered plants and animals.)

In addition to being embedded into the overt curriculum, connectionist social values were promoted through a variety of visual symbols at Harmony. During much of the school year, a hand-drawn poster of two children riding on a dove carrying a flower in its mouth, with the words *peace, friendship,* and *harmony* written in a circle around it in both English and Russian, was displayed on the door of the central office. Likewise, the T-shirt logo for Harmony's Spring Festival was a picture of the earth with arms and hands shaking across it, and had the same words, *peace* and *harmony*, in both English and Russian. On several of the students' lockers were stickers of the United States and Soviet Union flags crossed with *peace on earth* written underneath them. Harmony's old van and a number of faculty cars had bumper stickers on their fenders such as "Question Authority," "Think Globally, Act Locally," "Split Wood, Not Atoms," "Love Your Mother (earth)," and "El Salvador is Vietnam in Spanish." At any given time during the year we observed, there were posters on the school bulletin board in support of the Nicaraguan revolution, Tibetan liberation, defense funds for midwives, or pubic forums on freedom of speech. During this same year, the school custodian was convicted of civil disobedience related to the Iran-Contra scandal for publicly stealing a "John Poindexter" street sign in Odon, Indiana, that had been put up to glorify Poindexter's actions.

Our suggestion that elementary schools openly teach children connectionist values (moral compassion, social responsibility, globalism, antiracism, antisexism) is based on the assumption that curricula can never be value neutral. Efforts to present a position of neutrality only obscure and mystify the values that do indeed exist in conventional schools, and thus make it difficult for the public to debate what is being taught to our children. Certain social, political, and economic interests will always be served at the expense of other interests through the curricular content and activities found in a given school or classroom. For example, although Harmony's curriculum devoted considerable attention to concerns of race, gender, internationalism, and ecology, it did relatively little (although still far more than in most traditional schools) with issues of class and labor (an occasional unit or individual report on labor leaders, the union movement, or unemployment), perhaps because most of the faculty at Harmony came from upper-middle-class backgrounds and took their former class privileges for granted.

Given the recent rise in conservative ideology in our country, in which the interests of women, minorities, labor, the poor, children, and peoples of nonindustrialized nations have been marginalized, it is particularly important that direct curricular efforts be made to balance the prevailing values and attitudes found in the larger societal context. However, as will be discussed in more detail in a later section of this chapter, it also is important that, when directly teaching children certain social values over others, one does not let these curricular practices degenerate into indoctrination.

SOCIAL ACTION AND COMMUNITY SERVICE PROJECTS

Although it is good to encourage children to adopt community values and develop greater sensitivity to and compassion for the needs of other people and the ecological balance of our planet, if kept on an intellectual level, these values and sensitivities rarely become genuinely meaningful. Schooling for critical democracy suggests that young people will be given opportunities to experience how their actions can potentially impact upon the local, national, and international community in which they live. In spite of President Bush's calls for a new feeling of "volunteerism," there are few efforts made in traditional schools to help children see or experience a meaningful connection between their education and the development of a more compassionate world. As Giroux and McLaren (1986: 237) state,

> It is an unfortunate truism that when communities are ignored by teachers, students often find themselves trapped in institutions that . . . deprive them of a relational or contextual understanding of how the knowledge they acquire in the classroom can be used to influence and transform the public sphere. Implicit in the concept of linking classroom experiences to the wider community is the idea that . . . students and teachers can engage in a process of deliberation and discussion aimed at advancing the public welfare in accordance with fundamental moral judgments and principles.

At Harmony, there was a strong tradition of getting children involved in community activities as a way to heighten their sensitivity to the world around them and motivate them to act upon their developing sense of social responsibility. The students often made weekly field trips into the community as part of their ongoing studies. A number of Exploration and Creation courses specifically focused on the local community, as the following course descriptions illustrate:

Bloomington Works!	Ever wonder what happens inside a hospital? Ever wonder how people can drink water from Lake Monroe? Ever wonder where poop goes after you flush the toilet? Come and find out! We'll be traveling all over town to find the answers. (Elementary)
Old Friends	Visit the Fontanbleu Nursing Center. We'll take turns bowling, decorating, visiting, and sharing. We'll learn about what life was like long ago and the difficulties of elderly people today. (All grades)
Recycling	Let's start a recycling program at school. We'll meet as a committee and discuss how to start. We'll visit recycling centers and discuss options for our homes and the city of Bloomington. (Elementary and middle schools)

Guest speakers from the community were also a frequent resource for learning within the building. Course assignments at Harmony often included activities such as writing the federal government questioning its policy on endangered animals and passing out petitions to preserve American Indian burial sites in Indiana. During Program and Family meetings, students discussed whether they should avoid using plastic bags (since plastic is not biodegradable) to carry their lunch food, signed (on a volunteer basis) a banner to be used at an anti-nuclear testing demonstration, and set up a pen pal correspondence program with children from South Africa. Sixth graders had to perform at least ten hours of community service as one of their graduation requirements in order to, as Dan stated to the students on several occasions, "give something back to the community for their support for our school."

In addition, students at Harmony participated in several direct social action projects for various causes. Take, for instance, the following:

> Today some students from the middle school came into the elementary Family Meeting and asked if anyone wanted to participate in the "Rhino Campaign." It seems that there had been this sculpture of a rhinoceros in front of a local art gallery for the last twelve years. Children loved to play on it, but the artist had recently announced that he was removing it because one of his other sculptures had been destroyed by vandals. Harmony's students decided to "prove that young people can treat art responsibly" and organized a campaign to "keep the Rhino in Bloomington." The students negotiated with the artist to buy the sculpture for $6,000. After several months and numerous fund-raising events organized by Harmony's students, the artist sold his sculpture to them for $5,200. In placing the sculpture on the school grounds, the students made a conscious decision to face it towards the neighborhood as a symbol that "the Rhino belongs to the community" rather than just the school. (Summary of field notes)[2]

One parent shared the following story as an example of the unique types of community activities found at Harmony.

> Several years ago, the elementary school was in Washington, D.C., on a field trip, and there was a protest march against nuclear weapons and power. Over 200,000 people were there, and through a fluke, Harmony students got to lead the entire march.

Harmony's students had numerous opportunities to use their knowledge of the world and their artistic, communicative, and organizational talents to, as one fourth-grade girl said, "make the world a better place to live."

Although these projects were significant, there was a need to integrate more dialogue into these activities. Although on several occasions teachers mentioned that it was important for the students to feel a sense of responsibility to people outside of their family and school, there was a conspicuous absence of substantive discourse related to several of these social action projects. As a result, a number of students only superficially participated in them. For example, several students mentioned taking part in the "Rhino Campaign" only because it gave them opportunities to "hang out" with their friends. These students seemed unaware of the broader purposes involved. Five out of the twelve sixth graders looked at the "community service" graduation requirement as simply "job training" rather than as part of a reciprocal relationship between themselves and the community in which they lived. Without substantive discourse, students can too easily miss the significance of working to "make the world a better place."

This need for dialogue, however, did not go unnoticed by Dan and other staff members. The following spring, the faculty decided to organize the first annual Social Action Day at the school. As part of this schoolwide project, students volunteered to find a sponsor and go on a one-day fast for "progressive schools." (The money raised was donated to the National Coalition of Alternative Schools.) On the day in question, the school sponsored a symposium and workshops on "nonviolent civil disobedience" that included representatives from various environmental, peace, civil rights, and feminist organizations. However, although these types of forums are valuable, they cannot substitute for dialogue that is blended into specific projects. Integrating substantive dialogue into social action projects provides powerful opportunities for children to examine abstract notions such as 'social justice,' 'freedom,' and 'liberation' within a specific historical and social context, and thus make them meaningful.

VOICE

One of the most important characteristics of democratic living is the feeling that one is free to express himself or herself. Giving "voice" to individuals is essential to critical democracy. Perhaps it is for this reason that many scholars interested in democratic schooling have illustrated the way in which the "voice" of women, Afro-Americans, labor, children, and other marginalized groups of people has been systematically silenced in our society (Giroux, 1986; Lewis & Simon, 1986; Smith, 1978). As Giroux and McLaren (1986: 235) state, "Voice . . . refers to the means at our disposal —the discourses available to us—to make ourselves understood and listened to, and to define ourselves as active participants in the world." Although the notion that education should provide for a diverse expression of ideas is widely accepted in our society, in fact, conventional schools are largely locations of silence where only a few voices (predominantly through textbooks that express the interests of white, middle- and upper-class men) can be heard.

Perhaps the first observation at Harmony that attracted our attention was the freedom that students and teachers felt to express themselves. There was no dress code to follow or censorship of students' or teachers' ideas. One statement that was repeated by almost every student and teacher in the school was "At Harmony, I can be myself." If a student did not want to participate in activities with overt political implications, there was verbal support for his or her decision, and active efforts were made to find him or her alternative activities.

As previously illustrated, students' "personal knowledge" was often actively integrated into class sessions. Individual children who seemed shy and withdrawn might be asked to share their opinions during class discussions, and if necessary these individuals would be counseled in an effort to help them feel more confident and comfortable in expressing themselves. For example, one day after an impromptu class debate, Dan said,

> Did you notice Patti speaking during the discussion? A year ago she would never have talked in class. Each year there are a number of girls and a few boys who are terrified to speak in public. I'm not sure why that is; sometimes it's because of the family dynamics. It takes some of these kids a long time and individual counseling to give them the self-confidence necessary to express themselves. When I see someone like Patti come out of her shell, it makes me feel that we are doing something really worthwhile.

We took special note of the tremendous quantity of verbal interaction that occurred at Harmony. Although there were many times when students would be hard at work and little noise could be heard, in general Harmony was not a quiet place. The children at this school were given daily opportunities to "tell their story." As one parent who had children in both Harmony and the public schools told us,

> I've gone on lots of school trips, and the one thing that I've noticed about Harmony kids is how much more verbal they are. They're not afraid to ask questions and tell you what they think. On the last trip, the museum guide told me that Harmony students asked more questions and were more willing to talk than any other group of students he had ever seen. However, what's interesting is that I've heard the same thing a number of times.

When teachers would engage students in class discourse, they were never observed expressing disapproval of students who disagreed with their views. To the contrary, it often seemed that students who disagreed with a prevailing sentiment within a given discussion received special attention, and protection if needed, by the teacher. Take, for instance, an exchange that occurred in an Exploration class on recycling:

> Julie asked the students why they thought it was important to conserve and recycle resources. After several students provided reasons, Tommy strongly disagreed that "we" (students) can really make a difference. "Look at the pollution around us," he challenged the class. "You're telling me that if I (as an individual) don't use plastic or recycle cans, it's really going to make a difference. Get real." At this point, several students began to

argue with Tommy all at the same time, and Julie had to interrupt them by saying that Tommy was entitled to his views. The class then continued their discussion with more decorum. Tommy was given numerous opportunities to speak since he was the only student who expressed this point of view against several other students and the teacher. (Summary of field notes)

While creating an atmosphere that was respectful of students' and teachers' voices at Harmony was evident, what was not given enough notice was students' lack of attention to what was being said. We often observed teachers ignoring students during meetings and class sessions who were not listening to their fellow students' ideas. Occasionally, these inattentive students would disrupt the dialogue in progress and not be confronted about their interruption. At times, teachers' ignoring of students' inattention was rationalized by a libertarian philosophy. As one teacher said, "As long as they don't disrupt others from working, I don't think we [teachers] should *force* them to pay attention to everything that is going on. Kids have to realize for themselves why learning is important, and this won't happen if we impose it on them." However, it is our view that freedom of expression must be a two-way street. Critical democracy needs individuals who are able and willing to honestly express what they believe, but it also needs people who listen carefully and critically to what others say.

Viewing schools as locations where teachers' and students' voices can be heard is easy to support. However, given the inevitable constraints of time, space, and energy, allowing for a wide diversity of voices is more problematic. In the previous two sections of this chapter, it has been argued that connectionist values take precedence over other social values given the individualism that dominates our society. Although teachers who see education as a means of promoting critical democracy in our society need to have a clear commitment to these connectionist values, it is important that they not be imposed upon students. As Dewey (1946) notes, imposing ideological changes on people might alter societal structures; however, in the process it distorts human intelligence and thus undermines the process of establishing genuine forms of democracy. If critical democracy is to be fostered, then any change of consciousness among children must not be obtained by silencing other voices that come from different perspectives. In advocating that elementary curricula be designed to promote critical democracy, it is, as mentioned in the previous chapter, important to avoid establishing curricular content and practices that result in social conformist rather than community values. For example, Kessen (1975), Peshkin (1986), and Rose (1988) provide several illustrations of schools with a "community" emphasis where children memorize "correct" answers to moral questions and issues. To be genuinely effective and democratic, one must try to influence children's values in the direction of a connectionist orientation in an atmosphere in which children can freely examine a diversity of convictions without fear of intimidation. The question of whose "voices" should be heard was an ongoing dilemma for the staff at Harmony. Take, for instance, the faculty discussion related to the "Nonviolent Civil Disobedience" symposium:

> In discussing which national and local organizations should be contacted to see if they would be willing to participate in the symposium or workshops, Dan and Steve suggested that a "pro-life" organization be invited (although a feminist organization had already been agreed upon, it was not specifically a "pro-choice" group). Alison strongly objected to this suggestion. Dan thought that since the symposium was dealing with nonviolent strategies for social change, a group's particular ideological orientation should not be considered when decisions were made about who should be represented in the symposium. Alison, however, pointed out that the symposium was supposed to address nonviolent strategies for *progressive* [her emphasis] social change, and that "anti-abortion" groups did not meet that criterion. In addition, she objected to a recent, widely distributed pro-life movie, "Silent Scream," which reflected pro-life groups' willingness to be dishonest in their efforts to sway public opinion. Alison argued that this type of overt dishonesty could not be considered a form of nonviolence. After a few other teachers spoke, it was clear that Alison's position was widely supported by the staff, and Dan withdrew his suggestion. (Summary of field notes)

Although this particular voice was not given an opportunity to be heard in the above situation, in general Harmony's faculty was particularly sensitive to providing a "fair hearing" of opposing viewpoints. Often guest speakers were invited to classrooms or schoolwide functions to present differing points of view on a given issue. Dan once told us, "Since many of our parents, and therefore their children, have liberal beliefs, I and other teachers often find ourselves arguing from a conservative perspective to ensure it gets a fair hearing." As Kelly (1986) illustrates, this practice of "fair hearing" is necessary when teachers make a commitment to an openly ideological curriculum. The dilemma of making Harmony a place where different voices could be freely heard while at the same time promoting connectionist social values was clearly reflected in Steve's comment, "I wish our students left here with a greater political commitment. I don't mean we should *indoctrinate* them, but I would like it if they left here a little more committed to being politically active."

This freedom to express and hear a diversity of voices is particularly important when children are involved in the types of overtly value-laden curricula and social action projects found in Harmony. Although the purpose of Harmony's curriculum was to help children become more compassionate, sensitive, and active, there is an important difference between teaching from a connectionist perspective and engaging in social activism (Liston & Zeichner, 1987). Although the two roles of democratic teacher and social activist have many things in common (the distribution of knowledge, the challenging of taken-for-granted societal values, the promotion of alternative visions of people and society), there is a crucial distinction. The former is primarily concerned with the emotional and intellectual integrity of his or her students, whereas the latter is primarily concerned with a particular social or political agenda. Recognizing that the curriculum will always promote political interests of some sort does not give teachers license to turn schools into institutions of ideological activism. Taking the responsibility to involve young people in the types of curricula and social action projects found at Harmony requires careful introspection on the part of elementary teachers to constantly check against potential abuses of the power inherent in the role of educating young and highly impressionable children.

REFLECTIONS: CRITICAL THINKING, FEMINIST PEDAGOGY, AND DEMOCRACY

Although an examination of elementary curriculum for critical democracy raises several ideas worthy of discussion, given the limitations of space, only two can be discussed here. In this chapter, it has been suggested that curricular issues and practices within elementary schools are perhaps the most important of all aspects related to the education of children for critical democracy. Yet when one examines the literature on democracy and elementary education, one finds that most of it is limited to discourse on "interpersonal relationships." When curricular practices and issues are mentioned, they often amount to little more than calls for more "critical thinking" among students.

To many individuals, critical thinking is the archetypal goal of schooling in a democracy. Currently there is a plethora of documents and curriculum packages and guidelines designed to foster "critical thinking" within schools. However, as McLaren (1988) points out, "critical thinking" as discussed in the vast majority of this literature has been stripped of its historical, political, cultural, or social context. As such, it simply has come to mean "the development of cognitive skills in order to solve increasingly complex intellectual problems" (McLaren, 1988: 3). A few recent examples include Flynn's (1989) description of an instructional model that teaches students how to "analyze, synthesize, and evaluate ideas"; McFarland's (1985) presentation of two instructional strategies to teach students how to define a "point of view" and to distinguish "relevant from irrelevant" information; and Norris's (1989: 26) argument for using "improved" multiple-choice, critical thinking exams that evaluate students' abilities to identify "knowledge of criteria for judging credibility . . . to apply the criteria in context, and . . . to weigh and balance conflicts among the criteria when they point in different directions."

At Harmony, the notion of critical thinking took on a more complex and substantive meaning. First, cognitive abilities were never taught out of context, as separate content. Research skills (library referencing, note taking, rough draft writing) were always integrated into the study of some broader subject. These skills were strictly seen as a *means* to learning rather than the end product of learning. Similarly, cognitive talents (generating and synthesizing ideas, developing reasons and finding support for one's views) were naturally integrated into class discussions and assignments. In other words, Harmony resisted the dominant trend in education (and the technocratic rationality from which it emerges) to reduce all educative experiences to learning isolated skills. More important, at Harmony the notion of critical thinking could not be separated from the social and moral consequences of one's contemplations. At Harmony, the notion of critical thinking implied establishing links between one's individual actions and thoughts and the social, historical, and cultural contexts within which one lives: that is, critical thinking implied, not only reading the word, but reading the world (Freire & Macedo, 1987).

By failing to place "critical thinking" within an overtly democratic context, conservative and libertarian educators have been able to neutralize the potential effectiveness of this notion for generating substantive reforms in our schools. As a result, the numerous critical thinking strategies being offered today actually inhibit the development of schooling for critical democracy by turning our attention in the wrong direction. We do not need young people who are simply capable of developing their powers of rationality so that they can obtain the greatest power possible when they enter our market economy. What is needed are young people who have learned to use their minds critically in order to recognize those powers that inhibit and those that work towards the creation of a more compassionate, caring, and socially just world, as well as the moral courage to participate with those in the latter group. The curriculum found at Harmony would suggest that calls for more "critical thinking" in our schools should not be automatically viewed as synonymous with democratic education.

The curriculum found at Harmony provides insight into popular educational practices such as "critical thinking," and it also invites some discussion of feminist pedagogy. As mentioned in the first chapter, our society promotes a rationality that boys more than girls are socialized to embrace. As several scholars (Belenky et al., 1986; Gilligan, 1982; Harding & Hintikka, 1983; Janssen-Jurreit, 1980; Keller, 1985) have noted, this masculine ethos promotes several intellectual and epistemological values, such as objectivity, order and control, technical and mechanical reasoning (memorization), competition, utility, sequential logic, efficiency, knowledge as absolute (right and wrong answers), the categorization of knowledge and time, and quantitative evaluation. As a result of patriarchy, the legitimation of this masculine ethos has implied a repudiation of a more feminine rationality that values intuition, subjectivity, collectivity, emotions, nurturance, personal interaction, and empathy. Numerous educators (Acker, 1989; Apple, 1986; Goodman, 1988a; Grumet, 1981; Strober & Tyack, 1980) have illustrated the way in which teaching has gone through a process of "feminization" (transition from a male to a female occupation) in the United States, and how, as a result, the power to decide what happens in schools and classrooms has shifted from teachers to those who occupy positions as school board members, administrators, textbook authors, curriculum developers and evaluators, and educational researchers. Since the vast majority of these latter positions are occupied by men, it is not surprising or difficult to see the influence of this masculine ethos at work in our elementary schools.

Grumet (1981) suggests that even though most teachers (especially at the elementary level) are women, they have had to suppress their own natural inclinations about what and how to educate children and have thus become "pedagogues for patriarchy."

> Women, . . . as teachers, have contributed our labor and our children to institutional and social organizations that have extended their own subordination and contradicted the essential character of their own experiences of nurturance. It has been widely argued that schooling supports the dominance of men in society first by exaggerating those characteristics that distinguish male from female gender and then by gradually establishing success norms that favor males, linking their achievements and world view to ideologies that dominate both the economy and the state. (Grumet, 1981: 174-175)

In her analysis of the relationship between schools and families, Lightfoot (1978: 70) notes that both mothers and teachers "are required to raise [teach] children in the service of a dominant group whose values and goals they do not determine [and] to socialize their children to conform to a society that belongs to men."

The implication of these authors' work is that, if left to their own devices, most teachers (male teachers would not be automatically excluded from this group since men who choose to teach at the elementary level often share many feminine values) would create curricular practices and ideas much different from those currently found in conventional schools. As awareness has grown of the ways in which this masculine rationality has influenced the education of our children, several educators have forged an alternative, feminist pedagogy (Bunch & Pollack, 1983; Clinchy, Belenky, Goldberger, & Tarule, 1985; Goodman, 1987b; Lather, 1984). For example, Clinchy and her colleagues (1985) refer to this pedagogy as "connected education" in which the students are affirmed as capable "learners," students' personalized knowledge is legitimated in the context of what is being studied, educational goals and expectations are collaboratively developed by teachers and students, and teachers express faith in their students' talents and abilities.

> Connected teaching is personal. Connected teachers present themselves as genuine, flawed human beings. They allow students to observe the imperfect processes of their thinking. Connected teachers take a personal interest in their students. They want to know how each individual student is thinking. But connected teaching is not "soft." It is rigorous. And it is objective, although not coldly impersonal. . . . They trust their students' thinking and encourage them to expand it. (Clinchy et al., 1985: 42, 44)

Although their assessment of feminist pedagogy is based on studies of postsecondary education, in examining the curriculum at Harmony, we were struck by the similarities. At Harmony the teachers had the power to determine the curriculum, and they created one whose characteristics (collaborative learning, expansive knowledge base, connectionist values, social action, voice) reflected those values associated with a feminine ethos. Since prospective teachers' values are carefully screened prior to employment at Harmony (see Chapter 3), one can only speculate what might happen on a broader scale if elementary teachers were sanctioned to create the curriculum found in our schools.

As previously mentioned, what is taught to children through both the content and practices associated with the curriculum represents the heart and soul of schooling. The truth of the above statement is clear once put into a larger societal context. As Kliebard (1986: 1) stated, "I have always regarded the curriculum of any society or any period as a significant cultural artifact since what a society consciously and deliberately tries to teach its young is a major indication of what a society values." The curricular issues and practices that emerged from Harmony's elementary school can serve as a catalyst for rethinking curriculum reform in terms of democracy and its relationship to individuality and community. However, developing curricular practices for critical democracy requires more than just a conceptual framework. As will be more fully discussed in the next and final chapter of this book, it is equally important to see how intentions can be manifested in given situations. The portrait of a connectionist curriculum for elementary school presented in this chapter provides a modest, but necessary and long overdue, beginning.

6

Creating an Elementary Pedagogy for
Critical Democracy:
Conclusions and Suggestions

This book has called for viewing elementary education as a vehicle for promoting critical democracy in our society. In doing so, it has argued that educators need to conceptualize this goal within the dialectical tension that exists between the social values of individuality and community. It has been suggested that educational initiatives for critical democracy in the United States must focus on cultivating a connectionist perspective within children (and the adults who work with them) to counterbalance the individualism that dominates our cultural and political institutions. The organizational structure and policies, interpersonal dynamics, instructional practices, and curriculum content of elementary schooling must help move children towards values of social bonding, caring, responsibility, and justice as well as help them embrace antisexist, antiracist, and proglobal environmental attitudes. At the same time, educators must avoid those practices which undermine students' moral and intellectual autonomy. As stated in the first chapter, the traditional approach to radical school reform with its emphasis on "individual liberty" does not offer the vision needed for a compassionate, just, and democratic society to be built or sustained.

This project has represented two different but intricately related searches. As mentioned in the second chapter, one search concentrated on finding an elementary school with an explicitly democratic ethos as a guide for its activities. Once a school was located, this part of the search was extended into the corridors and classrooms of a particular building to investigate the way in which this ethos was interpreted and manifested in the educational lives of its students, administrators, and teachers. By spending an extended period of time observing people who were struggling to create a democratic elementary education, we hoped that we could gain insights useful to us and other educators with similar interests. The second search represented our attempt to find a way to articulate our experiences and newly discovered understandings of the relationship between elementary education and democracy. In particular, this search focused on ways to explicate a

163

meaningful association between the macro and micro "worlds" of educating young children in our society.

As a result of these searches, this book reflects our endeavor to envision and discuss one way in which elementary schooling can be created to promote critical democracy. In this final chapter, we offer a number of concluding suggestions to further enhance the establishment of an elementary pedagogy for critical democracy and to thus contribute to the discourse now going on in our universities, schools, and society. In particular, it is being suggested that a new language and set of political strategies must be fashioned in order to advance our education and society towards critical democracy.

TOWARDS AN EDUCATIONAL LANGUAGE OF DEMOCRATIC IMAGERY

Language has great power. To some degree, it can simultaneously reflect, illuminate, mystify, and create social reality. Through language, people's thinking can be galvanized in new directions or reestablished in accordance with previously held beliefs. As Pinar (1988) recently noted, during the last twenty years, critical discourse on education has proliferated within academic circles; however, it has received practically no attention in elementary schools or society at large. During the last decade, conservatives have set the agenda and tone for public debate regarding education in our society. Certainly, the primary reason for the impotence of critical educational discourse in schools and society is that it has to a large extent challenged those who dominate the cultural, political, and economic sectors of our society to relinquish much of their privilege and power. Obviously, reform proposals and reports such as *A Nation at Risk* that sustain the dominant interests in our society will be more widely discussed by the public than reports that substantively challenge these interests. However, this lack of attention does not mean that critical educators are powerless or totally blameless for the apparent absence of critical voices beyond the symbolic walls of academia. As Giroux and McLaren (1989: xiii) note,

> The success of the conservative educational agenda also points to a fundamental failure among progressive and radical educators to generate a public discourse on schooling. . . . One major problem facing the recent outpouring of critical discourse on schooling is that over the years it has become largely academicized. . . . In effect, critical and radical writings on schooling have become ghettoized within the ivory tower, reflecting a failure to take seriously the fact that education as a terrain of struggle is central to the reconstruction of public life and, as such, must be understood in vernacular as well as scholarly terms.

To understand what we must do to reverse our lack of influence, we must examine our recent linguistic history.

Starting in the early seventies, a few educators began to seriously question the role of schooling in a democratic society. This work quickly grew into what has come to be called a "language of critique" within education. Apple (1979) articulates its purpose.

> First, it aims at illuminating the tendencies for unwarranted and often unconscious domination, alienation, and repression within certain existing cultural, political, educational, and economic institutions. Second, through exploring the negative effects and contradictions of much that unquestionably goes on in these institutions, it seeks to "promote conscious (individual and collective) emancipatory activity." That is, it examines what is supposed to be happening in say, schools if one takes the language and slogans of many school people seriously; and it then shows how these things actually work in a manner that is destructive of ethical rationality and personal political and institutional power. (Quoted in Mazza, 1982)

Given this goal, this language of critique has provided educators with numerous insights. For example, it has uncovered the myth that schools in our society serve as the "great equalizer" which allows children from all social and economic backgrounds to compete fairly in our marketplace economy. The early work of Bowles and Gintis (1976) and, later, the work of Oakes (1985) illustrate the way in which schools actually limit the cultural, social, and economic mobility of our children, thus reproducing the existing inequalities found in our broader society. These works have also exposed the way in which conventional schools in our society transmit a "hidden curriculum" that undermines most of our children's sense of self-esteem, efficacy, and compassion and that profoundly narrows whose "voices" (men versus women, whites versus people of color, industrialists versus laborers, militarists versus peace activists) and what epistemological and social values are expressed in classrooms. In addition, this language of critique has carefully examined the theoretical frameworks that have been used as heuristic devices to understand schooling and society. For example, there has been active and at times acrimonious debate concerning the value of correspondence, phenomenological, neo-Marxist, feminist, and poststructuralist theories, to name a few, and their usefulness to the scholarly discourse in education.

Although this language of critique has provided educators with a significant departure from the mechanistic and administrative language that has dominated traditional educational discourse in our society, it has a couple of major weaknesses. As previously mentioned, one problem is centered on the linguistic complexity that runs rampant through this scholarship. There is more to this question of linguistic complexity than simply the propensity to create sociological jargon. As the early critical theorists in the Frankfurt School point out, unique linguistic structures and terminology are at times required to move us beyond the everyday langauge that binds us to everyday conceptions of social reality and action. Terms such as *hegemony, repro-duction,* and *cultural capital* have been extremely useful in conceptualizing the relationship between schools and the broader society within which children are educated.

It is reasonable to assume that it may take two or in rare cases even three readings of some sociological analyses to fully grasp the entire meaning of a given author, especially if she or he is addressing subtle and complex phenomena. It is not being suggested that educational scholars must always express themselves in everyday language. However, when the linguistic structure and terminology of this scholarship prevent the vast majority of like-minded scholars (let alone classroom teachers) from having little more than the slightest notion of what is being said after several readings, then it becomes at best a form of self-indulgent expression in which the author simply writes for his or her individualistic pleasure and professional aggrandizement (even though its stated purpose is the "emancipation" of teachers and their students) and at worst a form of psychic oppression. Take, for instance, the following paragraph written by Wexler and his colleagues (1987: 242) in which they call for a new educational movement that questions the dualistic thinking found in traditional rationality and that legitimates contradiction, ambiguity, and paradox as central features of this new education:

> The free play of the signifier in the polysomic movement of language shatters the linguistic conventions of a hierarchical, paternal order. A careful but fearless approach to polysomy points towards that ambiguity which the intransitive sign suppresses. Paradox that plays with expressive excess and contradictory conversation are themselves signs of a new educational practice. Paradox and contradiction are the forms of a pedagogic relation that encourage multiple interpretation. Collective identity formation through writing, the communicative production of ambiguity and the pluralizing effect of contradiction animate education as a social relation.

Even if one accepts the value of what is being said, it is hard to imagine many elementary, secondary, or university instructors (even those with radical sympathies) feeling a sense of enlightenment from the above passage or others like it. Rather, they are usually faced with the dilemma of either discounting its relevance to their own work or concluding that they must not be intelligent enough to decipher its meaning. In either case, the exper-ience is less than emancipatory. Christian (1987: 55, 56) cogently examines this problem in her analysis of literary criticism and its relationship to Afro-American literature and is worth quoting at length.

> I feel that the new emphasis on literary critical theory is as hegemonic as the world which it attacks. I see the language it creates as one which mystifies rather than clarifies our condition, making it possible for a few people who know that particular language to control the critical scene. . . . As a student of literature, I am appalled by the sheer ugliness of the language, its lack of clarity, its unnecessarily complicated sentence constructions, its lack of pleasurableness, its alienating quality. It is the kind of writing for which composition teachers would give a freshman a resounding F. . . . In their attempt to change the orientation of Western scholarship, they, as usual, concentrated on themselves and were not in the slightest interested in the worlds they had ignored or controlled. Again I was supposed to know *them*, while they were not at all interested in knowing *me*. Instead they sought to "deconstruct" the tradition to which they belonged even as they used the same forms, style, language of that tradition, forms which necessarily embody its values.

Whether it is found in sociological, literary, or educational discourse, the intellectual elitism that is embedded in much of this language of critique significantly undermines its own liberatory intentions.

Secondly, the language of critique unfortunately reifies the academic tradition of building individual careers at the expense of one's colleagues. Often, the way to be "successful" in academia is to "stand out" from the crowd and be a "leader in the field." One of the most effective and quickest ways to achieve this recognition is to emphasize the faulty thinking of one's colleagues (who share one's general ideological commitments) rather than to address issues regarding the schooling of young people. Such educators and sociologists are more interested and spend more energy in developing their special "brand" of educational criticism at the expense of fellow critical scholars than in establishing meaningful dialogue in which people can collaboratively learn from one another. Obviously, it is necessary to illuminate how the ideas of one's colleagues need to be expanded, reexamined in light of other assumptions, or refined in light of different information. For example, the criticisms of the "correspondence theory" as used in Bowles and Gintis's (1976) early work and the use of notions such as "hegemony" led to a more fully developed understanding of the relationship between schools and society. In addition, there is a need to recognize the points at which similar ideological schools of thought become distinct from one another. This distinction is necessary not only for the sake of clarity and insight, but also for political reasons. For example, as feminist and anti-racist critiques have emerged within the discourse of criticism, it is useful to draw clear lines of distinction between these languages and the more general radical language of critical theory vis-a-vis the Frankfurt School. Drawing these distinctions is important in order to protect these new languages from being dominated by more traditional languages of criticism that happen to reflect the voices of mostly white males. However, within the discourse of criticism there exists a particular strand that seems focused primarily on gaining an intellectual advantage over others which has at times been ill-tempered and mean-spirited. It seeks to silence or arrest the work of a particular individual or individuals by questioning their basic motives and integrity, rather than to advance a mutually supportive development of ideas. As Giroux (1988b: 206) states,

> Instead of developing a political project and ethics that . . . connect schools and other institutions to forms of ongoing struggle, these newly emerging strains of critical educational theory appear to be suffocating in ideological narcissism, tied more closely to the self-serving tenets of vanguardism and despair than to anything else.

This intellectual sectarianism diverts attention away from those who are seriously interested in building a democratic pedagogy. Our inability to speak to our ideological colleagues in ways that nurture our collective interests ends up isolating us from each other and reifies the power of those who already have it. We must, as Apple (1979) suggests, learn how to stand on each other's shoulders rather than nip at each other's ankles.

Finally, this language of critique has tended to weaken the resolve of many critical educators by emphasizing the way in which schools serve the dominant interests within society at the expense of marginalized groups such as children, women, the poor, people of color, people with disabilities, and homosexuals. Because this language emphasizes the way in which the interests of the most powerful members of society dominate the lives of individuals and groups of people within various institutions such as schools, it has covertly undermined people's sense of potential agency and power. At first, this language was helpful in that it brought to conscious awareness the relationship between schooling and the broader social, historical context within which education takes place. However, its failure to take note of the way in which individuals and groups oppose various forces of social, political, and educational domination eventually reified those very interests. This reification of the supposed power structure within schools and society demoralized, and thus weakened, our ability to develop a language and social strategy to counter these dominant influences. The language of critique eventually degenerated into a "discourse of despair" by promoting the view that people with a critical consciousness are basically unable to exert a meaningful impact within our society: that is, it accentuated the way schools act as agencies for social reproduction by teaching young people and their teachers to be passive in their response to a curriculum and organizational structure that serve those who dominate our market economy and culture. Although the reification of power relationships in schools and society that emerged as a by-product of the language of critique was unintentional, as scholars we must seriously reflect upon our primary goals for engaging in academic discourse. Although the language of critique has provided important insights into the dynamics of educational and social power, because of its emphasis on providing a macro analysis, it has failed to provide a meaningful alternative vision to the organizational structure and curriculum of conventional schooling. Focusing on the critique of schooling and society while ignoring alternative visions and realities has resulted in "a series of self-alienating options in which our . . . presence is [limited to] bystanders, historians or critics . . . with only marginal or rhetorical connections to the confused and frustrating politics of our own time and place" (Williams, 1980: 238). In addition, as Christian (1987: 58) points out, there are very real dangers in not situating our theorizing within visions of practice.

> My fear is that when Theory is not rooted in practice, it becomes prescriptive, exclusive, elitist. . . . An example of this prescriptiveness is the approach the Black Arts Movement took towards language. For it, blackness resided in the use of black talk which they defined as hip urban language. So that when Nikki Giovanni reviewed Paule Marshall's *Chosen Place, Timeless People*, she criticized the novel on the grounds that it was not black, for the language was too elegant, too white. Blacks, she said, did not speak that way. Having come from the West Indies where we do, some of the time, speak that way, I was amazed by the narrowness of her vision. The emphasis on *one way* to be black resulted in the works of Southern writers being seen as non-black since the black talk of Georgia does not sound like the black talk of Philadelphia.

Unintentionally, a language of critique that is not rooted in visions of actual practice can potentially slip into dogma.

In response, Giroux (1988b) and his colleagues (Peter McLaren, Roger Simon, and Stanley Aronowitz) have called upon critical educators to move beyond the language of critique and have initiated the development of a "language of possibility." Rather than just criticize schools, society, and each other, the language of possibility calls upon critical scholars to create a discourse that is at first accessible and then provides others with a *vision* of hope and promise grounded in principles of empowerment, equality, and democracy. These principles are seen as promoting "the enhancement of human possibility" and the transformation of "human capacities and social forms" which "requires an education rooted in a view of human freedom as the understanding of necessity and the transformation of necessity" (Simon, 1987: 372, 373, 375). A language of possibility would then "enable students [and teachers] to do more than simply adapt to the social order but rather to . . . transform the social order in the interests of social justice, equality, and the development of a socialist democracy." Further, it would provide a basis for working "towards founding a redemptive and radically utopian social imagination grounded in hope" (McLaren, 1988: 3, 9).

Two primary visions have emerged from this language of possibility. The first is a picture of schools as "democratic public spheres" (Giroux, 1988b).[1] This concept emerges from Giroux's understanding of the English clubs, journals, coffeehouses, and periodicals that were used in the seventeenth and eighteenth centuries to question the autocracy of that society.

> The classic public sphere . . . defines social criticism as part of a larger discourse concerned with cultural politics and public morality and in doing so invokes the Enlightenment principles of rational argument and free exchange of ideas to challenge notions of authority rooted in superstition, tradition, and absolutist decrees. The classic public sphere established a legacy in which writing, the study of literature, and social criticism had a broadly civilizing function. (Giroux, 1988b: 207)

A vision of schools as democratic public spheres is offered as an alternative to viewing schools as merely institutions that prepare young people for their place in a competitive market economy.

> Instead of defining schools as extensions of the workplace or as frontline institutions in the battle of international markets and foreign competition, schools as democratic public spheres are constructed around forms of critical inquiry that dignify meaningful dialogue and human agency. Students learn the discourse of public association and social responsibility. Such a discourse seeks to recapture the idea of critical democracy as a social movement that supports individual freedom and social justice. Moreover, viewing schools as democratic public spheres provides a rationale for defending them along with progressive forms of pedagogy and teacher work as essential institutions and practices in the performance of an important public service. Schools are now defended in a political language as institutions that provide the ideological and material conditions necessary to educate a citizenry in the dynamics of critical literacy and civic courage, and these constitute the basis for functioning as active citizens in a democratic society. (Giroux, 1988b: xxxii)

With these "democratic public spheres," Giroux hopes to provide us with an alternative to the dominant vision of schools as "training centers" for a technological workforce.

Giroux also presents a vision of teachers as "transformative intellectuals" to replace the dominant notion of teachers as educational "technicians," "managers," or "professionals." As "transformative intellectuals" teachers can potentially play a significant role in creating schools as "democratic public spheres."

> Teachers need to develop a discourse and set of assumptions that allow them to function more specifically as transformative intellectuals. As intellectuals, they will combine reflection and action in the interest of empowering students with the skills and knowledge needed to address injustices and to be critical actors committed to developing a world free of oppression and exploitation. Such intellectuals are not merely concerned with promoting individual achievement or advancing students along career ladders, they are concerned with empowering students so they can read the world critically and change it when necessary. (Giroux, 1988b: xxxiv)

He goes on to state the following:

> Viewing teachers as intellectuals also provides a strong theoretical critique of technocratic and instrumental ideologies underlying an educational theory that separates the conceptualization, planning and design of curricula from the processes of implementation and execution. It is important to stress that teachers must take active responsibility for raising serious questions about what they teach, how they are to teach, and what the larger goals are for which they are striving. This means that they must take a responsible role in shaping the purposes and conditions of schooling. . . . If we believe that the role of teaching cannot be reduced to merely training in the practical skills, but involves instead, the education of a class of intellectuals vital to the development of a free society, then the category of intellectual becomes a way of linking the purpose of teacher education, public schooling, and inservice training to the very principles necessary for developing a democratic order and society. (Giroux, 1988b: 126)

Building upon Giroux and his colleagues' vision, Purpel (1989) proposes that teachers be seen as "educational prophets." These individuals have a deep devotion to sacred, humane values such as "peace," "justice," "love," "compassion," and "equality." These prophet/teachers consistently look upon these values as the core against which to examine their everyday practices. This vision represents a rich alternative to the dominant view of teachers in our society as educational managers who "get children through" a standardized curriculum within preestablished time limits.

The language of possibility has provided visualizations of alternative educational realities that are noteworthy and that have been absent within the language of critique. However, as mentioned in the first chapter, these visualizations have too often remained at an overly abstract level of discourse. For instance, one might suggest that Giroux's emphasis on teachers' use of their intellect (as opposed to their wisdom, intuition, and ethos of caring) reflects a narrow, masculinist perception of the human characteristics needed to change schools or society. Others might assume that "transformative intellectuals" are little more than social activists who recruit children to engage in civil actions reflective of leftist perspectives on various issues. One might question the degree to which social activism is or should be equated with the education of children. Without providing vivid images of "transformative intellectuals," it is difficult to understand the potential impact this vision has for schools and society.

Similarly, the previously mentioned work by Purpel (1989) lays out a vision of morality and spirituality as a guide for the education of our children. In doing so, he provides several insights that illuminate the way in which popular terms such as *excellence* have been used to reestablish what we have referred to in this book as an ideology of individualism, The book is filled with calls for an education that will fight human "misery," "hunger," "poverty," and "war," and help build a society based upon values of "love," "compassion," "joy," "equality," and "community." However, he stops short of illuminating what this education might actually look like within a real or even imaginary school. In his defense, he states, "It is surely not for me to provide the last word on what the broad educational framework ought to be, never mind the absurdity of an expectation that I or anyone else could also provide a detailed blueprint of implementation and practice" (Purpel, 1989: 156). Although a "blueprint" may in fact be inappropriate, it is perhaps irresponsible to expect others to tackle the difficult task of implementation if he is not willing to confront it himself. Unfortunately, what we end up with is vague visions and "coded" generalizations of education with which few individuals would disagree.

Purpel and Giroux are not alone in their unwillingness to provide substantive images of critical educational practices, and this failure is not a trivial oversight. As Gore (1989) suggests, the substance of the language of both critique and possibility has left many educators "paralyzed." How does one translate the previously stated goals and aspirations into actions within schools? Is it even possible to "transform the social order" through schooling, and if not, does that mean that teachers are a failure or the "system" too overpowering? What steps can or should be taken to reach the educational ambitions that are so eloquently articulated? The inadequacy of providing a discourse that can be digested by the educational community is not simply academic. To the contrary, it has had potentially negative political and educational consequences.

Although the language of possibility and in particular expressions such as *democratic public spheres, transformative intellectuals,* or *educational prophets* offer critical alternatives to traditional and conservative perceptions of schooling, one must not confuse the words with the values and visions that initially called them forth. One way in which dominant influences within society and the field of education maintain their hegemony is by usurping the meaning of new words and phrases that gain a certain degree of popularity and threaten the status quo. Take, for instance, the term *empowerment* that is increasingly being used in reference to teachers, students, and educational programs. Initially this notion was generated as a reaction against educational practices that reduce students and teachers to passive consumers and managers of the normative knowledge and skills needed to fulfill the labor needs of our society as presently constituted. However, because of the failure of critical scholars to create a discourse of "empowerment" grounded in the actual lives of teachers and students, conservative and mainstream educators have been able to use this term to justify their own agenda. As mentioned in Chapters 3 and 4, *empowerment* now often refers to providing special training programs or skill curricula that give students and teachers more "power" to take advantage of the opportunities offered by our corporate economy. Conservative forces have been able to usurp this term for their own ends by providing concrete illustrations of practice as presented in their work (e.g., Maeroff, 1988). Since it is easier to "act" within the discourse provided by conservative educators who are more than willing to describe in detail what should be taught and how people should act, their impact on current educational practices is not surprising. By removing the political and cultural context from which "empowerment" emerged, conservative and traditional educators have effectively crippled it as an effective expression for critical change. Visions of schooling that have surfaced from the language of possibility are not immune to such cultural and linguistic power maneuvers. For this reason, if no other, democratic educators must illustrate practices that reflect their lofty goals.

What is needed is to build upon the language of possibility by developing an educational language of democratic imagery, that is, a theoretical language which is informed by and rooted in images of real (or hypothesized) people involved in tangible actions that take place in actual settings. This then requires the development of a language that is visual as well as verbal. An educational language of democratic imagery would situate theoretical discourse within a given phenomenon. As we look back over the previous five chapters, it becomes obvious that this book represents one effort to develop such a language.

There are several aspects of this language that need to be more fully discussed. An educational language of democratic imagery implies the importance of historical and cultural context. As Clandinin and Connelly (1984: 5) note, a language of imagery can be seen as

> knowledge embodied in a person and connected with the individual's past, present and future. . . . [Image] reaches into the past gathering up experiential threads meaningfully connected to the present. And it reaches

> into the future and creates new meaningfully connected threads as situations
> are experienced. . . . Image carries intentionality.

A language of democratic imagery prevents critical discourse within
education from becoming lost in self-indulgent generalizations, coded
language systems, and sacrosanct idealism. It guards against discourse that
is so removed from social reality that it loses its potential for contributing
ideas to those for whose benefit it is supposedly written. Critical educators
need to take the time and make the effort to directly and explicitly address
the question of *how* (either hypothetically, based upon observations, or as
a result of reflecting upon one's own practices) individuals or groups of
people can potentially act within educational settings to advance the
democratic ideal. This willingness to *portray* the meaning of critical discourse
rather than just "talk about" it gives teachers and others interested in
democratic pedagogy an opportunity to learn through vicarious experience.
People's ability to visualize the actions that occur in one setting and to apply
this visualization to their own circumstances is a potentially powerful skill
through which democratic education can be expanded. Unfortunately, the
vast majority of critical discourse has often seemed to be more interested
in the glamor of abstract theorizing than in examining opportunities to tap
into the vicarious learning of others.

It is important to note that there is some danger in creating an
educational language of democratic imagery. First, it is important that this
discourse of imagery not be seen as a mindless backlash against the linguistic
complexity found in the discourse of critique in which the former is presented
as a morally superior form of scholarship over the latter. Giroux (1989: 132)
expands upon this point:

> The call to writing in a language that is touted as clear and accessible has
> become the political and ideological equivalent of a moral and political
> vision that increasingly collapses under the weight of its own anti-
> intellectualism. Theory is now dissolved into practice under the vote-
> catching call for the importance of focusing on the concrete as the all-
> embracing sphere of educational strategy and relevance. To argue against
> these concerns is not meant as a clever exercise intent on merely reversing
> the relevance of the categories so that theory is prioritized over practice,
> or abstract language over the language of imagery. Nor am I merely
> suggesting that critical educators mount an equally reductionist argument
> against the use of clear language or the importance of practice. At issue
> here is the need to both question and reject the reductionism and exclusions
> that characterize the binary oppositions that inform the overly pragmatic
> sentiments.

It is important that this call for a language of imagery not be viewed as "the
answer" for all individuals interested in educational inquiry. In calling for

the development of a discourse of imagery, it is not being suggested that educational scholarship must reflect a narrow and particularistic style. The languages of critique and possibility continue to make valuable contributions to our understanding of education. Perhaps it would be more helpful to recognize that some forms of scholarship are valuable for certain audiences, types of questions being explored, and value systems upon which they are based. Scholars do not always need to situate their discussions in a context specific setting in order to generate important insights about education. At the same time, practitioners in schools do not always need to have visual illustrations of ideas drawn out for them in order to be useful in their own deliberations about schooling. In recommending, as this chapter does, that educational scholarship ground itself through the use of visual narratives can be used to justify a form of essentialism that is counter-productive to the free exchange of ideas.

In suggesting the need to develop a language of democratic imagery, we are not proposing that it replace abstract theorizing as the new pinnacle of scholarly work. Rather, we encourage the development of a scholarship that is inclusive of both verbal and visual expression in our efforts to make what we say meaningful.

Second, in calling for more detailed illustrations of people working in classrooms and schools as a basis for our analytical and theoretical discourse, we are not suggesting that we should provide "cookbook" descriptions of "how it should be done." As previously mentioned, the dominant language within education today is one of management and control, and school-based personnel are familiar with responding to research or other types of scholarly literature with a "show-me-how-to-do-it" attitude. When an "expert" provides details of how schools can be run, how classrooms can be structured, what types of instruction can be used, or what curriculum can be taught, there is the assumption that those who read such work should merely "turn around" and implement these practices. However, to present practice in these terms negates the dialectical relationship between theory and action, and it reduces the reader to a passive consumer of ideas. The call to develop an educational language of democratic imagery is made with an understanding that one's purpose is not to ask others to mimic what is presented but to learn from the images provided and to apply what is vicariously experienced to one's own particular situation and limitations.

One problem in establishing schools as instruments of democratic ideals is that our very understanding of democracy has become so wilted that finding a moral foundation upon which to base our efforts seems increasingly difficult (MacIntyre, 1984). In recent years, for instance, notions of schooling for democracy have been tied to corporate and military interests that implicitly and explicitly neglect alternative visions of democratic schooling such as those found in the writings of Thomas Jefferson, Horace Mann, or John Dewey, let alone those voiced by more critical scholars. As Wood (1988) and Beyer (1988) argue, if we are to create a democratic pedagogy, then we must give serious attention to competing notions of democracy. We need to clearly articulate a vision of democratic arrangements that promote participatory action among people and a commitment to the elimination of all forms of racial, gender, sexual preference, and class oppression, or to what this book has referred to as "critical democracy." However, our notions of democracy and the moral foundation upon which it is built cannot be discussed in a vacuum. Concepts such as 'equity', 'freedom', 'justice', or 'liberty' have no meaning outside of a specific historical and social context. As previously stated, to understand democracy within our society we must analyze the impact individualism has had in subverting the democratic ideal in our society. Furthermore, we must go beyond the languages of critique and possibility towards a language of imagery in order to bring these democratic concepts to life within educational settings. Otherwise they become mere slogans without substantive meaning.

STRATEGIES FOR PROMOTING CRITICAL
DEMOCRACY THROUGH ELEMENTARY EDUCATION

Given the above discussion, a number of strategies that are based upon our observations at Harmony and that can be used to promote critical democracy in our society are worthy of particular attention. As stated in the first chapter, critical democracy will not emerge in our society through the transformation of educational practices alone. Schooling cannot be seen as an isolated compartment of society, as Peterson (1990: 5) eloquently illustrates.

> Take the case of the few school districts or municipalities in our country where progressive pro-equity forces have taken power. Leaving aside for a moment the obvious problems such districts face with massive bureaucracies and uncooperative educators, let's speak to the more fundamental problem of resources that such schools lack. For example, there is currently a progressive mayor, county executive and school superintendent in Milwaukee. But there is little money to do what needs to be done. Last year, a consultant group said it would take $500 million to rebuild the run-down schools in our city and to increase classrooms so class size could be reduced, full day kindergarten could be provided, and every school would have an art room, music room, and library. Five hundred million seems like a lot—but in fact it's less than the cost of one B-2 bomber. You know—those low flying offensive jets that military people say are going to be ineffective. And the Congress, which itself is bulging with millionaires, has ordered the construction of 132 such mechanical death birds. If instead Congress had established a national School

Reconstruction Fund, the 132 largest cities in the country would get 500 million dollars each to rebuild their schools. Think of the jobs it would create, the better learning conditions it would foster, the community centers for our alienated youth it could provide. But no, class interests and the obsession with militarism directly impact on what progressives can do in education.

Obviously, efforts need to be made in all spheres of society if our democracy is to become more caring and participatory in nature. However, as Peterson (1990) goes on to state and illustrate, it would be self-defeating to suggest that society must change before schools can change or before teachers or other educators can act. Each person needs to work for democracy in those areas of society that are most accessible, and for educators that is in schools.

Although most public school personnel do not have as much power and flexibility as teachers and administrators in independent schools such as Harmony, democratically motivated educators have been able to create within traditional institutions what Boyte (1980: 24) has referred to as "free social spaces" that have some "insulation from elite control." For example, Dorothy Fadiman's (1990) recent documentary *Why Do These Kids Love School?* portrays eleven schools[2] (both public and private) that have established, to various degrees and in different ways, many of the connectionist educational practices and values we observed at Harmony. As Wood (1988: 184) suggests, teachers and administrators have been able to create "islands of democracy" in some classrooms and schools around the country in spite of the tremendous forces working against such projects. The images of practice that emerge from our observations at Harmony can be used as one of several potential guides for others interested in establishing these "free social spaces" or "islands of democracy" in their own educational settings. Images that appear in Chapters 3 and 4 can help building administrators and teachers establish democratic power relationships among themselves, between themselves and students, and among the students. Images related to curriculum and instruction that were portrayed in Chapter 5 can aid those who are attempting to determine curricular content and learning experiences within a given elementary school or classroom that will promote democratic sensibilities among our young people. Although this book has provided several images upon which to build educational strategies, there is one aspect of Harmony's elementary schooling that has not been directly addressed, and yet seems particularly important. Perhaps the reason that we have been reluctant to mention it until now is that this facet of democratic schooling is difficult to clearly identify even when it is observed and difficult to describe in a manner that one can vicariously understand. Given this warning, there existed within Harmony's elementary school a subtle, delicate, and loving spirituality. While not wanting to sound overly simplistic or romantic, we would say that the life-affirming intellectual and emotional connection that existed among the teachers and students gave substance to Harmony's democratic ideology and practices. Although it is possible, as was done in Chapters 3, 4, and 5, to articulate the actions and ideas of people, the key to what makes Harmony a meaningful democratic alternative was the spiritual nature of its enterprise.

With regard to the images of power relationships and curriculum and instruction in this book, it is crucial that readers understand these images within their particular context. The type of elementary schooling that we observed at Harmony seemed emancipating for the children and teachers who attended this particular school. In our interviews, the teachers articulated their appreciation for the occupational autonomy they were able to exercise and for the intellectual and affective challenges that teaching at Harmony presented to them. Several themes emerged from student interviews, such as the following. *Work and Fun*: The students at Harmony often mentioned that they enjoyed their schoolwork. They referred to class assignments as "fun," "interesting," and "important." However, they also commented that assignments were "difficult" or "hard." In the minds of these students, the distinction between "work" and "fun" was not sharply drawn. *Students as Learners*: Students unanimously expressed the belief that they were "capable of learning," that their work was "appreciated" by their teachers, and that they were "knowledgeable" people. *Interpersonal Relationships:* Students enthusiastically spoke about the personal relationships they had at school. At Harmony the majority of students felt "part of" the school, as opposed to "apart from" it. In particular, they spoke of being "cared for" by the teachers, administrators, and other students, and of their own responsibility for themselves and to others. Clearly, it seemed that Harmony's elementary school has been able to create a meaningful educational experience for this particular heterogeneous group of children. However, educational programs cannot be reproduced like fast-food franchises. One cannot divorce an ideology or even a set of practices from those who are actually working within a given situation. Much of the success of Harmony's elementary school depends upon the unique blend of students, parents, faculty, and administrators involved in it. In fact, Steve has often been asked to help establish similar schools in other communities, but as of this date, these efforts have not been successful. In addition, schools that serve a more homogeneous population of children would need to establish programs suited to such a situation. For example, schools with large numbers of students from traditionally marginalized groups of people in our society might best be served by a curriculum that directly confronts (both historically and in the present) the oppression that these groups of people face in our society to a greater degree than what we witnessed in Harmony's elementary school (see Chapter 5). While we suggest that educators can vicariously learn from the images that emerged from Harmony's elementary school, it is extremely important that one does not view them as reforms suitable to all children in all situations. As previously mentioned, the language of imagery implies the importance of context in proposing any educational procedures.

Although Chapters 3, 4, and 5 provide numerous images that can be used in creating "islands of democracy" in our schools, it is equally important to articulate what actions can help facilitate the growth of democratic pedagogy across broader domains in our society. Creating an educational language of democratic imagery is one task before us that might help loosen the grip that conservative educators have had on the educational agenda in our society during this last decade. To facilitate the development of this language, several alliances should be strengthened. One obvious connection is between the teachers and administrators in schools such as Harmony and scholars within universities interested in critical or democratic pedagogy. Individuals who are trying to create democratic schools and classrooms often feel isolated, and this isolation makes it difficult for them to receive professional affirmation for their work and new ideas through which they can grow. It seems to us that critical educators in universities could provide some of this support. During the time we spent in Harmony, the teachers and administrators seemed to appreciate our presence. We provided these individuals with a lens through which they could see themselves, become aware of new ideas, or recognize concepts that they were intuitively acting upon but that lacked clear articulation. For example, according to Dan, recent attempts to rewrite Harmony's mission statement were significantly influenced by what was written in early drafts of this book. In particular, the struggle to balance the values of individuality and community, which were largely intuitively acted upon, became more explicit, allowing for greater overt discussion of the way in which these values do (or should) guide the work of these individuals. As we looked back over the year we spent at Harmony, it seemed to us that the teachers in this school might have benefited from being more exposed to the discourse currently being generated from critical scholars in education. Although we do not want to suggest that the theory making that these teachers were clearly engaged in (see Chapter 3) is inferior to the scholarly theorizing that occurs in colleges and universities, there is valuable substance in this scholarship. For instance, given the values of caring and social responsibility that guide the experiences inside Harmony's walls, it seems to us that the recent scholarship in feminist pedagogy might be particularly useful. Unfortunately, these teachers, like most, are engaged in occupations that give them little time or energy for graduate study. If these connections are to be fostered, then it is up to those with more flexible working conditions (scholars) to form these ongoing relationships. Perhaps one idea would be for every scholar who is committed to democratic pedagogy to "adopt" a teacher, administrator, or school in which to invest his or her time. By "adopt" we do not want to imply a paternalistic attitude. Rather, we simply mean that, as scholars, we would take a special interest in the lives of a few individuals who are attempting to develop educational projects for critical democracy.

The purpose of forming this alliance, however, is not simply to offer support to these courageous individuals. In addition, it seems to us that, as educational scholars who are interested in democratic pedagogy, we have much to learn from those who are involved directly with this enterprise. Unfortunately, several critical educators have mentioned to me that they "oppose" alternative schools (even ones driven by democratic values) because they feel that these schools somehow undermine the struggle to change public schools. Although this may provide them with a moral reason to keep their distance, their conclusion has little basis in fact. There is little indication that, of all the forces that influence what public education does or does not do in our society, alternative schools such as Harmony have obstructed efforts to bring about progressive change in conventional schools. In fact, if the number of democratic alternative schools sharply increased in our society, there is some indication that the public schools would respond in kind. One only has to look at the impact that more traditional private schools in urban settings have had on the public school system. For example, a number of school systems in the country currently are looking for ways to offer programs that would draw children back into the public school system (e.g., magnate schools). One can only speculate, of course, but if schools like Harmony suddenly emerged all over the country, then the subsequent impact upon public education might be positive.

In any case, the need to form alliances between critical scholars and individuals who work in settings such as Harmony is crucial. As previously mentioned, it is relatively easy to take the "high moral ground" that academia provides and espouse noble-sounding ideals related to schools and society. However, if we, as critical educators, are to have any credibility outside of the extremely narrow confines of our own professional world, then we had best spend time with those who teach children. If we do not begin to speak in a language of imagery, especially one in which those images are grounded in an actual setting, then we should not complain when no one listens to us.

In addition to forming closer ties between those educators in academia and those teachers and administrators in either public or private schools who are committed to democratic education, we need to establish other networks. As previously mentioned, a conservative ideology has captured the momentum of educational thinking and practices in our country. As a result, educators who wish to develop pedagogical ideas, values, and practices that promote critical democracy need to see their work as part of a broader social and political movement. Although individual teachers can act within their own classrooms and small groups of educators can create schools such as Harmony, we also need to build coalitions of educators working together for critical democracy. Currently, Harmony School is actively involved in the National Coalition of Alternative Community Schools. Steve has been particularly interested in getting this group to develop a more overtly democratic (as opposed to simply humanitarian) orientation towards education. In addition, he has pushed this organization to form bonds with those who are responsible for the creation of progressive alternative programs within public schools. However, as a group, the National Coalition of Alternative Community Schools has traditionally failed to go beyond the individualistic orientation common to its "free" school roots. Recently, three examples of coalitions with a more overtly democratic orientation have emerged in our society. The Institute for Democracy in Education (Wood, 1986), the Democratic Schools Collaborative (Berlak, 1985), and a group of teachers who work within the Milwaukee public school system (Peterson, 1990) have formed in order to bring teachers, administrators, university professors, and other interested parties together to share ideas and practices that enhance democratic possibilities within educational settings. These coalitions sponsor seminars, conferences, newsletters, and such journals as *Democracy and Education, Democratic Schools,* and *Rethinking Schools.* In addition, members of these organizations have engaged in overt political actions to resist the implementation of the conservative agenda in particular school districts (Peterson, 1990). Establishing these affiliations cannot be overemphasized. In discussing her work filming various progressive schools around the country, Ms. Fadiman stated,

> One thing that was very surprising to me was that none of these schools knew the others existed. They are so busy educating the children in their buildings and fighting to stay alive, often in the face of hostile central administrators, that they are unaware that there are other schools like them. Each one felt isolated, they thought that they were all alone, the only school of its kind perhaps in the entire country.[3]

The isolation of teachers and administrators working in schools with democratic visions must cease. The longer these educators remain secluded from each other, the longer it will take to initiate democratic reforms on a broader scale within our society's schools.

Finally, since the schooling of children cannot by itself transform our social consciousness, it is important for us to connect with citizens outside of educational settings as part of a broad-based effort to democratize our society. Connections need to be made with and work done inside women's organizations, unions, consumer associations, ecology groups, political parties, and local community organizations to help situate their concerns within a critical democratic framework (Barber, 1984; Boyte, 1980, 1984; Gran, 1983). Only by working together can we make critical democracy a reality.

Perhaps it is appropriate to conclude this book by putting its content into a temporal perspective. The last decade has been demoralizing to many educators who only a few years before the escalation of the Vietnam War were filled with hope that our society had made a strong commitment to the values of community, caring, social justice, and political participation for all of our citizens. It seemed that although much work lay ahead to fulfill the democratic ideal, the direction in which we were moving was clearly marked. Since then, changes in the executive and particularly the judicial branches of our government have made it difficult to maintain the optimistic vision of a society in which the well-being of children and adults will take precedence over industrial and military interests. However, we must remember that as a species we are relative newcomers to this planet. Human history is filled with periods of both promise and despair. As Henry Giroux has so often pointed out, we must not succumb to the recent turns of events as if societal situations were permanently cast in stone. To the contrary, now, perhaps more than ever, is the time to situate our work within a politics of hope. Although democratic and progressive elements within our society have been on the defensive during this last decade, they have not disappeared. The work of the teachers and administrators at Harmony's elementary school illustrates the tenacity of at least a small number of individuals who have maintained a commitment to educating children for the "common good." As one of the members of the 1950s blacklisted folk music group The Weavers stated at a reunion concert a couple of years after Reagan took office, "Don't despair, we've been through times like this before, and we'll persevere." The spirit within human beings from which concepts such as compassion, social equity, intellectual freedom, and caring emerged has not atrophied. Now is the time to reassert our dreams about how schooling can help young people develop their intellectual and creative talents, moral character, and civic courage, which will be needed to face the difficult tasks of defining and creating the "good life" for the many species of plants and animals that share this small planet, as it moves into the next century.

NOTES

NOTES TO CHAPTER 1

1. "We" refers to the author and two project assistants, Xiaoyang Wu and Jeff Kuzmic, who became involved with the people and events at Harmony's elementary school from July of 1987 to June of 1988.

2. Manicas (1985) notes that Dewey is perhaps the most widely interpreted (and misunderstood) philosopher of our modern age. His work has been characterized as nostalgic and irrelevant (Mills, 1969), in the mainstream of pluralistic, liberal democracy (Damico, 1978; Mills, 1969; Novack, 1975), a humanistic form of Marxism (Hook, 1966), a reflection of United States intellectual imperialism (Cornforth, 1955; Wells, 1954), and in the best tradition of anarchism (Manicas, 1985). As used in this context, his political philosophy is at the heart of critical democracy.

3. There are many complexities related to developing a concept of critical democracy and of establishing such a democracy within modern society. However, it is not within the realm of this particular project to sort out these complexities and questions. The reader is encouraged to examine several works in the field of political theory (Barber, 1984; Crenson, 1983; Dahl, 1982; Gran, 1983; Pateman, 1970).

4. I first heard the term *connectionist* in an invited address given by Michael Apple at the 1987 American Educational Research Association meeting. In this lecture, Apple noted that he saw himself as a "connectionist," as he pointed out that we would not have been able to have that particular discussion if it were not for miners who were willing to work underground to obtain coal in order to provide energy for the electricity to the building.

NOTES TO CHAPTER 2

1. Smith and Heshusius (1986) cogently argue why this type of blending should not be ended. From their perspective, rather than result in a new, more informative model of educational research, this merging would succeed only in "closing down" or stifling the type of dialogue that keeps educational research dynamic. Their contention is, of course, that there is nothing inherently "wrong" with intellectual "wars," and that these conflicts may even be the source of our best work.

2. Some notable exceptions to this statement are Lesko's (1988) study of girls in a Catholic high school and McLaren's (1986) study of boys in a Catholic middle school.

183

3. The term *interpretive* is being used in this book to refer to a whole family of phenomenologically based research approaches, including ethnographic, naturalistic, qualitative, participant observational, symbolic interactionist, and constructionist inquiry. Although these approaches are slightly different from each other, they have many similarities. As Erickson (1986) points out, the term *interpretive* is used because it (1) is more inclusive than other terms, (2) avoids the implication that this research is merely antiquantitative (as connoted by the term *qualitative*), and (3) emphasizes the key similarity among all of these approaches—a central interest in understanding and interpreting the constructed reality of social life. However, as previously discussed, our own orientation to our work took a much broader focus than that found within this strictly "interpretive" frame of reference.

NOTES TO CHAPTER 5

1. There have been several critiques of this position. Aronowitz and Giroux (1988) offer a particularly insightful analysis that exposes the way in which Bloom's and Hirsch's call for curricular reform is fundamentally reactionary and antidemocratic.

2. See the editorial "Rhino Fever: Catch It" in the June 1988 issue of *Kappan* for a more detailed description of the students' efforts.

NOTES TO CHAPTER 6

1. Giroux's vision is similar to Maxine Greene's notion of "public space" as discussed in her most recent book, *The Dialectic of Freedom* (1988).

2. The eleven schools depicted in this film are Central Park East II, East Harlem, NY; City Magnet, Lowell, MA; Clara Barton, Minneapolis, MN; Davis Alternative Elementary, Jackson, MS; Graham and Parks, Cambridge, MA; New Orleans Free School, New Orleans, LA; Tanglewood Open Living School, Golden, CO; Bailey Alternative High School, Jackson, MS; St. Paul Open, St. Paul, MN; Central Park East Secondary School, East Harlem, NY; Peninsula School, Menlo Park, CA.

3. Presentation and lecture of *Why Do These Kids Love School?* on March 29, 1990, Indiana University, Bloomington, IN.

REFERENCES

Acker, S. (1989). *Teachers, gender, and careers.* New York: Falmer.

Adler, R. (1977). *Research on the effects of television advertising on children.* Washington, DC: U.S. Government Printing Office.

Albert, S. (1977). Temporal comparison theory. *Psychological Review,* 84 (6), 485-503.

Almond, G., & Verba, S. (1963). *The civic culture: Political attitudes and democracy in five nations.* Princeton, NJ: Princeton University Press.

Althusser, L. (1969). *For Marx.* London: Penguin.

Anderson, G. (1989). Critical ethnography in education: Origins, current status, and new directions. *Review of Educational Research,* 59 (3), 249-270.

Anyon, J. (1979). Ideology and United States history textbooks. *Harvard Educational Review,* 49 (3), 361-386.

Apple, M. (1979). *Ideology and curriculum.* London: Routledge & Kegan Paul.

Apple, M. (1986). *Teachers and texts: A political economy of class and gender relations in education.* London: Routledge & Kegan Paul.

Apple, M., & Teitelbaum, K. (1986). Are teachers losing control of their skills and curriculum? *Journal of Curriculum Studies,* 18 (2), 177-184.

Aronowitz, S., & Giroux, H. (1988). Schooling, culture, and literacy in the age of broken dreams: A review of Bloom and Hirsch. *Harvard Educational Review,* 58 (2), 172-194.

Barber, B. (1984). *Strong democracy: Participatory politics for a new age.* Berkeley, CA: University of California Press.

Baron, D. (1979). A case study of praxis. *Journal of Curriculum Theorizing,* 1 (2), 46-53.

Barrett, N. (1979). Women in the job market: Occupations, earnings, and career opportunities. In R. Smith (Ed.), *The subtle revolution: Women at work,* 31-61. Washington, DC: Urban Institute.

Barthes, R. (1972). *Mythologies.* New York: Hill & Wang.

185

Bates, F. (1970). Power behavior and decentralization. In M. Zald (Ed.), *Power in organizations*, 175-176. Nashville: Vanderbilt University Press.

Bateson, G. (1958). *Naven*. Stanford, CA: Stanford University Press.

Bazeley, E. (1969). *Homer Lane and the little commonwealth*. New York: Schocken Books.

Becker, H., Geer, B., Hughes, E., & Strauss, A. (1961). *Boys in white*. Chicago: University of Chicago Press.

Belenky, M., Clinchy, B., Goldberger, N., & Tarule, J. (1986). *Women's ways of knowing: The development of self, voice, and mind*. New York: Basic Books.

Bellah, R., Madsen, R., Sullivan, W., Swidler, A., & Tipton, S. (1985). *Habits of the heart: Individualism and commitment in American life*. Berkeley, CA: University of California Press.

Bennett, W. (1984). To reclaim a legacy: Text of report on humanities in higher education. *Chronicle of Higher Education*, November 28, 16-21.

Berger, P. (1975). *Pyramids of sacrifice: Political ethics and social change*. New York: Anchor.

Berger, P., & Luckmann, T. (1967). *The social construction of reality: A treatise in the sociology of knowledge*. Garden City, NY: Anchor.

Berlak, A. (1988, April). *Teaching for outrage and empathy in the liberal arts*. Paper presented at the annual American Educational Research Association meeting, New Orleans.

Berlak, H. (1985). *Education for a democratic future*. St. Louis, MO: Public Education Information Network.

Berman, K. (1982). The worker-owned plywood cooperatives. In F. Lindenfeld & J. Rothschild-Whitt (Eds.), *Workplace democracy and social change*, 161-175. Boston: Porter Sargent.

Beyer, L. (1988). Schooling for the culture of democracy. In L. Beyer & M. Apple (Eds.), *The curriculum: Problems, politics, and possibilities*, 219-238. Albany: State University of New York Press.

Blau, P. (1970). Decentralization in bureaucracies. In M. Zald (Ed.), *Power in organizations*, 150-174. Nashville, TN: Vanderbilt University Press.

Bloom, A. (1987). *The closing of the American mind: How higher education has failed democracy and impoverished the souls of today's students*. New York: Simon & Schuster.

Blumberg, A. (1980, April). *Teachers, other teachers, and principals: Welds and cracks in the couplings*. Paper presented at the annual American Educational Research Association meeting, Boston.

Blumer, H. (1969). *Symbolic interactionism: Perspective and method.* Englewood Cliffs, NJ: Prentice-Hall.

Bowers, C. (1982). The reproduction of technological consciousness: Locating the ideological foundation of a radical pedagogy. *Teachers College Record*, 83 (4), 529-557.

Bowles, S., & Gintis, H. (1976). *Schooling in capitalist America.* New York: Basic Books.

Boyte, H. (1980). *The backyard revolution: Understanding the new citizen movement.* Philadelphia, PA: Temple University Press.

Boyte, H. (1984). *Community is possible: Repairing America's roots.* New York: Harper & Row.

Brady, L. (1985). The supportiveness of the principal in school-based curriculum development. *Journal of Curriculum Studies*, 17 (1), 95-97.

Braverman, H. (1974). *Labor and monopoly capital.* New York: Monthly Review Press.

Bronfenbrenner, U. (1970). *Two worlds of childhood: U.S. and U.S.S.R.* New York: Russell Sage Foundation.

Bryan, J. (1975). Children's cooperation and helping behaviors. In E. Hetherington (Ed.), *Review of Child Development Research*, volume 5, 127-181. Chicago: University of Chicago Press.

Bunch, C., & Pollack, S. (1983). *Learning our way: Essays in feminist education.* Trumansburg, NY: Crossing.

Burawoy, M. (1979). *Manufacturing consent.* Chicago: University of Chicago Press.

Bussis, A., Crittenden, E., & Amarel, M. (1976). *Beyond surface curriculum.* Boulder: Westview.

Cagan, E. (1978). Individualism, collectivism, and radical educational reform. *Harvard Educational Review*, 48 (2), 227-265.

Callahan, R. (1962). *Education and the cult of efficiency: A study of the social forces that have shaped the administration of the public schools.* Chicago: University of Chicago Press.

Campbell, J. (1988). *The power of myth.* New York: Doubleday.

Canter, L., & Canter, M. (1976). Assertive discipline: A take charge approach for today's educator. Seal Beach, CA: Canter & Associates.

Caputo, J. (1987). *Radical hermeneutics: Repetition, deconstruction, and the hermeneutic project.* Bloomington, IN: Indiana University Press.

Carlson, D. (1982). "Updating" individualism and the work ethic: Corporate logic in the classroom. *Curriculum Inquiry*, 12 (2), 125-160.

Carnegie, D. (1936). *How to win friends and influence people*. New York: Simon & Schuster.

Chafel, J. (1988). *Autonomous versus social orientations of achievement in children: A plea for future research*. Unpublished paper, Indiana University.

Christian, B. (1987). The race for theory. *Cultural Critique*, 6 (1), 51-63.

Cicourel, A. (1973). *Cognitive sociology*. London: Penguin.

Clandinin, D. J., & Connelly, F. M. (1984). *Teachers' personal practical knowledge: Image and narrative unity*. Working paper. Toronto, Canada: The Ontario Institute for Studies in Education.

Clews, H. (1907). *Individualism versus socialism*. Address delivered in the Columbia Theater, New York.

Clinchy, B., Belenky, M., Goldberger, N., & Tarule, J. (1985). Connected education for women. *Journal of Education*, 167 (3), 28-45.

Cornforth, M. (1955). *Science versus idealism*. London: Lawrence & Wishart.

Courtney, R. (1982). *Re-play: Studies in human drama and education*. Toronto: Ontario Institute for Studies in Education.

Crenson, M. (1983). *Neighborhood politics*. Cambridge, MA: Harvard University Press.

Crozier, M. (1964). *The bureaucratic phenomenon*. Chicago: University of Chicago Press.

Dahl, R. (1982). *Dilemmas of pluralist democracy*. New Haven, CT: Yale University Press.

Damico, A. (1978). *Individuality and community: The social and political thought of John Dewey*. Gainesville: University of Florida Press.

D'Amico, R. (1978). Going relativist. *Telos*, 67, 135-145.

Darling-Hammond, L. (1985). Valuing teachers: The making of a profession. *Teachers College Record*, 87 (2), 205-218.

Dennison, G. (1969). *The lives of children: The story of the first street school*. New York: Random House.

Densmore, K. (1987). Professionalism, proletarianization and teacher work. In T. Popkewitz (Ed.), *Critical studies in teacher education: Its folklore, theory and practice*, 130-160. New York: Falmer.

Dewey, J. (1922). *Human nature and conduct: An introduction to social psychology.* New York: Carlton House.

Dewey, J. (1927). *The public and its problems.* New York: Henry Holt.

Dewey, J. (1930). *Individualism old and new.* New York: Minton, Balch & Company.

Dewey, J. (1933). *How we think.* Boston: Heath.

Dewey, J. (1946). *Problems of men.* New York: Philosophical Library.

Dewey, J. (1966). *Democracy and education: An introduction to the philosophy of education.* New York: The Free Press.

Dietz, M. (1985). Citizenship with a feminist face: The problem with maternal thinking. *Political Theory,* 13 (1), 19-37.

Dreyfus, H., & Rabinow, P. (1983). *Michel Foucault: Beyond structuralism and hermeneutics.* Chicago: University of Chicago Press.

Duffy, G., Roehler, L., & Putman, J. (1987). Putting the teacher in control: Basal reading textbooks and instructional decision making. *Elementary School Journal,* 87 (3), 359-366.

Durkheim, E. (1933). *The division of labor in society.* London: Collier-Macmillan.

Durkheim, E. (1957). *The elementary forms of the religious life.* London: Allen & Unwin.

Eckstein, H. (1973). Authority patterns: A structural basis for political inquiry. *American Science Review,* 67 (4), 1142-1161.

Edwards, R. (1979). *Contested terrain: The transformation of the workplace in the 20th century.* New York: Basic Books.

Eisner, E. (1979). *The educational imagination.* New York: Macmillan.

Eisner, E. (1983). Anastasia might still be alive, but the monarch is dead. *Educational Researcher,* 12 (4), 13-24.

Ellsworth, E. (1988, October). *Why doesn't this feel empowering? Working through the repressive myths of critical pedagogy.* Paper presented at the annual Curriculum Theory and Classroom Practice conference, Dayton, OH.

Elshtain, J. (1981). *Public man, private woman: Women in social and political thought.* Princeton, NJ: Princeton University Press.

Emerson, R. W. (1929). New England reformers. In *The complete writings of Ralph Waldo Emerson,* Vol. 1. New York: Wise & Co.

Erickson, F. (1986). Qualitative research on teaching. In M. Wittrock (Ed.), *Handbook of research on teaching,* 119-161. New York: Macmillan.

Ewen, S. (1976). *Captains of consciousness: Advertising and the social roots of the consumer culture*. New York: McGraw-Hill.

Fadiman, D. (1990). *Why do these kids love school?* San Jose, CA: Dorothy Fadiman and KTEH-TV.

Fay, B. (1977). How people change themselves: The relationship between critical theory and its audience. In T. Ball (Ed.), *Political theory and praxis: New perspectives*, 200-233. Minneapolis: University of Minnesota Press.

Fay, B. (1987). *Critical social science: Liberation and its limits*. Ithaca, NY: Cornell University Press.

Feldstein, S. (1979). *The land that I show you: Three centuries of Jewish life in America*. Garden City, NY: Anchor.

Finkelstein, B. (1984). Education and the retreat from democracy in the United States—1979-198? *Teachers College Record*, 86 (2), 273-282.

Fiske, D., & Shweder, R. (1986). *Metatheory in social science: Pluralisms and subjectivities*. Chicago: University of Chicago Press.

Flanagan, J., Shanner, W., Brudner, H., & Marker, R. (1975). An individualized instructional system: PLAN. In H. Talmadge (Ed.), *Systems of individualized education*, 136-167. Berkeley, CA: McCutchan.

Flynn, L. (1989). Developing critical reading skills through cooperative problem solving. *Reading Teacher*, 42 (9), 664-668.

Foucault, M. (1977). *Discipline and punish: Birth of the prison*. London: Allen Lane.

Foucault, M. (1979). *The history of sexuality, Vol. 1: An introduction*. London: Tavistock.

Freire, P. (1973). *Education for critical consciousness*. New York: Seabury Press.

Freire, P., & Macedo, D. (1987). *Literacy: Reading the word and the world*. South Hudley, MA: Bergin & Garvey.

Fromm, E. (1956). *The art of loving*. New York: Harper & Row.

Frymier, J. (1987a). Bureaucracy and the neutering of teachers. *Phi Delta Kappan*, 69 (9), 9-14.

Frymier, J. (1987b, April). *State-legislated curriculum: Why be concerned?* Paper presented at the annual American Educational Research Association meeting, Washington, DC.

Gage, N. L. (1989). The paradigm wars and their aftermath: A "historical" sketch of research on teaching since 1989. *Educational Researcher*, 18 (7), 4-10.

Gee, J. (1989a). The narrativization of experience in the oral style. *Journal of Education*, 171 (1), 75-96.

Gee, J. (1989b). Two styles of narrative construction and their linguistic and educational implications. *Journal of Education*, 171 (1), 97-115.

Geertz, C. (1973). *The interpretation of cultures*. New York: Basic Books.

Giddens, A. (1971). *Capitalism and modern social theory*. London: Cambridge University Press.

Gilligan, C. (1982). *In a different voice: Psychological theory and women's development*. Cambridge, MA: Harvard University Press.

Giroux, H. (1978). Writing and critical thinking in the social studies. *Curriculum Inquiry*, 8 (4), 291-310.

Giroux, H. (1986). Radical pedagogy and the politics of student voice. *Interchange*, 17 (1), 48-69.

Giroux, H. (1988a). Postmodernism and the discourse of educational criticism. *Journal of Education*, 170 (3), 5-30.

Giroux, H. (1988b). *Teachers as intellectuals: Toward a critical pedagogy of learning*. South Hadley, MA: Bergin & Garvey.

Giroux, H. (1989). Schooling as a form of cultural politics: Toward a pedagogy of and for difference. In H. Giroux & P. McLaren (Eds.), *Critical pedagogy, the state, and cultural struggle*, 125-151. Albany: State University of New York Press.

Giroux, H., & McLaren, P. (1986). Teacher education and the politics of engagement: The case for democratic schooling. *Harvard Educational Review*, 56 (3), 213-238.

Giroux, H., & McLaren, P. (1989). Introduction: Schooling, cultural politics, and the struggle for democracy. In H. Giroux & P. McLaren (Eds.), *Critical pedagogy, the state, and cultural struggle*, xi-xxxv. Albany: State University of New York Press.

Giroux, H., & Penna, A. (1977). Social relations in the classroom: The dialectic of the hidden curriculum. *Edcentric*, 40-41, 39-46.

Giroux, H., & Simon, R. (1988). *Popular culture and critical pedagogy: Schooling and the language of everyday life*. South Hadley, MA: Bergin & Garvey.

Gitlin, A. (1983). School structure and teachers' work. In M. Apple & L. Weis (Eds.), *Ideology and practice in schooling*, 193-212. Philadelphia, PA: Temple University Press.

Givon, T. (1979). *On understanding grammar*. New York: Academic.

Glaser, G., & Strauss, A. (1975). *The discovery of grounded theory: Strategies for qualitative research.* Chicago: Aldine.

Goetz, J., & LaCompte, M. (1981). Ethnographic research and the problem of data reduction. *Anthropology and Education Quarterly,* 12 (1), 51-70.

Goffman, E. (1961). *Asylums: Essays on the social situation of mental patients and other inmates.* Garden City, NY: Anchor Books.

Goodlad, J. (1984). *A place called school: Prospects for the future.* New York: McGraw-Hill.

Goodman, J. (1980). *The blue plate: A study of a workers' collective.* Unpublished paper.

Goodman, J. (1985). Field-based experience: A study of social control and student teachers' response to institutional constraints. *Journal of Education for Teaching,* 11 (1), 26-49.

Goodman, J. (1987a). Factors in becoming a proactive elementary school teacher: A preliminary study of selected novices. *Journal of Education for Teaching,* 13 (3), 207-229.

Goodman, J. (1987b). Masculinity, feminism, and the male elementary school teacher: A case study of preservice teachers' perspectives. *Journal of Curriculum Theorizing,* 7 (2), 30-60.

Goodman, J. (1988a). The disenfranchisement of elementary teachers and strategies for resistance. *Journal of Curriculum and Supervision,* 3 (3), 201-220.

Goodman, J. (1988b). The political tactics and teaching strategies of reflective, active preservice teachers. *The Elementary School Journal,* 89 (1), 23-41.

Gordon, D., Edwards, R., & Reich, M. (1982). *Segmented work, divided workers.* New York: Cambridge University Press.

Gordon, T. (1974). *Teacher Effectiveness Training.* New York: Peter Wyden.

Gore, J. (1989). *Agency, structure and the rhetoric of teacher empowerment.* Paper presented at the annual American Educational Research Association meeting, San Francisco.

Gorz, A. (1982). Workers' control is more than just that. In F. Lindenfeld & J. Rothschild-Whitt (Eds.), *Workplace democracy and social change,* 397-412. Boston: Porter Sargent.

Gouldner, A. (1954). *Patterns of industrial bureaucracy.* Glencoe, IL: The Free Press.

Gran, G. (1983). *Development by people: Citizen construction of a just world.* New York: Praeger.

Graubard, A. (1972). *Free the children: Radical reform and the free school movement.* New York: Pantheon Books.

Greene, M. (1973). *Teacher as stranger: Educational philosophy for the modern age.* Belmont, CA: Wadsworth.

Greene, M. (1988). *The dialectic of freedom.* New York: Teachers College Press.

Greenspan, S. (1983). *The clinical interview of the child.* New York: McGraw-Hill.

Grimes, R. (1982). *Beginnings in ritual studies.* Washington, DC: University Press of America.

Gross, B., & Gross, R. (1969). *Radical school reform.* New York: Simon & Schuster.

Grumet, M. (1981). Pedagogy for patriarchy: The feminization of teaching. *Interchange,* 12 (2/3), 165-184.

Grumet, M. (1988). *Bitter milk: Women and teaching.* Amherst: University of Massachusetts Press.

Guerin, D. (1970). *Anarchism: From theory to practice.* New York: Monthly Review Press.

Habermas, J. (1970). *Toward a rational society: Student protest, science, and politics.* Boston: Beacon.

Habermas, J. (1973). *Theory and practice.* Boston: Beacon.

Habermas, J. (1975). *Legitimation crisis.* Boston: Beacon.

Hall, S. (1985). Signification, representation, ideology: Althusser and the post-structuralist debates. *Critical Studies in Mass Communication,* 2 (2), 91-114.

Hall, S. (1986). On postmodernism and articulation. *Journal of Communication Inquiry,* 10 (2), 45-60.

Hanson, R. (1985). *The democratic imagination in America: Conversations with our past.* Princeton, NJ: Princeton University Press.

Harding, S. (1987a). *Feminism and methodology.* Bloomington: Indiana University Press.

Harding, S. (1987b). Introduction: Is there a feminist method? In S. Harding (Ed.), *Feminism and methodology,* 1-14. Bloomington: Indiana University Press.

Harding, S., & Hintikka, M. (1983). *Discovering reality: Feminist perspectives on epistemology, metaphysics, methodology, and philosophy of science.* Dordrecht, Holland: Reidel.

Hartmann, H. (1984). The unhappy marriage of Marxism and feminism: Towards a more progressive union. In R. Dale, G. Esland, & M. MacDonald (Eds.),

Education and the state: Politics, patriarchy, and practice, Vol. 2, 191-210. New York: Falmer.

Hassan, I. (1987). *The postmodern turn: Essays in postmodern theory and culture.* Columbus: Ohio State University Press.

Haubrich, V. (1971). *Freedom, bureaucracy, and schooling.* Washington, DC: Association for Supervision and Curriculum Development.

Heath, S. (1983). *Ways with words.* Cambridge: Cambridge University Press.

Hemming, R. (1972). *Children's freedom: A. S. Neill and the evolution of the Summerhill idea.* New York: Schocken Books.

Henry, J. (1956). *Culture against man.* New York: Random House.

Hirsch, E. (1987). *Cultural literacy: What every American needs to know.* Boston: Houghton Mifflin.

Hochschild, J. (1984). *The new American dilemma: Liberal democracy and school desegregation.* New Haven, CT: Yale University Press.

Hofstadter, R. (1945). *Social Darwinism in American thought.* Philadelphia: University of Pennsylvania Press.

Homans, G. (1967). *The nature of social science.* New York: Harbinger Books.

Hook, S. (1966). *Reason, social myths and democracy.* New York: Harper Torchbooks.

Hostetler, J., & Huntington, G. (1971). *Children in Amish society.* New York: Holt, Rinehart & Winston.

Hubbard, R. (1979). Have only men evolved? In R. Hubbard, M. Henifin, & B. Fried (Eds.), *Women look at biology looking at women*, 7-35. Cambridge, MA: Schenkman.

Huber, R. (1971). *The American idea of success.* New York: McGraw-Hill.

JanMohamed, A., & Lloyd, D. (1987). Introduction: Toward a theory of minority discourse. *Cultural Critique*, 6, 5-12.

Janssen-Jurreit, M. (1980). *Sexism: The male monopoly on history and thought.* New York: Farrar.

Johnson, D., & Johnson, R. (1974). Instructional goal structures: Cooperative, competitive or individualistic. *Review of Educational Research*, 44 (2), 213-240.

Keller, E. (1985). *Reflections on gender and science.* New Haven, CT: Yale University Press.

Kellner, D. (1988). Postmodernism as social theory: Some challenges and problems. *Theory, Culture, and Society*, 5 (2/3), 239-270.

Kelly, T. (1986). Discussing controversial issues: Four perspectives on the teacher's role. *Theory and Research in Social Education*, 14 (2), 113-138.

Keniston, K. (1968). *Young radicals: Notes on committed youth.* New York: Harcourt, Brace & World.

Kessen, W. (1975). *Childhood in China.* New Haven, CT: Yale University Press.

Kleinfeld, J. (1979). *Eskimo school on the Andreafsky: A study of effective bicultural education.* New York: Praeger.

Kliebard, H. (1986, April). *What progressive education?* Paper presented at the annual American Educational Research Association meeting, San Francisco.

Kohl, H. (1968). *36 Children.* New York: Signet.

Kozol, J. (1967). *Death at an early age.* Boston: Houghton Mifflin.

Kuhn, T. (1970). *The structure of scientific revolutions*, Vol. 2. Chicago: University of Chicago Press.

Kuzmic, J. (1988, October). *Harmony high school: The paradoxes of creating an empowering educational environment.* Paper presented at the annual Bergamo Curriculum Theory and Classroom Practice conference, Dayton, OH.

Lanier, J., & Little, J. (1986). Research on teacher education. In M. C. Wittrock (Ed.), *Handbook of research on teaching* (3rd ed.), 527-569. New York: Macmillan.

Lasch, C. (1978). The culture of narcissism: American life in an age of diminishing expectations. New York: W.W. Norton.

Lather, P. (1984). Critical theory, curriculum transformation, and feminist mainstreaming. *Journal of Education*, 166 (1), 49-62.

Lather, P. (1986a). Issues of validity in openly ideological research: Between a rock and a soft place. *Interchange: A Quarterly Review of Education*, 17 (4), 63-84.

Lather, P. (1986b). Research as praxis. *Harvard Educational Review*, 56 (3), 257-277.

Lather, P. (1988a, April). *Educational research and practice in a postmodern era.* Paper presented at the annual American Educational Research Association meeting, New Orleans.

Lather, P. (1988b, April). *Ideology and methodological attitude.* Paper presented at the annual American Educational Research Association meeting, New Orleans.

LeCompte, M., & Goetz, J. (1982). Problems of reliability and validity in ethnographic research. *Review of Educational Research*, 52 (1), 31-60.

Lein, L. (1975). Black American migrant children: Their speech at home and school. *Anthropology and Education Quarterly*, 6 (1), 1-11.

Lesko, N. (1988). *Symbolizing society: Stories, rites and structure in a Catholic high school.* New York: Falmer.

Lewis, M., & Simon, R. (1986). A discourse not intended for her: Learning and teaching within patriarchy. *Harvard Educational Review*, 56 (4), 457-472.

Lightfoot, S. (1978). *Worlds apart: Relationships between families and schools.* New York: Basic Books.

Lightfoot, S. (1986). On goodness in schools: Themes of empowerment. *Peabody Journal of Education*, 63 (3), 9-28.

Lincoln, Y., & Guba, E. (1985). *Naturalistic inquiry.* Beverly Hills, CA: Sage.

Lindenfeld, F. (1982). Problems of power in a free school. In F. Lindenfeld & J. Rothschild-Whitt (Eds.), *Workplace democracy and social change*, 257-269. Boston: Porter Sargent.

Lindenfeld, F., & Rothschild-Whitt, J. (Eds.) (1982). *Workplace democracy and social change.* Boston: Porter Sargent.

Lipset, S., Trow, M., & Coleman, J. (1962). *Union democracy.* New York: Anchor Books.

Liston, D., & Zeichner, K. (1987). Critical pedagogy and teacher education. *Journal of Education*, 169 (3), 117-137.

Livingstone, D. (1987). *Critical pedagogy and cultural power.* South Hadley, MA: Bergin & Garvey.

Lloyd, S. (1987). *The Putney School: A progressive experiment.* New Haven: Yale University Press.

Lukes, S. (1973). *Individualism.* New York: Harper & Row.

Lyotard, J. (1984). *The postmodern condition: A report on knowledge.* Minneapolis: University of Minnesota Press.

Macaulay, D. (1976). *Underground.* Boston: Houghton Mifflin.

Macdonald, J., & Zaret, E. (1975). *Schools in search of meaning.* Washington, DC: Association for Supervision and Curriculum Development.

MacIntyre, A. (1984). *After virtue: A study in moral theory.* Notre Dame, IN: University of Notre Dame Press.

Maeroff, G. (1988). *The empowerment of teachers: Overcoming the crisis of confidence.* New York: Teachers College Press.

Manicas, P. (1985). John Dewey: Anarchism and the political state. *The Transactions of the Charles S. Peirce Society: A Quarterly Journal in American Philosophy*, 18 (2), 133-158.

Manthorpe, C. (1990). Feminism and science—Toward a human science? *Curriculum Inquiry*, 20 (1), 113-119.

Marcus, G., & Fischer, M. (1986). *Anthropology and cultural critique: An experimental moment in the human sciences.* Chicago: University of Chicago Press.

Maslow, A. (1976). *The farther reaches of human nature.* New York: Penguin.

Mayer, M. (1955). *They thought they were free: The Germans 1933-1945.* Chicago: University of Chicago Press.

Mayhew, K., & Edwards, A. (1966). *The Dewey school.* New York: Atherton.

Mazza, K. (1982). Reconceptual inquiry as an alternative mode of curriculum theory and practice: A critical study. *Journal of Curriculum Theorizing*, 4 (2), 5-89.

McFarland, M. (1985). Critical thinking in elementary school social studies. *Social Education*, 49 (4), 277-280.

McLaren, P. (1986). *Schooling as ritual performance: Towards a political economy of educational symbols and gestures.* London: Routledge & Kegan Paul.

McLaren, P. (1987). Schooling for salvation: Christian fundamentalism's ideological weapons of death. *Journal of Education*, 169 (2), 132-139.

McLaren, P. (1988). Language, social structure, and the production of subjectivity. *Critical Pedagogy Networker*, 1 (2/3), 1-10.

McLuhan, T. (1971). *Touch the earth: A self-portrait of Indian existence.* New York: Simon & Schuster.

Mead, G. H. (1934). *Mind, self, and society.* Chicago: University of Chicago Press.

Mead, M. (1949). *Male and female.* New York: Marrow.

Medler, K. (1972). Woman's high calling: The teaching profession in America. *American Studies*, 13, 19-32.

Meyer, J., & Rowan, B. (1978). The structure of educational organizations. In M. Meyer (Ed.), *Environments and organizations*, 78-109. San Francisco: Jossey Bass.

Miles, M., & Huberman, M. (1984). *Qualitative data analysis: A sourcebook of new methods.* Beverly Hills, CA: Sage.

Mills, C. W. (1969). *Sociology and pragmatism.* New York: Oxford University Press.

Montgomery, D. (1979). *Workers' control in America*. New York: Cambridge University Press.

Moore, S., & Myerhoff, B. (1977). *Secular ritual*. Amsterdam: Van Gorcum.

Moustakas, C. (1961). *Loneliness*. New York: Prentice-Hall.

Mouzelis, N. (1967). *Organization and bureaucracy: An analysis of modern theories*. Chicago: Aldine.

Myers, M. (1986). When research does not help teachers. *American Educator, 10* (2), 18-46.

Namenwirth, M. (1986). Science seen through a feminist prism. In R. Bleir (Ed.), *Feminist approaches to science*, 18-41. New York: Pergamon.

Nathan, J. (1983). *Free to teach: Achieving equity and excellence in schools*. New York: Pilgrim.

Neihardt, J. (1959). *Black Elk speaks: Being the life story of a holy man of the Oglala Sioux*. Lincoln, NE: Bison Books.

Neill, A. S. (1977). *Summerhill: A radical approach to child rearing*. New York: Wallaby.

Nelson, L., & Kagan, S. (1972). Competition: The star spangled scramble. *Psychology Today, 6* (4), 53-56, 90-94.

Nisbet, R. (1990). *The quest for community: A study in the ethics of order and freedom*. San Francisco: Institute for Contemporary Studies.

Noddings, N. (1984). *Caring: A feminine approach to ethics and moral education*. Berkeley: University of California Press.

Norris, S. (1989). Can we test validly for critical thinking? *Educational Researcher, 18* (9), 21-26.

Novack, G. (1975). *Pragmatism versus Marxism: An appraisal of John Dewey's philosophy*. New York: Pathfinder.

Oakes, J. (1985). *Keeping track: How schools structure inequality*. New Haven, CT: Yale University Press.

Okolo, C. (1984). *Conducting naturalistic interviews with children: Developmental factors affecting children's responses and their implications for the interview process*. Unpublished paper, Indiana University, Bloomington, IN.

Pateman, C. (1970). *Participation and democratic theory*. London: Cambridge University Press.

Pearson, P., & Baker, J. (1982). Seattle workers' brigade: History of a collective. In F. Lindenfeld & J. Rothschild-Whitt (Eds.), *Workplace democracy and social change*, 279-297. Boston: Porter Sargent.

Peck, M. (1983). *People of the lie: The hope for healing human evil.* New York: Touchstone Books.

Peck, M. (1987). *The different drum: Community making and peace.* New York: Simon & Schuster.

Perrow, C. (1976). *Organizational analysis: A sociological view.* Belmont, CA: Wadsworth.

Perry, S. (1978). *San Francisco scavengers.* Berkeley: University of California Press.

Peshkin, A. (1986). *God's choice: The total world of a fundamentalist Christian school.* Chicago: University of Chicago Press.

Peterson, B. (1990). The struggle for decent schools. *Democracy and Education,* 4 (3), 3-12.

Phillips, D. C. (1987). *Philosophy, science, and social inquiry: Contemporary methodological controversies in social science and related applied fields of research.* New York: Pergamon.

Pinar, W. (1975). Sanity, madness, and the school. In W. Pinar (Ed.), *Curriculum theorizing: The reconceptualists*, 359-383. Berkeley, CA: McCutchan.

Pinar, W. (1988). The reconceptualization of curriculum studies, 1987: A personal retrospective. *Journal of Curriculum and Supervision,* 3 (2) 157-167.

Popkewitz, T. (1981). Qualitative research: Some thoughts about the relation of methodology and social history. In T. Popkewitz & B. R. Tabachnick (Eds.), *The study of schooling: Field based methodologies in educational research and evaluation*, 155-178. New York: Praeger.

Popkewitz, T. (1983). *Change and stability in schooling: The dual quality of educational reform.* Victoria, Australia: Deakin University Press.

Popkewitz, T. (1984). *Paradigm and ideology in educational research.* New York: Falmer.

Popkewitz, T. (1987). *The formation of school subjects: The struggle for creating an American institution.* New York: Falmer.

Postman, N., & Weingartner, C. (1969). *Teaching as a subversive activity.* New York: Delta Books.

Purpel, D. (1989). *The moral and spiritual crisis in education: A curriculum for justice and compassion in education.* Granby, MA: Bergin & Garvey.

Putman, H. (1981). *Reason, truth, and history.* Cambridge: Cambridge University Press.

Rajchman, J. (1985). *Michel Foucault: The freedom of philosophy.* New York: Columbia University Press.

Ravitch, D. (1988). Tot sociology. *American Educator,* 12 (3), 38-39.

Ravitch, D., & Finn, C. (1988). *What do our 17-year-olds know?* New York: Harper & Row.

Rodriguez, R. (1982). *Hunger of memory: The education of Richard Rodriquez.* New York: Bantam Books.

Rose, S. (1988). *Keeping them out of the hands of Satan: Evangelical schooling in America.* New York: Routledge & Kegan Paul.

Roszak, T. (1969). *The making of a counter culture: Reflections on the technocratic society and its youthful opposition.* Garden City, NY: Doubleday.

Rothschild-Whitt, J. (1979). The collectivist organization: A alternative to rational-bureaucratic models. *American Sociological Review,* 44, 509-527.

Rothschild, J., & Whitt, A. (1986). *The cooperative workplace: Potentials and dilemmas of organizational democracy and participation.* Cambridge: Cambridge University Press.

Russell, R. (1982). The rewards of participation in the worker-owned firm. In F. Lindenfeld & J. Rothschild-Whitt (Eds.), *Workplace democracy and social change,* 109-124. Boston: Porter Sargent.

Sarason, S. (1971). *The culture of the school and the problem of change.* Boston: Allyn & Bacon.

Schlesinger, M., & Bart, P. (1982). Collective work and self-identity: Working in a feminist illegal abortion collective. In F. Lindenfeld & J. Rothschild-Whitt (Eds.), *Workplace democracy and social change,* 139-153. Boston: Porter Sargent.

Scholes, R. (1988). Three views of education: Nostalgia, history, and voodoo. *College English,* 50 (3), 323-332.

Schumacher, E. (1973). *Small is beautiful: Economics as if people mattered.* New York: Harper & Row.

Sennett, R. (1977). *The fall of public man.* New York: Alfred A. Knopf.

Sennett, R., & Cobb, J. (1972). *The hidden injuries of class.* New York: Vintage.

Shaheen, J. (1988). Democratic discipline, democratic lives. *Democracy and Education,* 3 (2), 1-8.

Shannon, P. (1987). Commercial reading materials, a technological ideology, and the deskilling of teachers. *Elementary School Journal,* 87 (3), 309-329.

Shor, I. (1986). *Culture wars: School and society in the conservative restoration —1969-1984*. Boston: Routledge & Kegan Paul.

Shor, I., & Freire, P. (1987). *A pedagogy for liberation: Dialogues on transforming education*. South Hadley, MA: Bergin & Garvey.

Silberman, C. (1973). *The open classroom reader*. New York: Random House.

Simon, R. (1987). Empowerment as a pedagogy of possibility. *Language Arts*, 64 (4), 370-382.

Simon, R. (1988). For a pedagogy of possibility. *Critical Pedagogy Networker*, 1 (1), 1-4.

Slavin, R. (1990). *Cooperative learning: Theory, research, and practice*. Englewood Cliffs, NJ: Prentice-Hall.

Smith, D. (1978). A peculiar eclipsing: Women's exclusion from man's culture. *Women's Studies International Quarterly*, 1 (4), 281-295.

Smith, J., & Heshusius, L. (1986). Closing down the conversation: The end of the quantitative-qualitative debate among educational inquirers. *Educational Researcher*, 15 (1), 4-12.

Spender, D. (1980). *Man made language*. London: Routledge & Kegan Paul.

Spender, D. (1982). *Invisible women: The schooling scandal*. London: Writers and Readers Publishing Cooperative.

Spradley, J. (1979). *The ethnographic interview*. New York: Rinehart & Winston.

Staub, E. (1971). Helping a person in distress: The influence of implicit and explicit "rules" of conduct on children and adults. *Journal of Personality and Social Psychology*, 17 (2), 137-144.

Strober, M., & Tyack, D. (1980). Why do women teach and men manage? A report on research on schools. *Signs: Journal of Women in Culture and Society*, 5 (3), 494-503.

Suls, J. (1986). Comparison processes in relative deprivation: A life-span analysis. In J. Olson, C. Herman, & M. Zanna (Eds.), *Relative deprivation and social comparison: The Ontario symposium*, Vol. 4, 95-116. Hillsdale, NJ: Lawrence Erlbaum.

Suls, J., & Mullen, B. (1982). From the cradle to the grave: Comparison and self-evaluation across the life-span. In J. Suls (Ed.), *Psychological perspectives on the self*, Vol. 1, 97-125. Hillsdale, NJ: Lawrence Erlbaum.

Suls, J., & Sanders, G. (1982). Self-evaluation through social comparison: A developmental analysis. In L. Wheeler (Ed.), *Review of personality and social psychology*, Vol. 3, 171-197. Beverly Hills, CA: Sage.

Talmadge, H. (Ed.) (1975). *Systems of individualized education.* Berkeley, CA: McCutchan.

Taylor, F. (1911). *The principles of scientific management.* New York: Harper and Brothers.

Teitelbaum, K. (1987). Outside the selective tradition: Socialist curriculum for children in the United States, 1900-1920. In T. Popkewitz (Ed.), *The formation of school subjects: The struggle for creating an American institution,* 238-267. New York: Falmer.

Tocqueville, A. de (1948). *Democracy in America,* Vol. 2. New York: Alfred A. Knopf.

Turner, V. (1969). *The ritual process: Structure and anti-structure.* Chicago: Aldine.

United States Department of Education. (1989). *Innovative projects for student community service: Guidelines for applicants.* Washington, DC: Office of Postsecondary Education.

Urban, W. (1982). *Why teachers organized.* Detroit, MI: Wayne State University Press.

Van Gennep, A. (1960). *The rites of passage.* Chicago: University of Chicago Press.

Varenne, H. (1977). *American together: Structured diversity in a midwestern town.* New York: Teachers College Press.

Ventriss, C. (1985). Emerging perspective on citizen participation. *Public Administration Review,* 47 (6), 433-440.

Verba, S. (1961). *Small groups and political behaviour.* Princeton, NJ: Princeton University Press.

Veroff, J. (1969). Social comparison and the development of achievement motivation. In C. Smith (Ed.), *Achievement-related motives in children,* 46-101. New York: Russell Sage Foundation.

Vivas, E. (1955). *Creation and discovery: Essays in criticism and aesthetics.* New York: Noonday.

Vygotsky, L. (1978). *Mind in society.* Cambridge: Harvard University Press.

Ward, S., Wackman, D., & Wartella, E. (1977). *How children learn to buy.* Beverly Hills, CA: Sage.

Warren, R. (1973). The classroom as a sanctuary for teachers: Discontinuities in social control. *American Anthropologist,* 75 (1/3), 280-291.

Weber, M. (1946). *From Max Weber: Essays in sociology.* New York: Oxford University Press.

Weick, K. (1976). Educational organizations as loosely coupled systems. *Administrative Science Quarterly*, 21 (1), 1-19.

Weiler, K. (1988). *Women teaching for change*. South Hadley, MA: Bergin & Garvey.

Weis, L. (1985). *Between two worlds: Black students in an urban community college*. Boston: Routledge & Kegan Paul.

Wells, H. (1954). *Pragmatism: Philosophy of imperialism*. New York: International.

Wexler, P. (1983). Movement, class and education. In L. Barton & S. Walker (Eds.), *Race, class, and education*, 17-39. Totowa, NJ: Croom Helm.

Wexler, P. (1987). *Social analysis of education: After the new sociology*. London: Routledge & Kegan Paul.

Wexler, P. (1988). Foreword. In N. Lesko, *Symbolizing society: Stories, rites, and structure in a Catholic high school*, ix-x. New York: Falmer.

Wexler, P., Martusewicz, R., & Kern, J. (1987). Popular educational politics. In D. Livingstone (Ed.), *Critical pedagogy and cultural power*, 227-243. South Hadley, MA: Bergin & Garvey.

White, H. (1981). The value of narrativity in the representation of reality. In W. Mitchell (Ed.), *On narrative*, 1-23. Chicago: University of Chicago Press.

White, R., & Lippitt, R. (1960). *Autocracy and democracy: An essay in experimental inquiry*. New York: Harper and Brothers.

Wiebe, R. (1967). *The search for order, 1977-1920*. New York: Hill & Wang.

Williams, R. (1980). *Problems in materialism and culture*. London: New Left Books.

Wirth, A. (1983). *Productive work — in industry and schools: Becoming persons again*. Lanham, MD: University Press.

Wise, A. (1979). *Legislated learning: The bureaucratization of the American classroom*. Berkeley: University of California Press.

Wolfgang, C., & Glickman, C. (1986). *Solving discipline problems: Strategies for classroom teachers*. Boston: Allyn & Bacon.

Wolf-Wasserman, M., & Hutchinson, L. (1978). *Teaching human dignity: Social change lessons for every teacher*. Minneapolis, MN: Education Exploration Center.

Wood, E. (1972). *Mind and politics: An approach to the meaning of liberal and socialist individualism*. Berkeley: University of California Press.

Wood, G. (1986, October). *Education for democratic empowerment: Theory into practice*. Paper presented at the annual Bergamo Curriculum Theory and Classroom Practice conference, Dayton, OH.

Wood, G. (1988). Democracy and the curriculum. In L. Beyer & M. Apple (Eds.), *The curriculum: Problems, politics and possibilities*, 166-187. Albany: State University of New York Press.

Wood, S. (1982). *The degradation of work? Skill, deskilling and the labour process*. London: Hutchinson.

Woodward, A. (1986). Over-programmed materials: Taking the teacher out of teaching. *American Educator*, 10 (1), 22-25.

Wu, Xiaoyang. (1988, October). *The roles and struggles of an elementary teacher in a school for democratic empowerment*. Paper presented at the annual Bergamo Curriculum Theory and Classroom Practice conference, Dayton, OH.

Yeatman, B. (1987, August). *A feminist theory of social differentiation*. Paper presented at the annual American Sociological Association meeting, Chicago.

Yesipov, B., & Goncharov, N. (1947). *I want to be like Stalin*. New York: John Day.

Zeichner, K. (1986). Social and ethical dimensions of reform in teacher education. In J. Hoffman & S. Edwards (Eds.), *Reality and reform in clinical teacher education*, 87-107. New York: Random House.

Zwerdling, D. (1982). At IGP, it's not business as usual. In F. Lindenfeld & J. Rothschild-Whitt (Eds.), *Workplace democracy and social change*. Boston: Porter Sargent.

INDEX